HISTORIC
BUILDINGS AT WORK

A GUIDE TO THE HISTORIC BUILDINGS OF SCOTLAND
USED BY CENTRAL GOVERNMENT

The Scottish Civic Trust

in collaboration with

Property Services Agency, Department of the Environment,
Scotland

1983

© Copyright 1983. The Scottish Civic Trust; PSA, Department of the Environment

Published by
THE SCOTTISH CIVIC TRUST

Printed by
David J. Clark Limited,
Cadogan Street,
Glasgow.

ISBN No. 0 9045 66 03 X

Front Cover: Royal Scottish Academy Edinburgh by W. H. Playfair, details from original drawing
(by courtesy of National Gallery of Scotland).

Cover Design: Russell Design Associates Ltd., Glasgow.

CONTENTS

PLATES

MAPS

FOREWORD

It gives us great pleasure to welcome this, the Scottish volume, in a series which arises from the report of the Working Party on Alternative Uses for Historic Buildings, chaired by Lord Montagu.

The historic buildings used directly by Central Government form a considerable part of Scotland's heritage and many of them deserve to be better known. No one can fail to be impressed by their variety and quality, and the range of modern purposes for which they are being successfully used. The volume mainly covers buildings maintained by the Property Services Agency (PSA), but also includes others, such as Edinburgh and Stirling Castles, which are looked after by the Scottish Development Department. We are keen that the Government should set an example by the standard of conservation of the historic buildings it uses or has in care. The high standard of adaptation and maintenance seen in the most notably successful examples (for instance, West Register House in Edinburgh) may not be found everywhere across the Government Estate. It is our hope that the contents of this volume will provide help and encouragement to occupying Departments in properly maintaining the many historic buildings which are in Government use, and will also enliven public interest in them. Historians, students, local amenity groups and others with special interests should find much information here which is not otherwise accessible.

The three volumes south of the Border are to be PSA publications. The fieldwork for this volume, too, has been mainly undertaken by PSA architects, but The Scottish Civic Trust and the Scottish Development Department's Historic Buildings and Ancient Monuments Inspectorates have edited and co-ordinated the entries. We are most grateful to The Scottish Civic Trust for undertaking the task of guiding the volume to publication.

GEORGE YOUNGER,
Secretary of State for Scotland.

TOM KING,
Secretary of State for the Environment.

INTRODUCTION

The Scottish Civic Trust is an independent organisation working to protect Scotland's architectural heritage and to encourage high standards of modern design. It was invited to edit and publish this volume by the Property Services Agency.

The Scope of the Register

The interest and variety of the 195 buildings included in this inventory has surprised even its compilers. They range, for example, from the prestigious National Museums, Galleries and Record Offices and other impressive public buildings such as Court Houses, Custom Houses and Military Barracks, through 19th century commercial blocks in which the Government leases space, down to humble farm-buildings taken over with estates acquired for other purposes. An appendix lists every building by type, so that they can be compared and contrasted. This is probably the only publication which brings together accounts of all the Scottish Court Houses and Custom Houses, except for the few no longer in that original use. Perhaps for the first time, the architectural and historic development of these characteristic civic buildings can be studied between the covers of a single volume.

All the buildings described in the Register are listed by the Secretary of State for Scotland as of special architectural and historic interest. This points to the fact that the Government faces the same obligations as every other owner of listed property, but over a wider spectrum. This responsibility chiefly falls on the Property Services Agency which, as the building and maintenance division of the Department of the Environment, has the day-to-day care of nearly all the buildings included in this volume. In some cases, where the Government is not the building owner, the PSA leases and maintains the premises, which may consist only of two or three rooms within a larger block. Scheduled Ancient Monuments are included only when directly in Government use (e.g. Edinburgh and Stirling Castles) or when they stand on part of a property serving some similar function (Rosyth Castle).

Buildings such as Post Offices, Railway Stations and Hospitals, owned and managed by other Government agencies, are not included but it is hoped to cover these in later, companion volumes.

Preparation of the volume

The survey was carried out by a small team of PSA Scottish Services architects with help from the James Taylor Partnership, Edinburgh. Checking and editing were undertaken jointly by members of the Historic Buildings Inspectorate of the Scottish Development Department and by The Scottish Civic Trust, which prepared the volume for publication. Most of the illustrations were specially taken by the PSA's photographic unit.

Surveying was done systematically and the occupancy and condition of every building was noted as a guide to future decisions on use and maintenance. Much useful architectural information was recorded which, for reasons of space, could not be included in the published text. Background research has revealed valuable historical evidence about the buildings and their architects, some of which is published here for the first time.

How to use the Register

The building descriptions, which make up the bulk of the volume, are arranged alphabetically by Region. Each Region is subdivided, in order of local government Districts (where these apply). Each building is then listed in order of its place name, and where more than one occurs in any city, town or village, in the alphabetical order of the street address. The index at the end of the volume includes every place name. Architects and artists are listed in a separate appendix. A further appendix groups all the buildings under their original uses.

Inclusion of a building does not imply that the public has right of access. Most defence establishments, for example, are normally inaccessible. Other properties can be visited by special arrangement. Some of the finest are public buildings in the fullest sense. These include the great national museums and galleries in Edinburgh and the public parts of the Castles at Edinburgh and Stirling.

Information regarding access can be obtained from:

PSA Scottish Services Secretariat, Argyle House, 3 Lady Lawson Street, Edinburgh EH3 9SD.

PROJECT TEAM

General Editors

The Scottish Civic Trust
John Gerrard, D.A.(Edin), R.I.B.A., A.R.I.A.S.
Maurice Lindsay, C.B.E., T.D., D.Litt.

Historic Buildings Division SDD
Anne Riches, M.A.

Property Services Agency
Project Architect   Sandy Leask, Dip.Arch., Dip.T.P., R.I.B.A., A.R.I.A.S.

Survey Team   Alex Aithie, R.I.B.A., A.R.I.A.S.
John Chalmers, R.I.B.A., A.R.I.A.S.
Gordon Macaulay
John Wheeler

James Taylor Partnership, Consultant Architects

Photography   Stewart Guthrie, A.I.I.P.
David Brown

Secretariat PSA   John Yellowlees, M.A., M.Phil.
Jean Miller

The Scottish Civic Trust   Sadie Douglas, Secretary

ACKNOWLEDGEMENTS

The project team wish to thank the following persons for their help and assistance in the preparation of this volume:
Catherine Cruft, Royal Commission on Ancient and Historical Monuments, Scotland;
David Walker, Principal Inspector, Historic Buildings Division, Scottish Development Department;
Iain MacIvor, Principal Inspector and Dr. Richard Fawcett, Inspector, Ancient Monuments Division, Scottish Development Department;
John Soutar, City of Aberdeen District Planning Department and
the staff of the Museums and Art Galleries of Aberdeen, Dunfermline, Inverness and Stirling.

We would also like to thank the occupiers of all the buildings visited, for their co-operation during surveys.

DESCRIPTIVE GUIDE

NOTES AND ABBREVIATIONS

Categories of buildings

When buildings are statutorily listed as being of special architectural or historic interest they are given categories. These categories are A, B and C(S). A number of buildings are listed C. This is a non-statutory category which is being phased out either by adding the buildings to the statutory list or by dropping them. The categories can be briefly defined as follows:—

A   Buildings of national or more than local importance, either architectural or historic, or fine, little altered examples of some particular date or style.

B   Buildings of primarily local importance, or good examples of some period or style which may have been altered in a minor way.

C(S)   Good buildings which may be considerably altered and other buildings which are fair examples of
C   their period, or in some cases buildings of no great individual merit which group well with others in categories A and B.

Some buildings are also protected under the Ancient Monuments Act; these are called scheduled monuments. Some of these buildings are held in trust for the nation by the Secretary of State. Those mentioned in this publication are Edinburgh Castle, Fort Charlotte, Fort George, Rosyth Castle and Dovecot and Stirling Castle.

Sources

Reference is normally made to source material at the end of each entry in the guide. Information on all entries is also given in the Scottish Development Department's descriptive lists of buildings of special architectural or historic interest. Four other sources have been used so frequently that they are not mentioned with individual entries. They are:

1. Biographical Dictionary of British Architects 1600–1840 (Colvin)
2. Dictionary of British Sculptors 1660–1850 (Gunnis)
3. The Old and New Statistical Accounts of Scotland c. 1790 and c. 1830–40
4. Ordnance Gazetteer of Scotland c. 1882–1900 (Groome)

Abbreviations:

APSD   Architectural Publication Society's Dictionary (ed. Papworth) 1848–92
QJRIAS   Quarterly Journal, Royal Incorporation of Architects in Scotland
RCAHMS   Royal Commission on Ancient and Historical Monuments Scotland
RSA   Royal Scottish Academy
SNMR   Scottish National Monuments Record
SRO   Scottish Record Office

Region	BORDERS
District	BERWICKSHIRE

Address:	1 Marine Parade, Eyemouth
Category:	C(S), in Eyemouth Conservation Area
Occupier:	Department of Agriculture and Fisheries
Use:	Offices
Holding:	Leased

This unpretentious mid-19th century building is situated near the entrance of Eyemouth Harbour and is currently occupied by Fishery Protection Officers and the Eyemouth Harbour-Master. It is also used by the Harbour Trustees as an occasional conference centre.

The building was originally constructed as a private dwelling-house, and has also been used as shop premises before conversion to offices. It is L-shaped in plan and two storeys high. The front elevation is faced in imitation bull-faced ashlar with rendered angle and window margins. Fenestration is by two sash windows to the left-hand advanced bay and a further three windows to the right-hand bay. The central doorway with a rectangular fanlight above is of early 20th century design and has an elliptical stained glass window. A small timber bracketted hood remains over this doorway.

The slated roof is hipped over the advance bay. The brick end stacks have new chimney cans.

Internally the building has been greatly altered and there is little evidence of the original finishes. All internal doors have been replaced. Entry to the first floor is by simple timber stair with straight balusters, capped with a Victorian-style mahogany handrail. A plaster centre-piece to the first-floor conference room ceiling is the only surviving decorative feature.

This building is an integral part of the harbour frontage and is related to a variety of similarly proportioned structures, collectively important in Eyemouth's fishing economy.

Region	BORDERS
District	ETTRICK AND LAUDERDALE

Name:	Sheriff Court
Address:	Ettrick Terrace, Selkirk
Category:	Recommended for Listing, in Selkirk Conservation Area
Occupier:	Scottish Courts Administration
Use:	Court House
Holding:	Crown

Selkirk Sheriff Court occupies a commanding site overlooking the town and is given added prominence by the boldly baronial design with a dramatic skyline of towers, corbelled turrets and crow-steps. It replaced the original classical Courthouse of c. 1810, situated in the Market Place, in which Sir Walter Scott meted out justice. The present Sheriff Court House was designed by David Rhind and was opened in July 1870, the costs being borne jointly by the county and the Treasury. The boldly executed baronial scheme reflects the period's interest in mediaevalism, inspired by Sir Walter.

This irregularly planned building is set into the hillside so that the basement level is wholly above ground level at the rear. Built of bull-faced rubble with polished ashlar dressings, there are two full storeys above the basement with attics inserted at random in the gabled roofs and in the tower and turrets. The building is entered from Ettrick Terrace by a platform bridging the basement area, through a round-arched doorway with a rope-moulded hood-mould firmly tied at either end to create knotted label stops. A canted oriel window rises through the two storeys above. The rope moulding is used again to great effect in the corbelling of the angle turret to the right of the entrance and on the corbelled turret clamped like a limpet to the massive circular tower at the north-east. This tower has an arcaded parapet above a corbel table, the latter bound together by more rope moulding from which project miniature dummy cannons. Sash and case windows of varying sizes, all set in chamfered margins, are used throughout the building. The attic windows all have crow-stepped gabled heads. Smart cast-iron railings contain the basement area, which is arcaded over to form a bridge on part of the west elevation.

Internally, the main interest is in the first-floor Court Room reached by a handsome staircase with twisted cast-iron balusters. The Court retains its hammerbeam roof and other original fittings, including the panel-fronted bench, the richly padded official seats and a cast-iron fireplace strategically placed to warm the sheriff. Portraits of the Duke and Duchess of Buccleuch (1806). Sir Walter Scott (1871) and Lord Napier & Ettrick (1896) hang in the court. The Sheriff's room and Jury room are reached from either side of the bench; the former has a simply-panelled inclined cornice and a marble chimney-piece enclosing an interesting cast-iron stove. The simply-fitted Jury room is within the circular tower. The basement housed the original police apartments and cells, the latter being connected by a tunnel under the street to the prison building. This building (not in the care of the PSA) continues the baronial scheme of the County Buildings.

References: *Border Advertiser*, 15 July 1870.
Hawick Advertiser, 16 July 1870.

Region	BORDERS
District	ROXBURGH

Name:	Sheriff Court
Address:	Castlegate, Jedburgh
Category:	B, in Jedburgh Conservation Area
Occupier:	Scottish Courts Administration
Use:	Court House
Holding:	Crown

The classical building which houses the Jedburgh Sheriff Court was originally the Roxburgh County Buildings. It occupies an important central site at the junction of Castlegate and Market Place, and dates from 1812. The architect's name is not recorded. It is now occupied only by the Sheriff Court and the Procurator-Fiscal, and provides spacious accommodation for both. In 1793, Sir Walter Scott pled his first case as advocate in the earlier Court House on this site. Although distinct from them in style, the Court House forms part of a historic group of buildings including the Town Steeple and the Old Jail, built in 1756. The Steeple is built over a pend known as Newgate, leading to a garden area and to the ancient Abbey. This building is separately listed in Category A.

The Court House is two storeys high, built in dressed ashlar stonework and is rectangular on plan with access from both Castlegate and Market Place. The twelve-bay elevation on the slope of Castlegate is designed in alternate blocks of three bays. Two of these are slightly advanced and articulated with Roman Doric pilasters and entablature. The parapet screens a pitched, piended and slated roof. The right-hand block contains three round-headed astragalled windows between the pilasters, which are coupled at the outer corners. In the other advanced block the windows are rectangular with recessed panels.

The entrance in this latter block is through an arcaded and balustraded porch. The recessed sections each have two windows flanking a central niche. The elegantly simple, symmetrical elevation to Market Place is three bays wide, articulated in the same manner as the Castlegate frontage by Roman Doric pilasters at the upper floor. The central bay and the twin-pilastered angles are slightly advanced. The ground-floor windows and the central doorway are segment-headed and those at first floor are round-headed, all with astragals.

Inside, a spacious inner vestibule leads from the Castlegate entrance to the cantilevered stone main stair which is elegantly designed with an iron balustrade and hardwood handrail. The stairway is lit from the rear elevation by two round-headed windows. The stairhall ceiling is semi-barrel in form. The rectangular Court Room has a small gallery with separate access and is top-lit through a panelled coved ceiling rich in classical detail, including ornamental scroll brackets. The Court Room contains a large portrait of the late William Oliver Rutherford of Edgerston, Sheriff of the County for sixty-one years. It was painted by Phillips of London and was presented by the Commissioners of Supply. Other accommodation includes a Library, Secondary Court, Jury Room, Witnesses' Rooms and service areas and accommodation for the Procurator-Fiscal. There is also a small caretaker's flat which is at present unused. The interior character throughout is consistent in style and period. All the work appears to be original, except for modern fire-resisting doors to the corridors.

References: Guide to Jedburgh & Vicinity (James Watson). Jedburgh—The Official Guide.

Region	BORDERS
District	TWEEDDALE

Name:	Sheriff Court
Address:	High Street, Peebles
Category:	B, in Peebles Conservation Area
Occupier:	Scottish Courts Administration
Use:	Court House
Holding:	Crown

This fine neo-Tudor building terminates the view at the west end of Peebles High Street, where it stands beside the Victorian Gothic Parish Church. The northern elevation overlooks Eddleston Water. The plainer jail block is attached to the rear. Behind, there is a walled garden bounded by the main wall of the Parish Church Hall. The site was apparently occupied by an older jail, demolished sometime between 1841–1843, and the present building was erected in 1844 to the design of Thomas Brown.

It comprises two principal floors, with attic and basement. The three-bay symmetrical east facade is very well constructed in smooth ashlar. Projecting pilasters, which rise above the first floor string course, are surmounted by hexagonal Tudor chimneys above the parapet where they incorporate shield motifs. The parapet is raked to form a steep gable above the central bay. The ground floor fenestration consists of paired windows with stone transoms on either side of the main entrance, linked by a continuous hood-mould. Each sash is divided into small panes. At first floor, the three evenly spaced tripartite windows are mullioned and transomed with straight hood-moulds. The north and south gables of the main block are terminated by further tall hexagonal stone chimney-stacks which accentuate the verticality of the building. The rear prison block has a piended slated roof with conventional ashlar chimney-stacks and earthenware cans.

On the ground floor the accommodation comprises the offices of the Sheriff Clerk and Procurator Fiscal and the prison cells. The first floor contains the Court Room, the Sheriff's offices and a library. The second floor is mostly vacant. The basement is occupied by the caretaker's flat. The central single-leaf entrance door, of six panels, has a rectangular fanlight above. The ground-floor offices have plain cornices but there are examples of dentil cornices and plaster friezes in the first-floor Sheriff's rooms. Windows have splayed ingoes which are timber-panelled with shutters. Doors are six-panelled, with original ebony handles and brass fittings. The Court Room has been refurbished but many of the original fitments nevertheless remain. The walls have vertical panelling to dado level with timber bench seats and desks incorporating ink-wells. The ornate Tudor-style panelled plaster ceiling incorporates a central cast-iron ventilator with an elaborate foliate grille. The open-well stair has spiral cast-iron balusters supporting a heavy timber handrail. It is side-lit by a double window with etched glass panes.

Region	CENTRAL
District	CLACKMANNAN

Name:	Burgh Chambers
Address:	14 Bank Street, Alloa
Category:	C, in Alloa Glebe Conservation Area
Occupiers:	Department of Transport, Customs & Excise, Department of Health and Social Security
Holding:	Leased

This building, erected in 1873–74 to a design by the Alloa architects, Thomas Frame & Sons, at a cost of approximately £4,000, was originally the Burgh Chambers. In 1952 the Burgh administration was transferred to Greenfield House and for some time the Chambers remained unoccupied. They were then altered to form Government offices.

Situated at the western end of the main town centre, this impressive Victorian Renaissance-style building occupies part of the former market place site. The original mercat cross now stands next to the front entrance.

The principal two-storey, three-bay elevation is constructed in rusticated ashlar at ground-floor level and smooth ashlar above. The projecting entrance bay is dominated by a Corinthian portico with dentil cornice. This is surmounted by the coat of arms of the former burgh set into an elaborate Baroque masonry surround.

The two tripartite ground-floor sash windows have stone mullions. The first-floor windows are plate-glass with the lower sash divided. They have alternating segmental and triangular pediments on brackets.

The building has a cornice and a panelled parapet with open balustrading over the central and end bays. The western projecting bay incorporates an arched vennel which leads to the rear walled courtyard of the former police station and cells. These are L-shaped on plan, constructed in random rubble. An external stone stair leads to the former witness rooms at the upper level. The main entrance door is double-leafed with square recessed panels and a semi-circular fanlight above. This leads to an imposing entrance hall with chequered stone flooring and green dado-height ceramic tiling.

The main open-well stone stair has a simple cast-iron balustrade with a mahogany handrail. The stairway is lit by a stained glass window at the first landing level and a lantern-light above.

The building has been substantially altered internally for use as offices. The Department of Transport occupies part of the ground floor and some rooms at the rear remain unused. The first-floor accommodation was extended in 1952 to incorporate rooms in the adjacent building for the use of the Department of Health & Social Security. The Customs & Excise occupy the remaining accommodation at this level.

Some dentil cornices remain at first-floor level. On the ground floor a relocated timber screen with stained glass lights and a heavy panelled door give some indication of the original detailing.

References: *Alloa Journal*, October 12 1872
The History of Clackmannan (Rev. T. Crouther Gordon).
Buildings of Architectural and Historic Interest in Clackmannan District (Clackmannan District Council).

Name:	Sheriff Court
Address:	Mar Street, Alloa
Category:	B, in Alloa Glebe Conservation Area
Occupier:	Scottish Courts Administration
Use:	Court House
Holding:	Crown

The County Court was held in the neighbouring town of Clackmannan until 1822, when Alloa became the seat of justice. The Court then used the old Alloa Assembly Rooms, until the Tontine Hotel was acquired in 1842 and reconstructed to serve as a Courtroom and Prison. This also proved unsatisfactory and designs for a purpose-built Court House and County Buildings were commissioned from the Edinburgh architectural firm of Brown and Wardrop in 1863. They were completed and formally opened with great ceremony on 8th December 1865. Extensions added along Drysdale Street in 1910 and 1938 were designed by William Kerr of the Alloa architects John Melvin and Son. The Court House and its administration now occupy all of the original building. The extension contains offices for the Police.

Brown and Wardrop based their design approximately on 16th century Flemish and Scottish precedent. The building displays some very fine detailing, especially in the stonework entrusted to the local mason, John Mailer. The stone came from the Dunmore quarry, on the opposite side of the Forth. The main building consists of two tall storeys plus a part-basement and a clock tower constructed in finely dressed snecked rubble with a steeply-pitched slated roof.

The main seven-window frontage to Mar Street is 90 feet long. The high, buttressed central door-piece supports a massive stone balustraded balcony with corner pedestals on which sit carved lions supporting the shields of St. Andrew and St. George. Crowning the central bay is a decorated crow-stepped gable enclosing a bold carving of the Royal Arms between decorated angled finials. At the apex a lion rampant supports a weather vane. Two symmetrical crow-stepped gablets and tall hexagonal corner chimneys add to the liveliness of the skyline. All the subsidiary gables have triangular-coped crow-steps and finials and incorporate carved panels representing the 'heraldic bearings of the leading proprietors in the County'. That on the north gable displays the building's commencing date, 1863. Pronounced eaves and first-floor string courses tie in the design of the front and side elevations, the eaves string rising to frame the carved panels and the Royal Arms. The rectangular clock tower is placed at the north-east corner. Its roof is steep and nearly pyramidal, with a short ridge and a bargeboarded lucarne on the west face. The clock, supplied by Ritchie and Sons of Edinburgh, has faces on all four sides set into crow-stepped and crocketted gablets resembling those on the main frontages. Carved gargoyles occur where the gablets meet the parapet. A corbelled circular turret encloses the spiral stone access stair to the clock tower. At the north-east corner the tower is splayed and corbelled at ground level, beside a single-bay link containing the public entrance to the courtroom. The two-storey extension to Drysdale Street is plainer, but it reflects some of the main building details such as two and three-light windows and triangular copes to the crow-steps.

The staircase, with twisted iron balusters, leads from the entrance hall and is lit by a tripartite window. Portraits of the 12th Lord Mar and Lady Mar hang beside the stair-well, which has an ornate coved ceiling. The Courtroom, on the first floor, measures approximately 45 feet by 28 feet. Its principal feature is the timber hammer-beam roof with bracketted ornamental couples, moulded ribs and bosses. Old brass lamp fittings now decorate the underside of the roof ventilators. Behind the painted bench is the Royal Cypher. The room is lit by four side windows and a tripartite window in the end wall. The doors have shouldered architraves and the woodwork matches the quality of the roof. The Sheriff's Room, otherwise plain, contains a marble chimney-piece and a working speaking tube to the Sheriff Clerk's room on the ground floor. The other rooms are plainly decorated, but all have good panelled doors and window ingoes.

References: A Short History of Alloa—(Rev. T. Crouther Gordon 1936.)
Alloa Advertiser, 16 December 1865.

Region	CENTRAL
District	FALKIRK

Name:	Sheriff Court
Address:	Hope Street, Falkirk
Category:	B
Occupier:	Scottish Courts Administration
Use:	Court House
Holding:	Crown

Falkirk Sheriff Court was erected between 1866 and 1868 at a cost of £7,000. The building was designed in the baronial style by Thomas Brown, of the Edinburgh architectural firm of Brown and Wardrop and is prominently sited near the busy junction of Hope Street and West Bridge Street at the west end of Falkirk town centre.

This two-storey structure, with attic and basement, is faced in snecked rubble obtained from local quarries. It is irregular in form, appearing basically as a series of crow-step-gabled facades. The south elevation includes a high-spired circular turret and a smaller square tower with spirelet, angled above the former entrance to the police station. The windows are varied in design, with stone-mullioned tripartites to the ground floor and an assortment of pedimented, plain and arched windows to the upper floors. A series of tall ashlar chimney-stacks contributes to the building's picturesque skyline. Further detailed interest is provided by a number of ornate stone panels depicting historical and armorial subjects.

The accommodation is made up of offices, detention rooms and cells on the ground floor, with the Court Room, Sheriff's office and library on the first floor. The attic rooms were formerly used as a caretaker's flat and it appears that the basement area previously housed cells or detention rooms.

The principal stone open-well stair is notable for the extremely ornate cast-iron balusters and, at the first-floor landing, contrasting classical timber balusters, rail and newel post. A large rectangular lantern light is centred above, surrounded by an ornate coved ceiling. The single Court Room is almost completely unaltered with a fine double hammerbeam roof, original dado panelling, timber bench seating and other furnishings. The police station wing, which was added to the south elevation in 1870, was demolished before 1969.

This Court House survives as a bold and now somewhat isolated example of Victorian public architecture in this sector of the town.

References: *Builder,* January 1866
Falkirk Mail, May 1957
Falkirk Herald, August 1963

Name:	Grahame House
Address:	45/47 Vicar Street, Falkirk
Category:	B, in Falkirk Town Centre Conservation Area
Occupier:	Inland Revenue Office and Department of Employment
Use:	Offices
Holding:	Leased

This two-storey building, originally designed as Falkirk's Head Post Office, occupies a corner site with its main, west, elevation facing Vicar Street. It dates from 1893 and was designed in a late neo-Tudor manner by W. W. Robertson and W. T. Oldrieve, architects to the Office of Works in Scotland. The Gothic design is handsomely complemented by Sir George Washington Browne's neighbouring early Renaissance Bank of Scotland. Grahame House is rectangular in plan and is now connected at both floor levels with a modern office block at the rear. Little of its original internal character remains but the outside elevations have been completely retained and refurbished.

The three-bay Vicar Street elevation is nearly symmetrical. The centre bay is slightly advanced and gabled above the parapet. The ground-floor windows are mullioned and transomed; those above have cusped ogee heads set into square openings with hood-moulds. The doorways in the outer bays have four-centred heads. The centre bay is accentuated by a three-light oriel at first floor and the finialled, panelled parapet above incorporates the Royal insignia. The remaining first-floor windows have cusped lights and pretty ogee hood-moulds, linked by a string course.

The corner with Weir Street is emphasised by an elaborate corbelled octagonal angle turret with an ogee-capped Gothic cupola braced by diminutive flying buttresses. The detailing on the short return frontage is similar to the Vicar Street elevation. The masonry has weathered remarkably well, and the fine stone detailing seems to be in excellent condition.

Internally, little original character remains except on the first floor where the panelled doors, shutters and skirtings are intact. The ceilings are now obscured by suspended acoustic tiles. Most of the office work is done within the new building to the rear, the first floor of the former G.P.O. being used for record storage.

Region	CENTRAL
District	STIRLING

Name:	Queen Victoria School
Address:	Dunblane
Categories:	A and C(S)
Occupier:	Ministry of Defence
Use:	Boarding School
Holding:	Crown

After the Boer War, it was realised that the education of the sons of men serving in H.M. Forces was unsatisfactory, due to families being continually on the move. In 1901, a scheme was therefore promoted, following English and Irish precedents, to build a boarding school in Scotland to commemorate the Scottish servicemen who fell in the South African War. It was not until the autumn of 1902 that the idea took definite shape. It was then decided that the school should serve the dual purpose of commemorating Scotland's fallen servicemen and the recently deceased Queen Victoria. A committee was formed, funds were raised by public subscription and Dunblane was chosen as the site because of its central location, healthy situation and excellent railway facilities. Plans were invited in competition from six Scottish architects. A committee chaired by Sir Rowand Anderson appointed John A. Campbell of Glasgow as architect for the project, which included separate buildings for the School (Main Building), Gymnasium, Hospital, Swimming Bath, Library, Science Workshop and homes for the Headmaster, Adjutant and other staff. Construction started in 1906 and was completed by 1913.

Boarding School (Main Building) Category A
The Main School Building provided places for 276 boys. It was completed in 1908 and officially opened by King Edward VII. It consists of a massive four-storey E-plan block with a main west front twenty-five bays wide. It is harled with freestone dressings to the windows and ground floor of the thirteen-bay advanced centre section and to various features of Scots Renaissance character which relieve the basic austerity. These include a boldly consoled balcony over the powerful mannerist entrance archway and a corbelled third-floor parapet. Above the small central balcony is a Roman Doric window aedicule with segmental pediment and Royal Coat of Arms. Flanking it and on the balcony balustrade are the Arms of Edinburgh, Glasgow, Aberdeen and Dundee, in recognition of the subscriptions raised in those cities. The end bays of the centre block

break through the eaves with angle tourelles linked by balustrades. All the windows are sash and case. Circulation areas are lit by semi-circular arched windows at the junction of the "E".

The roof is slated and steeply pitched with crow-stepped gables and with balustrades at the junctions of the wings. A tower stair at the west end gives access to the masters' rooms. On the south gables, corbelled square turrets project above the eaves.

Semi-circular steps lead into the entrance hall, which has seven stone arches of Overwood stone with carved foliate bosses and sculptured soffits. Within the arches leaded glass is fixed in ornate wooden screens. The entrance hall leads to the circulation areas, reception halls and dining room, the latter with circular piers supporting a beamed ceiling. On the left of the entrance hall is a fine boardroom with mahogany dado panelling. A large reception hall, with lantern lights and a beamed ceiling is also entered from the vestibule. All other internal spaces are plainly detailed.

Memorial Chapel   Category A

The Chapel, also designed by Campbell, occupies a prominent position on the crest of the hill beside the approach to the School buildings. A line of cypress trees leads the eye to the square tower which is capped by a low octagonal slated spire.

The building, influenced in its general form by the medieval church at St. Monance in Fife, is late Scots Gothic in style. The plan is cruciform consisting of three bays, the central crossing tower and one further bay. The walls are grey-harled with stone dressings and the three gable windows are filled with bold curvilinear tracery. The main entrance is through a low porch at the south-west corner, embellished by a small niche above the entrance door and two pinnacles. The tower, reminiscent of designs by Sir J. J. Burnet, is the most prominent feature of the building.

Access to the organ gallery is by a stone spiral stair, octagonal in plan, with an ogee roof. This forms an effective external feature seen from the south-west in conjunction with the square tower. There is a small gallery at the south end of the nave, also approached by a spiral stair from the south-west porch.

Internally, the building is simple with a high exposed roof of dressed rafters and purlins which spans the nave and the two wide aisles. The supporting arcade is round-arched. The walls generally are white but the entrance vestibule is all of dressed stonework. The pulpit is in stone with Gothic style sculpture. The stained glass in the chancel window includes a representation of the four evangelists.

Infirmary   Category C(S)

The Infirmary, known originally as the Hospital, was built in 1908. It is attributed to Harry B.

Measures, of The War Office, London, but it is likely that he simply supervised John A. Campbell's scheme.

The accommodation comprises a single-storey ward block, linked to an asymmetrically designed two-storey building of domestic character, containing medical and dental treatment rooms, convalescent room, offices and kitchen, with a flat for the matron on the upper floor.

The building is harled with stone dressings in Scots Renaissance style. Part of the two-storey block is corbelled over the ground floor. It also has a dormer window, crow-steps and a pyramidal roof. All windows are twelve-pane sash and case, the wards having an additional hopper window for ventilation above the standard window openings.

The interior is plain, with clinical finishes to the wards and treatment rooms. On the upper floor, the matron's flat is domestic in character with plain wooden staircase and simple cornices.

Headmaster's House   Category C(S)

A two-storey, three-bay detached building, roughly square on plan and pleasantly situated in a clearing off the approach avenue from the north.

The walls, up to first-floor level, are in snecked, squared rubble, rounded at the angles. Above, they are harled with corbelled angles. Windows are astragalled sash and case. A canted bay window projects to the right of the central entrance door.

Internally, a flat arch marks the bay window in both the lounge and the dining room. The internal details are very simple.

The house is characteristic of architect-designed early twentieth century detached suburban houses, distinguished particularly, in this case, by the piended roof with wide overhanging eaves.

Wall and Gates   Category C(S)
The whole school is surrounded by a high stone wall built in random rubble with a dressed freestone coping weathered in one direction.

There are two similar entrances to the site, flanked by large double piers in random rubble, circular on plan, with a string course and domed cap. The double gates are in wrought-iron, supported on a tracked wheel. The ironwork is simple and functional, apart from a circular feature at the head of each gate. The two gates frame, respectively, the school's title and coat of arms, both of which are painted in appropriate colours with some gilding.

Address:	1 Corn Exchange Road, Stirling
Category:	B, in Stirling Town Centre Conservation Area
Occupier:	Customs and Excise
Use:	Offices
Holding:	Leased

This building is L-shaped in plan and situated on a dominant corner site. It is one of the most ornate structures in Stirling, and shares Corn Exchange Road with other architecturally important buildings such as the Old Council Chambers and Stirling Public Library. The frontage is on the main route to Stirling Castle, close to a commanding statue of Wallace in full regalia.

The property was completed in 1901 for the Clydesdale Bank, the ground floor serving as the place of business and the upper two floors being occupied by the Bank Manager and servants. The upper floors have been continuously let to HM Customs and Excise since 1937.

The architect responsible for the design was James Thomson of Glasgow. The main building contract was let to Bailie Gourlay. The style adopted was Early French Renaissance with an arched frontage and richly sculptured stonework. The Roman Doric columned main entrance to the telling room has richly carved oak panelling and extensive use is made of Sicilian marble for both walls and floors. There are two stained glass windows in this area, one bearing the arms of Stirling, the other those of Glasgow.

The building is three storeys high with further accommodation in the roof space, which was formerly the servants' flat. The plinth is in Peterhead granite surmounted by rusticated Locharbriggs red sandstone at ground floor level. The upper storeys are in sandstone ashlar with a balustraded balcony at first floor level. The window bays are framed by pilasters, those on the top floor having elaborate pedimented dormer heads.

The secondary entrance leading from Corn Exchange Road was formerly the private entrance to the Bank Manager's house, but now leads to the Customs and Excise Offices. The first floor is reached by an open-well stone stair with heavy oak balusters and newel posts. The walls are lined with recessed oak panelling to dado level and the stair is pleasantly lit by two flower-patterned stained glass windows.

The main public rooms have unusual curved bay windows with floral bracketted friezes. Cornices are plain but the plastered ceilings are more ornate. Most fireplaces have been blocked but the original chimney-pieces remain intact. The style of the surrounds is mainly classical and they are constructed of mahogany and marble.

The building fabric is generally in excellent order with few additions or alterations.

References: *Stirling Journal and Advertiser*, November 20th 1901
Stirling Sentinel, December 5th 1944

Name:	Forthside House
Address:	Forthside, Stirling
Category:	B
Occupier:	Ministry of Defence
Use:	Vacant
Holding:	Crown

Forthside was originally the mansion house of an estate lying outside Stirling along the south bank of the River Forth, east of the town centre. It is a handsome classical country house dating from c. 1815. The architect is unknown. It was later sub-divided into two separate dwellings.

The house is two storeys high, over a raised basement. The three-bay main elevation is symmetrically composed, the centre bay being very slightly advanced. The bays are articulated by Roman Doric pilasters, paired at the angles, supporting a deep entablature and parapet. The roof, hidden behind the parapet, is piended and slated. The facade is finished in finely dressed ashlar and there are moulded string courses at ground and first-floor levels. The central entrance is approached by a flight of steps with a simple iron railing at each side. The entrance is framed by a Greek Doric porch, consisting of a pair of fluted columns on each side of the stairhead and paired pilasters beside the doorway. Above the original wide, nine-panelled door is a good semi-circular fanlight with a delicate pattern of curved astragals. The un-ornamented windows have also retained their astragals. The four-bay side elevations, which share pilasters only at the angles, are much simpler in design although the window proportions are similar. These elevations have been stuccoed and lined as ashlar and the rear elevation has been harled, though it is not certain whether this was originally intended.

Although in a dilapidated state, the interior has retained some fine classical features such as ornamental plaster friezes and cornices, door-pieces and low, panelled dadoes to the walls of the main rooms. These are particularly well preserved in the inner hall. The stone stair, with its iron balustrade and hardwood handrail, is approached through an outer hall which has retained a plaster centre-piece to the ceiling. The inner hall is particularly spacious. Some polished marble chimney-pieces have been retained although the flues have been blocked up.

The setting of the building is largely overgrown but originally the house was at the head of an impressive approach drive flanked with mature trees. It is now partly affected by dry rot and is very badly in need of repair and an appropriate new use.

Name:	Carlton House
Address:	15 Snowdon Place, Stirling
Category:	B, in King's Park Conservation Area
Occupier:	Ministry of Defence
Use:	Offices
Holding:	Crown

Carlton House is a sizeable mid-Victorian detached villa, situated in the heart of one of Stirling's most elegant residential areas. Two storeys and basement in height, the house has a stable block and an extensive garden.

The symmetrical three-bay front elevation is built in ashlar with a channelled basement and neatly tooled quoins, and features an unusual porch with Ionic columns modelled on an original design by the French Renaissance architect, Philibert De L'Orme. The entrance is reached by a wide flight of steps oversailing the raised basement. The sophisticated Renaissance detailing is continued around the first-floor central window. The flanking bays have full-height canted windows. The side and rear elevations are less suave. Flanking screen walls with gateways, channelled gate piers and up-swept copes seclude the rear garden.

Internally the house has many fine decorative features, notably in the large hall with its fine Ionic columns, pilasters and moulded ceiling. A pair of plaster heads of owls and rams embellish the seating of the beams.

The sitting room has a panelled ceiling and frieze and a fine mahogany chimney-piece with fluted Ionic columns. The other ground-floor rooms also possess good decoration. A polished black marble chimney-piece and a mahogany chimney-piece with fluted Ionic colonnettes remain in the dining room and ante-room, respectively. The stair-well half-landing window is a stained glass representation of Jeanie Deans, the heroine of Scott's '*The Heart of Midlothian*'. A wide cantilevered stone stair with iron balusters and hardwood handrail leads to the upper-floor bedrooms. These rooms are decorated with simple cornices and most retain plain marble chimney-pieces. All the window ingoes are shuttered and all the doors are panelled, with good architraves. The plainly decorated basement floor is mainly used for cooking and storage but it also houses a billiard room and a small sitting room.

The old single-storey stable block, now used as a garage and garden stores, is constructed in rubble with a slated roof. Traces of former living accommodation survive in the attic loft.

Name:	Stirling Castle
Category:	A, Scheduled Monument in Old Town Conservation Area
Occupier:	Ministry of Defence
Use:	Regimental Museum
Holding:	Crown

Stirling Castle resembles its sister fortress at Edinburgh, not only in its siting on a conspicuous volcanic rock but also in its long history, which is part of the history of Scotland itself. Occupying a site of vital strategic importance, it developed as a principal royal place of strength through the Middle Ages. It was a royal residence from an early date—Alexander I died at Stirling, almost certainly in the Castle, in 1124—and it enjoyed the particular favour of the Stuart Kings. As a strategically central fortress, its defences were strengthened at a time of crisis just after the 1707 Act of Union, and they were to see limited action in 1746 against siege by Prince Charles Edward. Its Palace continued in at least a nominal state of readiness for a Royal visit until 1707 but during the 18th century it was adapted, along with the rest of the Castle's buildings, for military use as the Georgian army took over all the accommodation. The alteration of the ancient architecture culminated in a most unsympathetic conversion of the Great Hall into barrack accommodation about 1800. In reaction to this and other enterprises, an appreciation of the importance of the Castle's buildings as historic architecture began to develop, ultimately leading in 1905 to the transfer of responsibility for the care of the Castle, as an ancient monument, to HM Office of Works.

As at Edinburgh Castle, the full visual impact of Stirling Castle lies in the accumulation of its parts, both buildings and defences, on its precipitous site. Stirling, however, has the distinction of possessing a group of Royal buildings which, individually, have the highest possible place in the architectural history of Scotland: James IV's Great Hall of c. 1500 (where the unhappy consequences of the barracks conversion are being unpicked from the ancient fabric), James V's richly detailed Renaissance Palace with its intact internal plan of 1540–42, and the Chapel Royal which appears in the form given to it in 1594 for James VI. Important defensive works include the new front and gatehouse (1500–1510) and the artillery fortifications beyond it (1709–14).

Reference: Stirling Castle guidebook (H.M.S.O.)
Footnote: Stirling Castle was formerly in the care of PSA as an ancient monument but since 1978 it has been in the care of the Secretary of State for Scotland and is maintained on his behalf by the Ancient Monuments Division of the Scottish Development Department. P.S.A. however, retains a responsibility for the areas used by the Army.

North elevation of the Palace.

SDD Ancient Monuments Division

CENTRAL/STIRLING

Name:	Sheriff Court
Address:	Viewfield Place, Stirling
Category:	B
Occupier:	Scottish Courts Administration
Use:	Court House
Holding:	Freehold

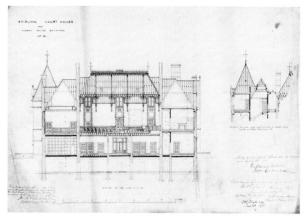

Scottish Record Office

Stirling Sheriff Court was built between 1874-76 to a design by Thomas Brown and executed by Wardrop and Reid. The style adopted is a mixture of late Gothic and early Renaissance. A matching two-storey west extension was added in 1912.

The main elevations are finished in smooth ashlar. The original symmetrical facade has a central entrance porch and advanced gabled wings with set-back corbelled angle turrets. The porch is Tudor-arched with elaborate crocketted decoration rising into the arcaded balustrade, the latter having panelled and crowned terminals over mock gargoyles.

The tall vertical sash windows are either two or three-light with stone mullions and transoms. The first-floor window pediments of the advanced bays and the two windows flanking the central bay are elaborately decorated with scrolls and central cartouches. The upper dormer windows are integral with the parapet and have bold, shaped pedimented heads. The advanced gables are crow-stepped with pitched roofs. The piended platform roof is topped with elaborate iron cresting.

Linked to the rear of the main building is the now disused prison and derelict warden's house now proposed for demolition.

Internally, the accommodation consists of two Court Rooms, offices, cell block, caretaker's flat and a substantial basement. The main Court Room is impressive with a fine single hammer-beam roof, original seating and a remarkable hooded canopy above the judge's bench. Cornices tend to be plain but the coved ceiling in the smaller court has a dentil frieze. A similar ceiling exists above the main open-well staircase.

The disused jail to the rear is two-storey, with a gallery constructed in cast-iron. Lighting is by a lantern-light running the full length of the gallery.

| Region | DUMFRIES AND GALLOWAY |
| District | ANNANDALE AND ESKDALE |

Name:	Highburn House
Address:	20 Scotts Street, Annan
Category:	B
Occupier:	Department of Health and Social Security
	Department of Employment
Use:	Offices
Holding:	Crown

It would be interesting to know for whom this very pleasant three-bay, two-storey house was built early in the 19th century. It is sited on the eastern edge of Annan, beside the main road to Carlisle, and must originally have been fairly isolated. There are still fields at the bottom of the garden.

The house is built of dressed, stugged, random coursed red sandstone, cream-painted at the front, with dressed margins, cornice and door-piece emphasised in warm brown. Sash and case windows retain astragals on both floors. The door has a simple, classical door-piece. A slightly lower, two-storey rear wing, added c. 1890, has a diamond gable-head chimney-stack. Also at the back of the house is a curious single-room building of brick with a small porch and its own pitched and slated roof.

The plainly detailed interior still has the feel of a home, despite the usual alterations to make offices. The previous owners kept their wine in a low ceilinged basement, where the stone racks are still visible.

| Region | DUMFRIES AND GALLOWAY |
| District | NITHSDALE |

Address:	44 Buccleuch Street, Dumfries
Category:	B
Occupier:	Department of Employment
Use:	Offices
Holding:	Crown

This was the main G.P.O. until the 1950's. The former ground-floor public office still exists above a basement of stores and small offices.

Dated 1887 in a panel over the entrance, the building has an asymmetrical two-storey street frontage, of red sandstone. Only the broad, projecting gabled entrance bay is of real note. It is linked to the adjacent Sheriff Court House (q.v.) by a banal modern infill section, faced in sandstone. Nothing of interest exists inside.

Name:	Sheriff Court
Address:	40, 42 Buccleuch Street, Dumfries
Category:	B
Occupier:	Scottish Courts Administration
Use:	Court House
Holding:	Crown

The architect David Rhind was commissioned to design Dumfries' new Court House in 1863. It is recorded that £6,069 was provided by the Government and £6,967 by the County, making a total building cost of £13,715. The difference in balance may have been accounted for by the architect's fee. These substantial funds account for the boldly detailed Baronial design. Built in squared red sandstone rubble with polished dressings, it was completed in 1866, and since then it has dominated Buccleuch Street. The asymmetrical front elevation has a prominent central tower, corbelled over the round-arched entrance. Smaller turrets clasp the angles and all have copper-covered conical caps. The elevation displays all the decorative trappings of the Baronial style; dummy cannons, rope mouldings, corbels and bold string courses. A taller, parapetted rear tower further emphasises the romantic massing of the building.

Internally, the Court House is largely unaltered, although the basement cells are no longer used as such, and in the large Courtroom the area under the gallery has been converted to house more witnesses' rooms and a temporary cell. This Court has an elaborate ribbed and coffered ceiling. To improve the acoustics, the walls are hung with curtains. Natural light enters only from windows behind the bench, the roof-lights having been covered in with an acoustic-tiled false ceiling. A fireplace near the Sheriff's seat can only have been intended for his benefit if he walked over to it, being inappropriately domestic in scale. The original "pews" are still used as the public seats. The other original fittings are little altered.

On the top floor is another smaller Courtroom with its original fittings. On both upper levels there are rooms for the Law Library, Sheriffs and Witnesses.

Reference: *Dumfries and Galloway Standard* 1863.

Address:	114 English Street, Dumfries
Category:	C (S)
Occupier:	Ministry of Defence
Use:	Careers and Information Office
Holding:	Leased

No. 114 is the west end of a pleasant two-storey, four-door, red sandstone domestic terrace. One of the doors has been built up. Unfortunately, another door has been removed and a somewhat inappropriate shop frontage inserted. One decently carved door opening remains at no. 118. The frontage is divided horizontally by a double string course and finished with a neat moulded cornice.

The interior is of no particular interest.

Name:	Queensberry House
Address:	147–151 High Street, Dumfries
Category:	C (S)
Occupier:	H.M. Customs and Excise (second floor only)
Use:	Offices
Holding:	Leased

H.M. Customs and Excise occupy the top floor of this undistinguished pair of three-storey, four-bay buildings, listed for their appropriate scale in the High Street rather than for their individual architectural merit. The buildings are united at ground-floor level by a modern bank frontage, designed regardless of the upper storeys. Above ground floor, the left-hand section is a plain red sandstone elevation of the 1950's. The right-hand facade is the best part of the group. This is a late Victorian design, also in local red sandstone ashlar, with pronounced individual cornices to the first-floor windows and a deep, bracketted eaves cornice. All the upper windows have been refitted with modern metal casements.

There is nothing of distinction internally.

Name:	Old Custom House
Address:	139 Irish Street, Dumfries
Category:	B
Occupier:	Manpower Services Commission
Use:	Offices
Holding:	Crown

A substantial early 19th century town house, built by Thomas Goldie, a Dumfries lawyer. The name "Old Custom House" may perpetuate an error, since old maps of the town show another Custom House further south in Irish Street. The house was the office of a bank before it was taken over by the Ministry of Labour in the 1930's. A brick extension has been built over part of the garden at the rear, and a further extension joins it to the neighbouring property to the south.

It is a tall, three-storey house with a raised basement, built in tooled ashlar, now painted. The centre bay is advanced and pedimented, with a clumsy mid-nineteenth century porch disguising the original entrance. The rusticated quoins, architraves and modillioned cornice are now over-emphasised by an unfortunate contrasting paint scheme. Narrow screen walls, two storeys high project north and south. Possibly, these once formed part of a courtyard.

Internally, the house consists of basement kitchens, with the principal rooms on the ground and first floors flanking a central timber stair. This stair, with some delicately worked pilasters and an archway in the entrance hall, is about all that survives of the original internal detailing, although more may remain above inserted ceilings.

Name:	Shambellie House and Lodge
Address:	New Abbey
Category:	B
Occupier:	Royal Scottish Museum
Use:	Costume Museum
Holding:	Crown

By the standards of many 19th century mansions, and certainly of those designed by its architect, David Bryce, this is a modest house, lacking adjacent stables or outhouses. It was designed in 1854 and redesigned, on a reduced scale, in 1856 for William Stewart, whose monogram and crest are carved on a panel above the entrance and also appear on the weather vane. The house is built of local coursed grey granite rubble with red sandstone dressings. The slates, as usual in the south-west of Scotland, come from Cumbria across the Solway. The external details are typical of Bryce, including corbelled turrets, a circular stair tower, canted windows and crow-stepped gables. The attics were completed by James Barbour of Dumfries in 1866. The planning is also typical of Bryce's design philosophy, derived from William Burn and based on the separation of public, family and servants' quarters. Only the circular stair, used by the servants, provides access to all floors, the timber main stair leading from ground to first floor only. The ground floor, reached by a shallow flight of steps within the front porch, consists of Library, drawing and dining rooms, all fairly small, which now house the collection of costumes gathered by Mr. Charles Stewart and gifted, together with the house, to the Royal Scottish Museum. The original fireplaces were replaced in the early 20th century. When first built, these rooms must have had a fine view of Sweetheart Abbey nearby, but this is now only visible over the trees, from the first-floor bedrooms. A first-floor bathroom has a primitive shower, operated by opening a plug in a slate water-tank above.

The house which can barely be glimpsed from the road, is surrounded by mature beechwoods and nearby is a famous plantation of Scots pine, planted in 1775–1780. At the entrance is a small gate lodge designed by Barbour in 1864. It is built in rock-faced granite and has prominent crow-stepped gables, latticed windows and a tiny turret on its north-east corner.

References: Mr. David Bryce 1803–1876: (Fiddes and Rowan). The Creation of Shambellie (A. Rowan).

22

| Region | DUMFRIES AND GALLOWAY |
| District | STEWARTRY |

Name:	Sheriff Court
Address:	High Street, Kirkcudbright
Category:	C (S), in Kirkcudbright Conservation Area
Occupier:	Scottish Courts Administration
Use:	Court House
Holding:	Crown

This imposing castellated Court House was constructed in 1868, replacing rudimentary facilities in the Tolbooth (q.v.). Its designer is unrecorded, but may well have been David Rhind, architect of the Dumfries Court House. The Court Room interiors at Dumfries and Kirkcudbright look very much alike. The architect had to incorporate an existing twin-towered cell block of 1815, at the rear of the site, and insert the whole into an area of the town consisting mainly of two-storey domestic buildings. The result, in terms of townscape, is somewhat overwhelming. The cost was £8,583.

The Court House is built in a greenish whinstone, used locally on other buildings, including the nearby Tolbooth. Red sandstone is used for dressings and the castellated parapets. The shallow, two-storey High Street facade is symmetrical, five bays wide with a three-storey central tower incorporating a three-window canted oriel. This front acts as a screen for the main rectangular courtroom block, set back from the street frontage with its own castellated parapet and hipped roof. Behind this, off-centre, rises the older, six-storey cell block tower, with a higher corner turret, which looks as if it might have been inspired by a mediaeval parish church in Devon or Cornwall.

The plan is asymmetrical, although the main entrance from the High Street is under the central oriel window. A staircase rises to the left and the former suite of Fiscal's offices on the right is now a Public Library with its own entrance. To the rear, in the older part of the building, is the Keeper's house, still in domestic use. Over the Library is the large Courtroom, entered by a lobby, with adjacent Sheriff's room and witnesses' rooms. All these are virtually unchanged. In the spacious upper hall hang two portraits of the Maxwells of Munches, a father and son, who, between them, served as Conveners of the Stewartry of Kirkcudbright for over 70 years. The Courtroom itself is lofty, with an impressive, elaborately decorated, coved and panelled ceiling. The floor is tiered for the public seating. The pine fittings, including the doors are original throughout, with only minor alteration. The tower and rooms above the Keeper's house are now used for storage.

References: Maxwell's Guide to the Stewartry of Kirkcudbright ed. 1873 (and subsequent editions).

Name:	Tolbooth
Address:	High Street, Kirkcudbright
Category:	A, Scheduled Monument in Kirkcudbright Conservation Area
Occupiers:	Department of Agriculture, & Fisheries and H.M. Coastguard
Use:	Offices and Storage
Holding:	Leased

The Tolbooth, with its unusual circular spire and pyramidal corner finials, terminates the north-south limb of the High Street. It is the focal point of this picturesque street, lined by pleasant houses, one or two of which are contemporary. Building began c. 1580. Alterations and additions were made in 1591, 1625 and 1751. According to tradition, it was built partly of stone robbed from Dundrennan Abbey, which became Crown Property in 1621. Two bells in the tower, dated 1646 and 1724, still strike the hours, but the original clock is now in the Stewartry Museum. The fully-rigged ship weather vane is said to commemorate the Battle of Trafalgar. The town cross originally stood in front of the Tolbooth, but the upper part has now been placed at the top of the fore-stair to the tower, leaving the base in the middle of the High Street with a lamp post clamped to it. A 19th century fountain once formed part of the base to the same stair, but the stone commemorating it is now almost illegible.

The rest of the Tolbooth consists of a long, three-storey range, narrow in breadth. The thick rubble walls have roll-moulded details to most of the windows. These still have housings for iron grilles, a reminder of the Tolbooth's role as the town gaol.

The interior is entirely modern, except for two vaulted rooms at the west end of the building. The slit window and evidence of a heavy, hung door suggest that the upper room was once a cell. The ground-level room is now a store, entered straight off the street. The present entrance to the upper levels is immediately next to the vaulted rooms. It leads to a modern stair and totally renovated offices, with small windows to north and south. There is evidence of a moulded surround to an older door in the centre of the High Street elevation. At the north-west corner of the building hang the "jougs". These primitive instruments of justice were used as recently as 1803, when they were fastened to the neck of Jane Maxwell, condemned for witchcraft and sorcery.

References: R.C.A.H.M.S. Kirkcudbright.
Dumfries & Galloway Antiquarian Society 1896–97.

| Region | DUMFRIES AND GALLOWAY |
| District | WIGTOWN |

Name:	Brewery House
Address:	23 King Street, Newton Stewart
Category:	B
Occupier:	Customs and Excise
Use:	Offices
Holding:	Crown

Until 1974, this modest early 19th century house was the home of the manager for the brewery, which occupies a narrow strip of ground between the road and the River Cree, less than a mile north of the town. The adjoining brewery building has been converted into flats, and the house now provides offices for H.M. Customs and Excise.

Because of the fall-away of the site, the house has two storeys to the front and three to the rear. Externally, the three-bay house is built of dressed Creetown granite, and is virtually unchanged. The front elevation is enlivened by a Doric portico, a simply moulded eaves cornice and scrolled skews. The timber central stair is unspoiled, with cast-iron balusters and a hardwood handrail from ground to first floor. There is a simpler, all-timber stair to the two-room attic. The public rooms still retain their simple cornices but all other original details have disappeared.

Address:	22 Victoria Street, Newton Stewart
Category:	C (S), in Newton Stewart Conservation Area
Occupier:	Department of Employment
Use:	Offices
Holding:	Crown

Originally an early 19th century house, this building stands in the centre of Newton Stewart in a terrace of houses and shops. It was later adapted as a bank, when the ground-floor windows were given their present appearance. The ground floor is built of bull-faced granite, the first floor and angles being of squared dressed granite with whinstone snecks in each vertical course, a local masonry characteristic. The attic has been enlarged by an assertive mansard.

The building is undistinguished internally, and has been listed for its group value rather than for individual architectural quality.

Name:	Sheriff Court
Address:	Lewis Street, Stranraer
Category:	B, in Stranraer Conservation Area
Occupier:	Scottish Courts Administration
Use:	Court House
Holding:	Crown

Designed by James Maitland Wardrop, of the Edinburgh firm of Brown and Wardrop, Stranraer Court House was built in 1872–3. The frontage lines up with substantial detached villas to the south and a distinctive contemporary church to the north. The depth of the site was also restricted and space had to be found not only for a Courtroom and attached offices but also for a Town Hall. By planning both Hall and Court at first floor, the maximum advantage was gained, but the space between them was limited, so that the main stair and first-floor landing are restricted and rather mean. The building is hybrid Tudor Gothic and Baronial in style, constructed in bull-faced, coursed masonry with ashlar dressings. Three equal, crow-stepped gables, two of which support thin Tudor chimney-stacks, give the main frontage a lively silhouette. The principal rooms on the first floor are lit by tall, plainly detailed lancet windows, arranged in groups of three in the front and end gables. Tucked away on the north elevation and hidden in long views by the neighbouring church, is a slender bell tower, square at the base with a pretty octagonal belfry and stone spire.

This sensitive detailing continues inside. The original Courtroom, well modernised in 1981, has a pleasant Tudor Gothic plaster ceiling. The Town Hall, which occupied the whole frontage at first floor, has recently been completely transformed internally in order to gain another smaller Courtroom and ancillary rooms, as well as rooms for the Sheriffs. The ceiling of the hall can still be seen from a small gallery.

The main stair has cast-iron, rather domestic, balusters with more elaborate wooden ones to the landing. At ground level are the Sheriff Clerk and Fiscal's offices, and what was formerly a Custodian's house, next to the bell tower. This house, which has since been used as offices, is now empty but is due for improvement in the near future. Two cells remain, with their original steel doors. A modern escape stair was added to the rear in 1981.

The cost was £7,000; good value for money in 1874.

I. Shambellie House, Dumfries and Galloway.

II. Stirling Castle, from the West.

SDD Ancient Monuments Division

III.   Stirling Sheriff Court, Principal Court Room.

IV.   Tulliallan Castle, Fife.

Region	FIFE
District	DUNFERMLINE

Name:	Sheriff Court
Address:	79 High Street, Dunfermline
Category:	A, in Abbey Conservation Area
Occupier:	Scottish Courts Administration
Use:	Court House
Holding:	Crown

Situated on the south side of Dunfermline High Street the Court House, and in particular its steeple, is one of the town's principal landmarks. The building has variously been known as the 'Guildhall', 'Spire Hotel', 'Cross Buildings' and 'County Buildings' and was erected by the Fraternity of Guildry in Dunfermline as a potential County headquarters for Fife. Cupar was chosen, however, as the County Town and it was only in 1848 that the building was taken over and adapted as the Court House for the western part of the 'Kingdom'. The main structure was completed to the design of Archibald Elliot in 1809, in a

handsome classical style, with the main facade constructed in ashlar, rock-faced in the basement and smooth above. The spire was added in 1810 but doors, windows and floors were not fitted until 1816, after the Guildry's financial troubles had forced its sale to Alexander Robertson. It was leased and fitted out as the Spire Hotel in 1820, continuing as such until becoming the Court House in the late 1840s.

Three storeys high, the Court House has a central two-storey advanced pedimented section housing the main entrance, with an arched Venetian window above. The elegant 132 ft. spire rises in stages behind the pediment. The wings are three bays wide, with an arcaded, rusticated ground-floor frontage, architraved sash and case windows with cornices at first floor and lower, more simply detailed windows above. Located to the right of the entrance is the 'B' listed Mercat Cross, formerly positioned in the centre of the High Street and re-erected here in 1868. The west elevation to Guildhall Street takes up the slope of the street with a basement, incorporating a shop. The ground floor at High Street level is treated as an open arcade with a wrought-iron balustrade, one bay of which leads into a central courtyard finished in granite setts.

There is accommodation for the Sheriff Clerk on the ground floor and for the Procurator Fiscal above. A former caretaker's flat occupies the second floor. The old police cells and stores are at basement level. Internally the building has been much altered. A central stone stair with cast-iron balustrade and plain timber handrail leads to all floors. The building contains two Courtrooms, one of which has been fully modernised. The rear Courtroom is, however, substantially unaltered with bench seating, a timber dado and heavy moulded skirtings. New court accommodation is being built in Dunfermline and is due for completion in 1983. No new use has yet been found for the existing building.

References: Royal Dunfermline. A Historical Guide and Pictorial Souvenir. ("Press" Office, Dunfermline).
Old Dunfermline (Robertson).
Clarke's Guide to Dunfermline and its Antiquities.

Name:	Hilton Farmhouse and Steading
Address:	Hilton, near Rosyth
Category:	C(S)
Occupier:	Ministry of Defence
Use:	Farm (Tenant)
Holding:	Crown

Farmhouse

The two-storey and attic house at Hilton farm, built around 1825, is fairly typical of the good quality late Georgian farmhouses built in Fife at this period. It is solidly built of dressed rubble stonework, harled on the rear elevation, with a slated pitched roof. The frontage is three bays wide. The ground-floor windows have architraves with cornices and all the windows, including the attic windows in the gables, are sash and case. The anta doorpiece contains a panelled double door and a diamond-glazed fanlight.

The internal vestibule door and screen is glazed, with a fanlight. On the ground floor, the dining room has a moulded cornice and panelled wood dado with panelled shutters to the window ingoes, a classical wooden chimney-piece and glazed cupboards. Most of these features are repeated in the first-floor drawing room. A neat geometric staircase with cantilevered stone stairs, wrought-iron balusters and hardwood handrail gives access to the upper floor. A small moulded cornice neatly finishes the junction of stair soffit and wall.

The four small attic rooms are reached by a curved stone stair with iron balustrade.

Some recent harled additions have been made at ground floor, to the rear of the main building.

Steading

A range of utilitarian farm buildings, built about 1825 and consisting of animal pens and storage on the ground floor with grain lofts over and a hexagonal horsemill adjacent on the east side. The main outbuildings are very well constructed in rubble stonework with flat-arched openings to the ground floor and milling area. The low-pitched roof to these buildings is slate covered. The horsemill is constructed of a low rubble wall with a roof of red pantiles. This part of the Steading was severely damaged by fire in June 1982.

None of the original machinery remains, but there is still sufficient evidence to visualise the spindle and drive-shaft mechanism.

Name:	Pitreavie Castle and Dovecot
Categories:	Castle B
	Dovecot B, Scheduled Monument
Occupier:	Ministry of Defence
Use:	Offices (Castle)
Holding:	Crown

Castle

The Castle at first appears to be almost entirely 19th century Baronial, but it incorporates an early 17th century tower house, visible on the north elevation as a U-plan, twin-gabled facade, with corbelled circular stair towers in the re-entrant angles. The original main entrance remains in the west wing, set into bold bolection mouldings with a pediment enclosing floral designs and the initials SHW with a star, the family crest, at the apex. The initials are those of Henry Wardlaw, created a Baron in 1634, the son of Sir Henry Wardlaw who was Chamberlain to Queen Anne and who was given charge of Dunfermline Palace when James II ascended the English throne. The entrance in the opposite wing led only to a vaulted cellar and has since been converted to a window. Gun-loops, to protect the entrances, survive. The house has undergone much alteration and extension, principally in 1885 when C. G. H. Kinnear of Kinnear and Peddie was architect for a major

c. 1890

recasting of the house. A new principal entrance was formed in the east wing of the north elevation, to which was added a flat-roofed, balustraded porch containing a finely carved pediment with the date 1885 and the initials HB, those of the new owner, H. Beveridge, a successful Kirkcaldy merchant. A large six-light stained-glass window was introduced in the gable above, to light the main staircase. This window has stone mullions and an ornamental pediment. Various original windows on the inner faces of the wings have been blocked.

The symmetrical south elevation was completely rebuilt in 1885. It faces over the garden with views towards the Firth of Forth. The two gabled bays, reflecting the original 17th century examples on the north front, are linked at ground and first floors by three bays articulated with engaged composite columns and forming a balustraded balcony to the central second-floor windows. The canted windows in the ground and first floors of the gabled bays are typically late Victorian. A tall, central chimney stack with four attached flues on a panelled plinth replaces the former boldly shaped wallhead gable and apex stack, a comparatively rare early Renaissance detail. The detailing used above the first floor is of typically Scottish Renaissance proportion, well displayed in the pedimented dormers and attic windows. A lower, three-storey wing in the same style projects to the east.

Internally the arrangements date from 1885. Of the original building all that can be seen is the entrance hall in the west wing, the iron yett and the mouldings on the edges of the newel. The stairs have been removed. The mouldings continue over the arch supporting the upper flight and have sophisticated chamfer stops. Immediately to the south lies the old kitchen, with the huge chimney arch still in situ, exhibiting an unusually fine array of masons' marks (also to be seen on the original south west quoins). The kitchen was converted to a gun room in the late 19th century, when it was panelled. Above the ground floor the planning and detailing are all Kinnear's. In the original house all the rooms either opened off the turnpike or were reached through each other. The social requirements of the 19th century dictated more independence, with the result that corridors link the wings at first and second floors. The 19th century grand stair rises in the east wing and has low-relief plaster decoration on the first-floor landing ceiling leading into the corridor which is barrel vaulted with plaster ribs and decoration. The L-plan drawing room occupies the south-west corner, with a bay window to the south and an inserted oriel to the west. The room is partly panelled and has an elaborate chimney-piece with brass fittings, excellent tiles and a handsome pilastered overmantel with shelves and niches; a deep frieze with putti and swags encircles the room. The library occupies the remaining two central bays and has another elaborate oak chimney-piece and good, built-in oak shelves with a decorative floral cove above. John Duncan painted two panels, representing Orpheus, for this room in 1897. They have now been covered over. The final room on this floor in the original building lies at the head of the stairs and is now known as the chapel. Panelled in oak it has improving texts in the frieze—"Whatsoever thy hand findeth to do, do it with thy might", "Except the Lord build the house they labour in vain that build it", "Now abideth faith, hope and charity but the greatest of these is charity"; this room has another good chimney-piece with tiles very like the work of William de Morgan. A dining room was added in the eastern addition; this is partly panelled and has a buffet built in to one end. The other end now links through to the modern accommodation. Above the first floor the rooms are plain and only the turnpike stairs survive from the original house. In the attic a billiard room was created with a large south-facing roof-light. Some partitions have been inserted, most noticeably in the original drawing room and in the attic but earlier details have scarcely been disturbed. A poorly designed modern mess has been added at the east.

Dovecot
This good example of the square, lean-to type with crow-stepped flank walls stands north-east of the Castle. It is harled with a slated roof, recently restored. There are nine entry holes in the roof-slope and a projecting, rat-deterrent string-course.

References: Castellated and Domestic Architecture vol. VII p.537 (MacGibbon & Ross).
(plan showing original state).
R.C.A.H.M.S. Inventory, Fife, Kinross and Clackmannan.
Royal Scottish Academy 1887.

Name:	Rosyth Castle and Dovecot
Address:	H.M. Dockyard, Rosyth
Category:	A, Scheduled Monuments
Occupier:	Vacant
Use:	Monuments
Holding:	Crown

Castle

In 1428, James I confirmed Sir David Stewart in his barony of Rosyth, which remained with this family until the failure of the male line towards the end of the 17th century.

Due to extensive land reclamation schemes, the Castle, which formerly occupied an island site accessible at low tide, is now wholly within the Admiralty Dockyard. The Castle consists of a tall tower of late 15th century date built of large squared rubble blocks, to which a substantial courtyard range was added on the west in the 16th and 17th centuries creating domestic and service accommodation. This later work is now very ruinous.

The rectangular tower, with its projecting stair turret, has vaulted ground and first floors with a further storey and a caphouse above. The roof level includes the remains of a parapet walk. The entrance is through an elliptical-arched opening on the south side, adjoining the staircase tower.

Two large windows with dressed mullions and transoms were inserted in the main wall in 1635.

The lower transom on the west side incorporates the inscription I.S.M.N. 1635, for James Stewart of Rosyth and Margaret Napier, his wife. The courtyard entrance, through another elliptical-arched gateway in the north range, is set forward from the main wall face. Above the gateway are two armorial panels. The lower, enclosed by a

R.C.A.H.M.S.

SDD Ancient Monuments Division

plain moulded border, is now wholly illegible. The upper, more elaborately framed, contains the Royal Arms of Scotland ensigned with a crown and the date 1561 within a garland flanked by the initials M (ARIA) R (EGINA), each beneath a crown. Below the garland is a unicorn couchant. It was in August of that year that Queen Mary sailed into the Forth on her return from France. Traces of stairs, large fireplaces and gun-loops can still be seen in the ruined remains.

Dovecot

Probably built in the 16th century, the Dovecot now stands outwith the Dockyard, close to the mainland road north of the Castle. It is roughly six metres square on plan, constructed of rubble stonework. The gables are crow-stepped and all four skew-putts are carved with human heads. The roof is a barrel vault covered with lapped stone slabs. The entrance, which faces north, has a quirked edge-roll at the arris and the lintel bears a now wholly illegible inscription. The south gable has a table off-set as an anti-rat device, and two flight holes. The Dovecot is in an excellent state of preservation.

Reference: R.C.A.H.M.S., Inventory Fife, Kinross and Clackmannan.

Name:	Tulliallan Castle, Blackhall Dovecot and Blackhall Lodge and Gateway
Address:	Kincardine on Forth
Category:	Castle A; Blackhall Dovecot B; Blackhall Lodge and Gateway B
Occupier:	Scottish Police Commission
Use:	Police College
Holding:	Freehold

Tulliallan Castle

On retirement from the Navy after a distinguished career, Admiral Sir George Keith-Elphinstone, created Viscount Keith in 1814, purchased the extensive estates of Tulliallan. This included the medieval Tulliallan Castle, then in a dilapidated condition.

The architect commissioned to design a fashionable replacement was William Atkinson (c.1773–1839), well known as a country house designer and as a pioneer of the Tudor Gothic style of which Tulliallan is a notable example. His best-known comparable Scottish commission was the reconstruction of Scone Palace, Perth, between 1803 and 1812.

Tulliallan Castle was built approximately a decade later between 1818 and 1820. It consists of two symmetrical three-storey battlemented main blocks with emphatic corner turrets and a projecting central tower, flanked by two-storey wings terminated by squat, square towers. The house is constructed in coursed ashlar with a moulded string course below the battlements.

Windows are mainly Georgian sash and case with rectangular hood-moulds but the towers have arched openings and late Gothic tracery.

The mansion is entered through a bold porte-cochere on the north elevation, with a rib-vaulted ceiling. The entrance hall has unfortunately been considerably altered. An original chimney-piece is now surmounted by an oak baronial-style overmantel decorated with the heraldic insignia and motto of the Keith family.

Internally, the only notable rooms are on the ground floor, overlooking the extensive lawns and shrubbery. The library is exceptional for its original fitments, centred on a marble chimney-piece with a fine arch-framed mirror above. The fretted detail over its cornice is continued above the bookcases. The handsome plaster ceiling is rib-vaulted, as are those in the two adjoining lounges. The principal open-well staircase rises through all three floors. It has fine cast-iron balusters, oak newels and handrail. The wall surface is painted to resemble ashlar, possibly the original decorative scheme, and the ceiling is rib-vaulted.

The house and estate were used during the 1939–45 war by the Polish Army and were purchased by 1949 by the Police Commission.

Blackhall Dovecot

This rectangular lean-to late 18th century dovecot forms part of the courtyard of the estate buildings at Blackhall, west of the mansionhouse. It is constructed in rubble with crow-stepped gables and a modern slated roof. It originally housed 596

stone nesting boxes, some of which are now replaced by wooden ones.

Blackhall Lodge and Gateway

This forms the former main entrance from the village of Kincardine. Built in 1908 to designs by Watson & Salmond, the arched gateway is attached to the two-storey lodge, distinctly Jacobean with English characteristics. The gateway itself, an impressive composition with a moulded gothic arch enclosing elaborate wrought-iron gates, is set into substantial masonry walls. A heavily coped parapet, raised at the centre to accommodate a heraldic plaque, is guarded by recumbent lions. Small pedestrian entrances flank the main gateway. The lodge is constructed in smooth coursed ashlar with a slated pitched roof. A two-storey canted bay with an elaborately shaped and scrolled gablehead breaks through the retaining wall. The windows in this bay and elsewhere are leaded casements.

References: *Alloa Journal* 17.6.1962
History of Tulliallan (David Beveridge).

Region	FIFE
District	KIRKCALDY

Name:	Custom House
Address:	Sailor's Walk,
	445 High Street, Kirkcaldy
Category:	A
Occupier:	Customs and Excise
Holding:	Leased

This characteristic 17th century block, possibly incorporating parts of an earlier building, is situated at the eastern end of Kirkcaldy High Street and faces directly across to the Old Harbour. It is reputed to be the oldest house in Kirkcaldy and was scheduled for demolition in the late 1940s. The National Trust for Scotland, with the aid of a grant from the Historic Buildings Council for Scotland and additional funds raised by public appeal, saved the building and restored it for use as office accommodation in the early 1960s. It has an irregular H-plan, with gables projecting to front and rear. The western gable to Sailor's Walk is corbelled out over the ground floor, retains its asymmetrical elevation and has a crow-stepped gable and a wide gable-head chimney-stack. The east gable has symmetrically arranged windows and plain skews. The roofs are pantiled. Before restoration, Sailor's Walk seems to have been rubble-faced, but the walls are now rather blandly harled.

The building was once divided into four dwellings; the East House, the High House, the Garret and the Laigh House. The East House is now occupied by the Customs and Excise on the two upper floors and by a bookshop on the ground floor. The Customs offices are reached by a side entrance from a cobbled lane, which gives access to a stone turnpike stair. Upstairs, a small rear room is finely panelled but the most imposing apartment is the Customs public office which has a painted beam-and-board ceiling. The boards are decorated in the usual style of foliage and the beam edges bear elaborate texts from the Old Testament. Particularly appropriate quotations read 'I will pay my dows (dues) unto the Lord, now in the presence of all his people', and the prayer 'Deliver my soul, O Lord, from Lying Lips and a Deceitful Tongue'. This painted ceiling was revealed beneath later plaster work, now removed. The room is dominated by a large stone fireplace with an inscribed lintel bearing the date 1676 and the initials BW. On the west wall is a stone tablet bearing the Royal Arms of Charles II. This was formerly positioned on the east elevation of the building but was re-sited during restoration. Two further offices are situated at second-floor level, one of which has been sub-divided.

References: National Trust for Scotland Guide (Jonathan Cape). Kirkcaldy's Oldest House—(pamphlet available at Custom House).

Region	FIFE
District	**NORTH EAST FIFE**

Address:	16 St. Catherine Street, Cupar
Category:	B, in Cupar Conservation Area
Occupier:	Department of Agriculture and Fisheries
Use:	Offices
Holding:	Leased

This is one of several similar Georgian-style domestic-scale properties occupying sites on the north side of St. Catherine Street opposite the former Fife County Buildings. It was built after 1820, and includes Bank premises on the ground floor, opening direct from the street. The Manager's house at first-floor level has access from the side. The building continues to operate as a Bank but the first-floor is now leased for the use of Government Veterinary Officers.

The plan is rectangular. The two-storey and attic elevation to St. Catherine Street is symmetrical, with a slightly advanced centre bay containing a delicately designed Roman Doric door-piece. Its cornice continues as a string course across the elevation at first-floor level. The frontage, clasped by broad angle pilasters, is five bays wide. All the first-floor, four-pane sash and case windows have shouldered architraves. The ground-floor windows have lost their original astragals. A deep parapet screens the canted attic dormers. The stonework over the front elevation is finely-dressed ashlar, with a moulded base course at ground-floor level. Access to the former Bank house is through a plain classical archway linking the building to the adjoining Episcopal Church.

Internally, extensive alterations have been made to adapt the upstairs premises for their present use, which includes facilities for animal post-mortems. Some original features remain, including moulded cornices to the ceilings and a centre-piece in the largest room. One polished marble and one painted timber chimney-piece, dado rails, sash and case windows with panelled shutters, panelled doors and moulded architraves also survive. The attic flat has been adapted as ancillary rooms.

Name:	Sheriff Court
Address:	26 St. Catherine Street, Cupar
Category:	B, in Cupar Conservation Area
Occupier:	Scottish Courts Administration
Use:	Court House
Holding:	Crown

The former County Buildings, containing the Sheriff Court, are made up of three sections facing north along St. Catherine Street. Although similar in character, they were all constructed at different dates. The three-storey west section, probably designed by James Gillespie Graham with detail alterations by Robert Hutchison, was built between 1815 and 1817. It is rectangular on plan with a frontage of painted ashlar stonework. The long, symmetrical elevation is punctuated by advanced bays, divided by Roman Doric pilasters above the level of the first floor. The ground-floor stonework is rusticated. The central entrance is emphasised by a fine Roman Doric door-piece with coupled columns at each side. Above it, at first-floor level, is a prominent Venetian window set under a fluted panel between the pilasters. A balustraded parapet over the end bays, linked by a plain parapet, screens the pitched and slated roof. All the windows have retained their astragals. This section, which contains the District Council Chamber, has been extensively altered inside, first by William Burn in 1836, later in 1872 and 1892 and again more recently.

The centre section of the terrace, which contains the Sheriff Court and is probably exclusively Robert Hutchison's work, dates from 1817. It has a five-window frontage, continuing the basic architectural treatment of the west section. The upper part of the elevation is much plainer and there is no parapet above the shallow cornice. Above the ground floor the window astragals have been replaced by plate-glass panes. The upper floors were altered internally by William Burn in 1836 when the Sheriff Court was provided to his design, but the character is consistent throughout. The Court Room has a particularly fine segmentally-arched panelled ceiling, the ribs terminating over Roman Doric pilasters on the walls. Arched pendentives occur between the pilasters at the junction of the walls and ceiling. The painted joinerwork is also of excellent quality, particularly the bench, with its front of prominent fielded panels. The Solicitors' area and the public benches are similar in character. The Library, the Jury and Witnesses' Rooms and the service areas reflect a similar attention to detail. Modern adaptations include new light fittings and an acoustic treatment to the rear wall of the Court Room. The Procurator-Fiscal is accommodated in the rear part of the building.

The east section, designed by Thoms & Wilkie in 1925, is in the ownership of North East Fife District Council. It continues the earlier three-storey design scheme, with rusticated ground floor and dressed ashlar stonework above. The end bays are advanced. They have Roman Doric pilasters at the corners and tripartite windows at first and second-floor levels, with a seven-window frontage between. The entrance on the central axis is emphasised at the first storey by a cornice above the centre window. There is a prominent continuous cornice with a plain parapet above. The stonework is unpainted.

Reference: "Historical Notes and Reminiscences of Cupar"
   Fife Herald.

Address:	22 East Shore, Pittenweem
Category:	B, in Pittenweem Conservation Area
Occupier:	Department of Agriculture and Fisheries
Use:	Offices
Holding:	Leased

The East Shore looks south across the harbour of this picturesque Fife fishing village to the distant Bass Rock, Berwick Law and the Lothians. 22 East Shore was built in the later part of the 19th century as a small two-storey and attic dwelling house, with ground-floor shop, forming part of a seafront terrace of houses and shops. The shop is at present used by the 'Fishermens' Mutual Association' to stock clothes, waterproofs and small items of fishing gear.

The frontage is of ashlar, in long narrow blocks at the first floor. The shop front now has three modern full-height small-paned windows but retains the original panelled door and fanlight.

The two-window first-floor frontage has a single window to the west and a large oriel window, with strong moulded corbelling and slated roof, over the entrance. The pattern is repeated at the attic floor by dormer windows with prominent decorated barge boards. All the windows are sash and case, generally with single-pane upper sashes and two-pane lower sashes. The slated roof has dressed stone skews.

Internally the building is plainly decorated and the shop interior has been drastically altered. The two small Crown offices in the attic are reached through the shop and by a timber winder stair. They have recently been updated and modern doors have been fitted within the original plain architraves.

Address:	3 Queens Gardens, St. Andrews
Category:	B, in St. Andrews Conservation Area
Occupier:	Department of Health and Social Security
Use:	Offices
Holding:	Leased

Queens Gardens is a fine Victorian classical domestic terrace built between 1859 and 1869. The house fronts are varied, but all conform in scale.

No. 3 was built in 1860 to designs by William Scott. It is two storeys high, with an attic, and is constructed in ashlar stonework. It has a pitched slated roof and slate-cheeked, pedimented dormer windows. The frontage is symmetrical, with a central entrance and a consoled door-piece combined with a balustraded balcony above. On the ground floor, there are two single windows on each side of the door-piece. These have plain surrounds with moulded panels beneath the cills.

The upper floor, divided from the ground floor by a band course, is more ornate. Tripartite windows flank a single central window. All are linked by a moulded cill course and have finely moulded architraves. A deep, moulded cornice boldly defines the eaves line. The entrance leads through a two-leaf door, with a fanlight above, to a vestibule with a glazed inner screen.

Internally, the house has been converted to offices, retaining the original character and decoration, except on the ground floor where poor quality office partitions have been introduced. All the main rooms on ground and first floors have good cornices, panelled doors and architraves. Chimney-pieces of plain marble or timber remain in all rooms, their fireplaces being blocked up. Window ingoes are shuttered or panelled. The stone stair to the first floor is geometric with an iron balustrade and hardwood handrail. The wheel stair from the first floor to the attic is wooden, and a fine example of its type.

Reference: St. Andrews Architects, (R. G. Cant).

ABERDEEN

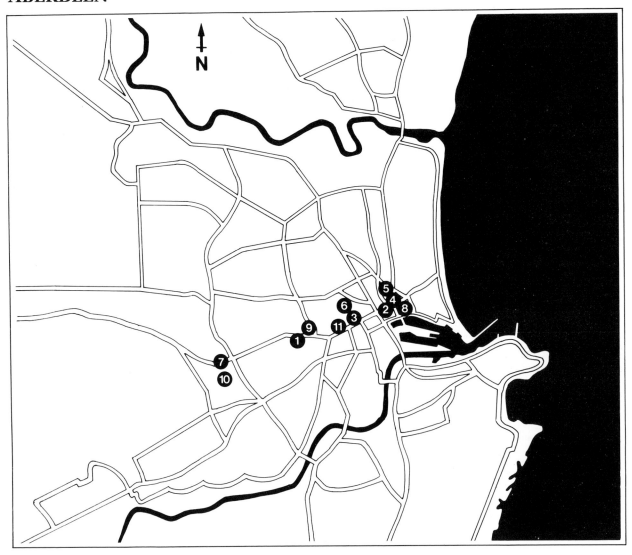

1. 34 Albyn Place
2. Sheriff Court House, Castle Street
3. 3 Golden Square
4. 27 King Street
5. 29 King Street
6. 23 North Silver Street
7. 226 Queens Road
8. 35 Regent Quay
9. 4 Rubislaw Terrace
10. St Lukes, Viewfield Road
11. 377 Union Street

Region	GRAMPIAN
District	CITY OF ABERDEEN

Address:	34 Albyn Place, Aberdeen
Category:	B, in Conservation Area 4
Occupier	Health and Safety Executive
Use:	Offices
Holding:	Leased

Albyn Place was laid out by Archibald Elliot in 1819, as a westward continuation of Union Street. The building development on the south is separated from the roadway by front gardens set behind an avenue of trees. Much of the original character of the area has remained, although these large detached mansion houses, built in the first half of the 19th century for the mercantile classes of the city, are now used for office and other non-residential uses.

Set in its own grounds, no. 34 is a classically proportioned detached mansion house dating from c. 1840. The street elevation is crisply framed by an entablature supported by panelled pilaster strips. The basic granite masonry is picked and built to regular courses with contrasting architectural details in ashlar, giving an overall refinement and balance to the design. The central entrance, reached by a short flight of steps, has a pilastered door-piece with a segmental pediment.

The pedimented tripartite windows on each side of the entrance are supported on volute brackets and have dressed margins continued below as apron panels. The central doorway has a larger, elliptical pediment. The upper-floor casement windows have projecting moulded architraves with small-pane astragals in the upper sash and vertical tripartite divisions below.

The plan of the interior accords with the symmetrical fenestration. The axial entrance hall leads to a stairway at the rear linking the upper floor with the basement. On the ground floor, the main public rooms flank the entrance and are noteworthy for the enriched classical detailing of the frieze and cornice mouldings which extend into the door architraves. The pine stairway is lit by a circular-headed, geometrical stained and painted glass window, seen to advantage from the hallway and entrance.

The building has suffered from the pressure of office development in this part of Aberdeen. A large single-storey extension has been added to the rear elevation, on the site of the original garden. At the front the garden has been hard-surfaced within the original low boundary walls. The ground-floor interior has been altered by sub-division of rooms and the main entrance is partitioned by a screen enclosing the stairway. The original fine quality of this house nevertheless remains very much in evidence.

Name:	Sheriff Court
Address:	Castle Street, Aberdeen
Category:	A, in Conservation Area 2
Occupier:	Scottish Courts Administration
Use:	Court House
Holding:	Crown

The Aberdeen Sheriff Court and Town House forms part of the magnificent block of civic buildings designed by the Edinburgh architects Peddie & Kinnear and built between 1868–74 to replace the previous Town House and Court House on this site. It resulted from a limited competition entered by three firms of architects.

Situated on the north side of Castle Street at its junction with Broad Street, the building is impressive both for its elevational treatment and for its dominant tower, which forms one of the most important city landmarks. The building accommodates the Sheriff Court, part of the City administration and the Society of Aberdeen Advocates. At the east end it incorporates the Tolbooth tower of 1629, a delicately detailed Scottish Renaissance timber and lead steeple. The complex was built at a cost of £50,000 and is constructed in Kemnay granite with an ashlar finish. The older Tolbooth was partly re-faced in squared sandstone in 1866 but its original, rougher east wall can still be seen from Lodge Walk, at the rear.

The style is the Scottish Baronial typical of Peddie and Kinnear's public buildings, with Flemish and French medieval influences, particularly notable in the corbelled tourelles and

turrets. Each facade is four storeys high, with a heavy semi-circular arcade on the ground floor beneath an arcaded gallery in front of the first floor. The arches are supported on thickset columns with bases and capitals. On the Union Street side, a mezzanine floor is lit by circular windows within the spandrels. A dominant double string course separates the two upper floors from those beneath, supplemented by a zig-zag string course below the square-headed fourth-floor windows. The main elevations are surmounted by projecting cornices and parapets. Tiny barge-boarded pointed dormer windows are set into the steeply pitched slated roof. Massive chimney-heads with gabletted copes and conical turret roofs are dominant features of the roof line. The massive square tower at the junction of the elevations is approximately 200 feet in height. It is embellished with turrets at each corner of the belfry stage, linked by corbelled parapets and is surmounted by a steeply pitched roof with bold gabled panels containing clock faces. The tower culminates in a decorative, crocketted leaded spire.

The main public rooms are at first-floor level with general offices and ancillary accommodation on the ground floor. The Town House, which also originally served the County Council administration, is entered through a circular-headed archway in the base of the tower. The entrance hall is tiled, and at the centre of the stair-well is a very grand marble statue of Queen Victoria by Alexander Brodie, originally at the

corner of St. Nicholas and Union Streets and removed here in 1888. The wide, pen-checked circular stairway is lit by armorial stained glass and photographs of former Provosts line the wall. The civic public rooms are behind the Castle Street facade. The most impressive of these is the Town and County Hall, 40 feet long by 25 feet wide with a timber hammerbeam roof and a panel-fronted gallery along one side. Adjoining this is the County Committee Room, a reception room of similar proportions with a fine ribbed plaster ceiling. The Society of Aberdeen Advocates' accommodation is also highly impressive. The reception rooms and ground-floor dining room are linked by a wide timber staircase entered between a pair of Corinthian columns. The first-floor library lies behind the Broad Street facade. These interiors still display their original decoration.

The Sheriff Court occupies the east end of the building, with its entrance in the centre of the Castle Street facade. A grand stairway rises up two flights to a landing from which the Sheriff Court is entered. Oversailing the main stairway is a gallery or bridge constructed behind the mezzanine, reached by a subsidiary double stairway, with plain sandstone parapets, which rises on each side of the main staircase. The ceiling over the vestibule is groin-vaulted, the ribs having foliate bosses at the intersections. The ceiling of the foyer, supported on foliage brackets, is formed of panels of diagonal timber lining within a framework of moulded timber beams. The walls are plaster-finished, with dressed sandstone margins and quoins. The foyer is lit by a tripartite window embellished with armorial stained glass incorporating the Royal insignia. The ceiling over the approach to the Sheriff Court is coffered, the beams resting on moulded brackets over pilasters. The dark varnished pine doors are four-panelled with panelled ingoes and architraves. The Principal Sheriff Court is square on plan with a raked floor. The public gallery is panel-fronted and supported by cast-iron columns. This Courtroom is lit by a series of high-level square-headed windows separated by moulded plaster panels. A high matchboarded dado on each wall incorporates the door-pieces, within which are set narrow dark-varnished panelled doors. The ceiling is coffered and coved at the perimeter, with beams supported on scroll brackets. The remaining three courtrooms have recently been modernised and lack any features of special interest.

References: Annals of Aberdeen 1818 (Kennedy)
        History of Aberdeen 1893 (Robbie)
        Aberdeen City Archivist—Record drawings available
        New and Old Aberdeen 1882 (Alec Smith)
        Aberdeen Journal, July 7th 1896, June 10th 1863, November 5th 1862
        Aberdeen Daily Journal, May 2nd 1905.

Address:	3 Golden Square, Aberdeen
Category:	B, in Conservation Area 2
Occupier:	Manpower Services Commission
Use:	Offices
Holding:	Leased

Golden Square was a development of the Hammermen Corporation of the Incorporated Trades of Aberdeen, and was laid out as a residential square by 1810. Building did not commence, however, until about 1820. The layout and design may have been by Archibald Simpson, but there seems to be no firm evidence for this. During the 19th century, residential use was gradually displaced by a predominance of professional chambers, which in turn have been altered to less select office accommodation. The original railings to the central private gardens have disappeared and these have been replaced by car parking, sadly detracting from the quality and spaciousness of the Square. The statue of the 5th Duke of Gordon, an early work of the Aberdeen mason, John Morgan, was moved to the centre of the Square from the Castlegate in 1951.

No. 3 was completed as a town house in 1841–42. Its early use was as a young ladies' school and by 1880 it was already being used for commercial purposes. The building, like the remainder of the Square is of two storeys with basement and attic. The frontage is of square ashlar granite, and the rear elevation is built of random rubble. A later brick-built three-storey extension with a flat roof has been added to the rear. The frontage is simple late Georgian, three bays wide with the entrance placed in the right-hand bay. All windows are now single-pane sash and casement. It would greatly improve the unity of the Square if the original six-pane astragals were restored. Original ornamental cast-iron railings survive in front of the narrow basement area and later, pedimented timber dormers of tripartite design are set behind the stone parapet.

Inside the building, the vestibule contains a columned timber screen, beyond which an open-well stairway, lit by a large lantern-light, curves upwards to each landing. The interiors are generally plain with simple cornices. Window shutters remain, but a large number of the original six-panel doors have been altered or replaced. The first-floor front public room, however, retains many of the original fittings. In the room above the entrance there are two well-made presses with classical architraves enclosing brass-edged cupboard doors which are finished in cross-banded veneered Spanish mahogany.

Address:	27 King Street, Aberdeen
Category:	B, in Conservation Area 2
Occupier:	Customs and Excise
Use:	Office
Holding:	Crown

No. 27 King Street was completed in 1833 as the County Record Office to a design of John Smith, Aberdeen City Architect. It passed into the ownership of the Customs and Excise in 1873. The main importance of the building lies in its townscape value, as part of a remarkable series of classical civic buildings, commencing with Archibald Simpson's Medico-Chirurgical Hall of 1818–20, now the Customs and Excise Office at 29 King Street (q.v.). Smith's North Church was built in 1828–9 and this Record Office and the simpler domestic buildings to the south followed in the 1830's. Although all the sites within the street were developed independently, the neo-Greek unity of style was maintained by the collaboration of Smith and Simpson, as the architects chiefly responsible.

The two-storey building is pleasingly proportioned, having advanced end bays on the front elevation with anta-pilasters supporting an architrave frieze and cornice. The parapet terminates in a balustrade concealing the pitched roof. The elevation is balanced by single-storey end bays. One is an arched gateway to the yard behind. The other houses the main entrance to the building. The wings emphasise the verticality of the main building without sacrificing the balance of the elevation. The composition is completed by the symmetrical window arrangement. The central ground-floor window has a consoled cornice, and the windows within the anta-pilasters have segmental heads. At first floor, the windows are square-headed sash and case. The building is entered up three steps to a single entrance door leading into a corridor connecting with the hall and stairway.

The interior contains many large public rooms on both ground and first floor, all of them plainly detailed. The impressive open-well stairway is entered through a colonnade, a feature continued on the first floor. The plasterwork of the Corinthian capitals is particularly fine. The ceiling over the stairway is coffered, with beams supported on volute brackets. The basement, entered underneath the main stairway, is constructed as a series of brick arches forming small cellars and was originally used for the storage of contraband.

Reference: Historical Walk About Aberdeen
(Cuthbert Graham).

Address:	29 King Street, Aberdeen
Category:	A, in Conservation Area 2
Occupier:	Customs and Excise
Use:	Offices
Holding:	Leased

The Aberdeen Medico-Chirurgical Society was founded in 1789 by a group of young doctors— including James McGrigor, later Director-General of the Army Medical Department—to provide basic teaching in the various branches of science including medicine. A subscription was begun in 1809 to finance a purpose-built hall to house the Society's library, together with a museum, lecture room and caretaker's flat. The hall was eventually constructed in 1820, at a cost of £2,000. Its designer was Archibald Simpson, Aberdeen's premier architect of the late Georgian period. The consistent development of this side of King Street is due to Simpson's collaboration with the City Architect, John Smith, who designed 27 King Street (q.v.) and the adjacent North Church.

The building is two storeys high with a basement area surrounded with a simple cast-iron handrail. The King Street elevation, built of granite ashlar, consists of a central tetrastyle giant Ionic portico ten metres high, supporting an entablature and pediment and flanked by symmetrical three-window wings.

The building is entered under the portico through double-leaf mahogany doors into the stair-hall where an open-well staircase rises in short flights to the first floor. There is fine plaster decoration in the stair-well, particularly notable in the barrel-vaulted coffered ceiling and in the Greek-key frieze. Elsewhere simple classical egg-and-dart and Greek-key mouldings are used, with palmette detail on walls and bead-and-reel ornament in door panels. The pen-checked open stair has a simple classical cast-iron balustrade capped by a slender mahogany handrail.

The austere interior is grandly scaled with exaggerated room heights and oversized doorways, in which double-leaf doors are extended by matching fixed panels. Each classical door-piece is enclosed by a moulded architrave capped by frieze and entablature. The former Medical Library is on the first-floor west side and extends the length of the portico frontage. There is a simple marble chimney-piece at each end of the room. At each side of the fireplace the motif of the Society appears in low relief plaster.

References: Archibald Simpson—Aberdeen Civic Society 1978.
Archibald Simpson and his times, in *Aberdeen Weekly Journal* 1918 (G. M. Fraser).

Name:	Migvie House
Address:	23 North Silver Street, Aberdeen
Category:	B, in Conservation Area 2
Occupier	Property Services Agency
Use:	Offices
Holding:	Crown

Migvie House is a detached two-storey town house with attic and basement, built in 1839 for Dr MacRobin, then Professor of Medicine at Marischal College. Little is recorded about the history of the building, but it is known that it has had various uses, including service as the Manse for West St Nicholas Church. The building came into the Government estate in 1914.

Standing within its own walled garden, the building forms part of the Georgian townscape around Golden Square and North and South Silver Street. A number of extensions have been added, including the single-storey Victorian wing attached to the north gable. That to the south has been demolished. In recent years the PSA has added a small extension behind the main stairway. Although now dwarfed by a modern building complex to the north, the street frontage, walled garden and entrance gates remain as original.

The three-bay facade is plain, punctuated by a recessed central bay. Ashlar granite is used on the frontage while the gables and rear elevation are in freestone. The central door-piece has a consoled cornice, pilasters and a simple fanlight over the door. The building is entered up a short flight of steps. The basement front windows each have a semi-circular area, formerly guarded by iron railings.

The building is symmetrical in plan with public rooms to the front on each side of the entrance hall. The stair is constructed with pen-checked stone treads, the slim baluster being cast-iron with Regency-style mahogany handrails. The interior contains noteworthy plasterwork details and doorways. The plasterwork in the east ground-floor room incorporates an anthemion frieze and cornice, the central ceiling rose has foliate decoration and the pedimented doorway also has an ornamental frieze. All the doors are six-panelled with delicate architrave detail. The original chimney-pieces have been removed and other non-structural changes have been made but otherwise the interior of the building remains largely unaltered.

Name:	Angusfield House
Address:	226 Queen's Road, Aberdeen
Category:	C
Occupier:	Property Services Agency
Use:	Offices
Holding:	Crown

Angusfield House, an Edwardian classical mansion of rather heavy proportions set within its own landscaped gardens, is one of the many substantial mansion houses built for the professional and merchant classes during the early 20th century, when Aberdeen was expanding westwards along Queen's Road. The property was designed by R. G. Wilson in 1904. According to the original plans it was built for William Gibb of Crookston Hall, near Glasgow, but the Street Directory for 1904–5 indicates that it was first occupied by Lachlan McKinnon, Advocate. The property was purchased by the Government in the 1940s as part of the Ministry of Defence estate.

The building is two storeys high with an attic lit by dormer windows. The stonework is generally picked dressed granite. Banded string courses, quoins and voussoir lintels are all in contrasting granite ashlar. The plinth is rusticated. Each main elevation has projecting bays with deeply pedimented gables. The principal elevation has symmetrical advanced two-bay gabled wings linked by a three-bay centre, the main feature of which is a projecting neo-Baroque entrance porch.

This has a broken segmental pediment, enclosing a cartouche, over a rusticated semi-circular headed doorway. Above the doorway is a circular key-stoned window embellished by swags. All the windows are astragalled sash and case, those to the ground floor having bold stepped voussoir lintels. Over the centre bay are three symmetrical elliptical-headed dormers. The high stone chimneys have bold cornices. The west facade includes a semi-circular bay window.

The interior is largely original. The public rooms are on the ground floor, entered off a central corridor. This is linked to a spacious oak-panelled entrance hall, now unfortunately partitioned to comply with Fire Regulations. An impressive stairway rises to the first floor. A second domestic stairway leads from the first floor to the domestic quarters in the attic. The internal detailing and finishes are excellent. The ground-floor west public room, has a semi-circular bay framed by a screen of Corinthian columns, and particularly fine plasterwork. The frieze and cornice are heavily decorated with naturalistic swags and garlands. The stairway, lit by a Venetian window, is constructed in pine and oak and has a fine balustrade with ornamental cast-iron balusters. Chimney-pieces remain intact. The geometrical stained glass is also notable, particularly that in the half-glazed entrance door.

The building's fine state of preservation is largely due to the sympathetic care of its present occupants.

Name:	Custom House
Address:	35 Regent Quay, Aberdeen
Category:	A, in Conservation Area 2
Occupier	Customs and Excise
Use:	Offices
Holding:	Crown

This three-storey and basement, five-bay town house was completed in 1772–3. It was built for James Gordon of Cobairdy, a local laird who took part in the 1745 Jacobite uprising, for which he was never pardoned. Two years later the premises were sold to "Theophilus Ogilvy, Collector of Customs at Aberdeen and his successors in office" and has remained a Crown property ever since. The building is typically mid-Georgian, having a symmetrical facade and a pedimented central doorway with Gibbs' surround. It is known that James Gordon's grandfather subscribed to Gibbs' *A Book of Architecture*, which may account for the similarity of the doorway details. The most likely source for design however, is, one of the popular contemporary pattern books. Although the building is now part of the harbour townscape of Aberdeen it originally occupied an open landscape setting on the banks of the Denburn estuary now incorporated within the dock area.

Constructed in ashlar granite from Loanhead Quarry, the facade has raised chamfered quoins and projecting margins to the twelve-pane sash and case windows. The roof is double-pitched and slated with skews and two pairs of tall stone chimneys. The Coat of Arms over the central first-floor window is of an interesting "bastard" type. It includes the Garter motto particular to those Scottish Arms instigated in the reign of Charles II, who appointed the first Board of Customs in 1671.

The building is entered by a short flight of steps which oversails the basement area. A straight-flight stairway with curved winders is situated at the rear behind the entrance hall. Evidence from the cornices suggests that the principal front room was originally entered direct and that the entrance corridor was formed later. The first floor also contains public rooms and the second floor originally consisted of bedrooms. The attic is lit by small windows in the gable and by iron roof-lights. The stone-flagged and part brick-vaulted basement was sub-divided and made lockfast for the storage of contraband. Much original interior detail remains. The public rooms were formerly panelled, but only the presses remain as evidence of this. Other original fittings include six-panel doors and architraves and acanthus leaf cornices. A number of minor alterations have been carried out in recent years without affecting the original layout. A small extension was added to the rear of the building in the early 1960s.

References: Jacobites of Aberdeenshire and Banffshire in the '45 (Alistair and Henrietta Tayer).
Granite City (Chapman and Riley).
Records of Customs and Excise.

Address:	4 Rubislaw Terrace, Aberdeen
Category:	B, in Conservation Area 4
Occupier:	Vacant
Holding:	Leased

A notice in the Aberdeen Journal of 31 March 1852 announced considerable interest in proposals by Mr Skene of Rubislaw to build a terrace of houses, resembling the style of Abbotsford, in a manner loosely described as "Scottish-Elizabethan". The newspaper article went on to mention as a special feature the "pleasure grounds" laid out as formal gardens in front of the terrace. Although the terrace remains externally intact, many of the interiors have been sub-divided and altered to offices, due largely to the demand for office space stimulated by the oil industry. Rubislaw Terrace was designed by MacKenzie and Matthews of Aberdeen, in association with the artist J. Giles. It forms part of Albyn Place, from which it is separated by landscaped grounds and an avenue of trees. It is raised above the level of Albyn Place by a balustraded retaining wall which runs the entire quarter-mile length of the terrace, a front access roadway being provided between the buildings and the gardens. Alternate crow-stepped gabled bays of the facade are emphasised by two-storey bay windows with balustraded parapets. The intervening wallheads are enlivened by smaller gabled dormers. This treatment provides verticality and an interesting rhythm to the elevation, through the skilful use of a few repetitive elements.

No. 4 Rubislaw Terrace lies between two of the advanced bays and is designed as a flat facade slightly set back and mirrored in plan with respect to no. 3. The plan arrangement provides two alternatives. One type is as no. 4, while the other superior house plan features the canted bay windows at ground and first floors. No. 4 is two storeys in height with attic and basement and is constructed in hammer-finished granite blocks built to regular courses. The window arrangement is asymmetrical. The principal windows of the public rooms at ground and first floors are tripartite. The main-floor windows are two-pane sash and case and the attic windows have four-pane lights. The entrance is set to one side and is approached by a stairway which oversails the basement and is guarded by an elaborate, probably original, cast-iron railing. To the right of the pilastered door-piece a narrow window provides daylight to the entrance hall. Between the ground floor and basement a granite ashlar string course gives a firm base to the front view of the terrace. A deep ashlar granite cornice projects one course below the wallheads. The wallhead gable and gablet dormer are also built in ashlar and are defined by raised mouldings and sculptured finials. The rear elevation, in granite rubble, is boldly gabled with regularly spaced square-headed sash and case windows. A stairway with an elaborate cast-iron railing oversails the basement area, linking the ground floor with the garden.

The house has now been sub-divided for two occupiers by separating the ground and basement floors from those above. It is entered through an open hall, from which a dog-leg stairway, lit by a large roof-light, rises through the upper floors. The stair is constructed of varnished pitch pine with heavy square-section newel posts and ornamental cast-iron balustrades. Pendents project underneath, as continuations of the newel posts. The most interesting surviving interior is the first-floor public room, originally the drawing room. The walls are formed as a series of panels defined by plaster mouldings above a low timber dado. The ceiling has an ornate cornice based on naturalistic motifs. The chimney-piece has unfortunately been removed. The doors throughout the house are four-panelled varnished pitch pine with a central dividing bead.

References: *Aberdeen Journal*, March 31 1852.
Aberdeen (G. M. Fraser).

Address:	377 Union Street, Aberdeen
Category:	C(S), in Conservation Area 2
Occupier	Ministry of Defence
Use:	Careers and Information Office
Holding:	Leased

Built at the turn of the century, No. 377 is one of the most dominant buildings within the block on the south side of Union Street between Bon-Accord Street and Bon-Accord Terrace.

It was designed in a vigorous Edwardian classical style by John Rust for the Refuge Assurance Co. Three storeys in height with attic and basement, it is constructed in granite ashlar. The ground floor contains shops on either side of the entrance, one of which is leased by the Army Recruitment Information Office. Although the shop frontages have changed over the years, the granite-built elements of the facade have remained intact. Cellars remain from the early nineteenth century building which previously occupied the site. The design respects that of the building on the east, continuing the eaves cornice and blocking course detail above the first-floor windows. The facade is symmetrical about the very mannered main entrance, which has an elliptical canopy supported on consoles. The first and second floors both have central windows with consoled pediments, balanced by canted bay windows. A dentilled cornice supports a balustraded parapet punctuated by a circular attic window and balanced by elaborate dormer windows with colonnettes and segmental pediment heads. The building has a mansard roof and massive stone chimneys on the end gables. These attic features give a vivid flourish to the skyline.

The internal plan of the building is designed around an open-well staircase with landings, opening onto individual rooms. The mosaic-floored entrance hall is half-tiled, with a decorative tiled border. The impressive doors have bevelled glazing within geometric astragals, and stained glass toplights. The Army Recruitment Office, which comprises a front display area with offices to the rear, has been completely modernised internally.

Name:	St. Luke's
Address:	Viewfield Road, Aberdeen
Category:	B
Occupier:	Ministry of Defence
Use:	Museum
Holding:	Crown

St. Luke's Viewfield is largely the creation of the Aberdeen artist, Sir George Ogilvy Reid RSA, whose works include the famous painting "The Gordon's Warning". The building was purchased in 1960 for use as the Gordon Highlander's Regimental Headquarters and Museum, offering limited access to the public.

The property comprises an irregular group of buildings set within a large mature walled garden. At its core is a small single-storey house of circa 1800, then known as Kepplestone Cottage. By 1864 the bay windows had been added and the house was enlarged again after being purchased, circa 1900, by Sir George Reid. Reid engaged a local architect, Dr. William Kelly and the two men collaborated to alter and extend St. Luke's to form a unique residence and linked studio, in the manner of the Arts and Crafts Movement.

The house is approximately L-shaped in plan and is linked to the studio by a lean-to extension with leaded glazed screen wall. Reid's first move was to provide the original cottage with bay windows on the south facade. Their bell-cast roofs and the central half-timbered porch with leaded glazing seem to be the work of Dr. Kelly. Kelly and Reid then created the two-storey extension, to the west, which has a large projecting oriel window as its principal feature on the south elevation. The east-facing studio, designed by Dr. Kelly, is set on

slightly higher ground, behind the two-storey wing of the house. It is two storeys high, rectangular in plan, with two enormous nine-light leaded windows set in timber transoms and mullions and terminating in gabled, bargeboarded dormer roofs. At the south-east corner is a circular stair turret with conical, slated roof. This partly obscures one of the studio windows and seems to have been an afterthought, added after 1923. Both buildings are harled, the original single-storey cottage having exposed stone margins to windows and quoins.

The interior of the house is mostly unremarkable, but the oriel window, lighting the main stairway in the two-storey extension, is inset with older armorial stained glass. On the ground floor, set to one side of the stairway, a corridor leads to a flight of stairs rising through the covered way into the Museum building. Along the corridor linking the house to the studio/museum are fragments of excellent 17th century Netherlands stained glass set into leaded glass panels.

The Studio, now the Regimental Museum, is, by contrast, a large double-storey open room with exposed timber trusses and varnished matchboard linings. It is embellished with an eclectic mixture of ornament, mostly obtained from other buildings, including the stained glass in the windows. Two Arts-and-Crafts chimney-pieces with inset painted panels are Reid and Kelly's work. This highly individual room now houses artifacts displaying the traditions and history of the Gordon Highlanders since 1754.

Within the garden is an earlier two-storey stable block entered at first-floor level by an outside stairway. This building, now in generally poor condition, is of painted rubble stonework with a pitched asbestos-sheeted roof.

Region	GRAMPIAN
District	BANFF AND BUCHAN

Address:	23–25 Castle Street, Banff
Category:	B, in Banff Conservation Area
Occupier:	Department of Employment
Use:	Offices
Holding:	Crown

This property, situated on the west side of Castle Street, was a domestic house until the early 1950s when it was purchased for use as an Employment Exchange. It is one of the many early-to-mid-19th century buildings of classical design which give the centre of Banff its special character. Built around 1846–50 to a design by Thomas Mackenzie of Elgin, no. 23–25 is a detached two-storey domestic building with later canted dormer windows set in a slated pitched roof. There are a number of later rear extensions. This building makes an important contribution to the townscape on the west side of Castle Street, beside the Free Trinity and Alvah Church, with its dominant portico, designed by the locally-born architect, James Raeburn.

The house has a simple, three-bay elevation with a central doorway. An additional doorway has been squashed beside the left-hand window, upsetting the symmetry. Contrasting stone finishes are used effectively on this main elevation. The walling is coursed squared rubble whinstone with sandstone ashlar margins and rusticated quoins. At first-floor level a broad sandstone band gives a dominant horizontal emphasis to the building, echoed in the eaves cornice. The ground-floor window margins are carried down to the base course, to form apron panels. The central door-piece is simple Roman Doric, framing an inappropriate modern door with offset glazed panels. The original astragalled window pattern remains at first floor but the ground-floor windows have been modernised.

The building has a simple little-altered plan, although most of the original internal doors and chimney-pieces have been removed. The plan is symmetrical about the entrance hall, which is entered directly from the street. A dog-leg stairway, constructed in timber with open stringers, rises the full height of the building. The cast-iron balustrade is of palmette-inspired design up to the first floor. The entrance hall retains its Victorian tiled floor and a dado of embossed wallpaper which continues throughout the stairhall. Because the building is narrow, the rooms leading off either side of the entrance hall and stairhall occupy its full width. The ground-floor room on the west has a beam supported on corbelled brackets spanning the centre and the room directly above has an intricate cornice frieze and intact centre-piece.

The building has been enlarged over the years. On the west part of the rear elevation a harled two-storey and attic extension has been added, together with a single-storey service wing at the south end of the rear elevation. The remaining original part of the rear elevation displays a random pattern of original window openings, in contrast to the regular street front.

At the back of the garden, beside the rear lane, is a two-storey stable block with a gabled loft door to the attic floor. Although much altered externally, the building displays an interesting carved panel set within a pediment and said to depict "Eve's expulsion from the Garden of Eden". This formed part of an earlier building of unknown origin.

Reference: Royal and Ancient Banff
(Banff Preservation Society, 1975).

Name:	Sheriff Court
Address:	1 Low Street, Banff
Category:	B, in Banff Conservation Area
Occupier:	Scottish Courts Administration
Use:	Court House
Holding:	Crown

Banff Court House is an imposing Italianate building situated at the south end of Low Street, on the edge of the town centre. It occupies the former site of a domestic building known as "Little Fillacap", the house of Byron's grandmother, Lady Gight, where the poet sometimes stayed in his youth. The Court House was designed by James Matthews of Aberdeen and was built in 1870–71 by the Glasgow firm of John Drysdale & Son, masons, at a total cost of £7,200. The Treasury met half of the expense, the remainder being provided by the County on a rental basis. It was opened by Sheriff Gordon on 28th January 1871.

The principal elevations, intended to be viewed obliquely from the south and east, are built in sandstone ashlar from Newton, Moray. These elevations are further unified by the window design, segmentally-arched on the ground floor and semi-circular headed on the first floor, and by a continuous balustraded parapet above a dentil cornice. The north and west elevations are more domestic in scale and are consequently harled. The building is two storeys in height, with a pitched slated roof contained behind the balustrade. The seven-bay front elevation to Low Street has an advanced three-bay centre from which projects a balustraded Corinthian portico at ground-floor level, providing an imposing and dignified main entrance. The south, return elevation is five bays wide. All the windows are architraved, two-pane sash and case. Those at first floor are linked by an enriched dentilled string course between the springing of each arched head. The balustrade incorporates chimney flues in panelled plinths, at the centre of both main elevations.

The building is symmetrical about the entrance hall. This leads into an enclosed vestibule, from which a corridor runs the length of the building parallel to the Low Street frontage. The Sheriff Court Room occupies the rest of the ground floor behind the vestibule. At the north end, a wide curved stairway rises to a central first-floor corridor, from which open a number of civic rooms including the County Hall, now the Banff and Buchan District Council Chamber, and a Caretaker's flat. The remainder of the upper floor contains the double volume of the Sheriff Court. The most important interiors belong to the Sheriff Court and the County Hall. The rest of the building is institutional, with high ceilings, plain cornices, six-panel doors and large areas of unrelieved plasterwork. The Court Room is essentially simple and little-altered. Rectangular on plan with a raked floor below the public benches, it is airy and spacious, lit at the west end by three full-height sash and case windows with steeply-sloping sills. The raised Judge's bench has a panelled front and is flanked on each side by a semi-circular-headed niche enclosing a six-panelled door. In the well of the Court there are more good panelled fronts. A most interestingly-detailed witness box is positioned on one side. It rises above the well of the Court and is enclosed all round. Its most remarkable feature is a curved panelled sounding board, supported by piers on moulded plinths and crowned with ball finials. The ceiling is coved and coffered in plaster.

References: Annals of Banff, Volume 1 (William Cramond, New Spalding Club).
Banffshire Journal, October 18th 1870 and January 24th 1871.

GRAMPIAN/BANFF AND BUCHAN

Name:	Dalrymple Hall
Address:	Seaforth Street, Fraserburgh
Category:	C(S)
Occupier:	Department of Transport
Use:	Offices
Holding:	Leased

Dalrymple Hall, a large building with an impressive square tower, is by far the most dominant building on the harbour front at Fraserburgh. It was built in 1881 to a design by Jenkins & Marr, in a style which can loosely be described as Scottish Baronial, and occupies a steeply sloping site at the east end of the town next to the now-defunct Great North of Scotland Railway terminus which was then the focal point of the town's communications and commercial activity. It was designed to provide, on the upper floors, a large public hall capable of seating 1,100 persons. This level is entered from the high ground behind the building. The more impressive harbour frontage contains the main entrance to the former cafe, now used by the Department of Transport's Driving Examiners and the Department of Health and Social Security's local office.

The building was constructed at a cost of £4,500 and is named after Captain John Dalrymple, a merchant of the town who had considerable trading interests in the Far East and who contributed more than half the expense. The hall, which is still in use, is owned and operated by Banff and Buchan District Council.

The building is massively proportioned and comprises a three-storey main block with a five-storey square battlemented tower attached. A thin circular turret with a conical slated roof rises like an index finger from the north-west corner of the tower. A three-storey curved frontage rises within the re-entrant angle of the tower and the main block and includes the cafe entrance at ground floor. The main frontage of the building is constructed in picked-face granite blocks built to regular courses. The building is characterised by baronial features such as advanced single-window bays with crow-stepped gables and projecting balustrades. The principal windows of the ground and first-floor elevations have elliptical-arched heads. The remainder are generally square-headed. The ground-floor entrance has a stilted lintol with a marble panel inscribed "Dalrymple Hall and Cafe", which is supported by polished Kemnay granite half-columns set into the reveals. The rear elevation faces south over the town. There is a large area of open ground to the front which is enclosed by a low stone wall. This is the frontage of the two-storey main hall. At the east end rises the tower which houses the main staircase and the hall entrance. This south elevation and its west gable are constructed in coursed whinstone rubble, in contrast to the ashlar with which the rest of the building is faced. A later iron fire escape has been added to this facade.

The plan is dictated by the two entrance levels. The upper two floors, which form the double-volume public hall, are entered through the tower by a dog-leg pitch-pine staircase. This also formerly provided a second access down to the cafe on the first and ground floors, and is now blocked off to accommodate its separate office use.

The main hall has a barrel-vaulted close-boarded timber roof but is otherwise plain. The public stairway has an ornate cast-iron balustrade and moulded pitch-pine handrail. The ground floor contains kitchens and anterooms associated with the cafe which have been sub-divided to suit the present use. Plain classical chimney-pieces, some of marble, remain intact.

This massive edifice is mainly important for its dominance in the townscape and on the skyline at the east end of the town and as a forceful reminder of Fraserburgh's Victorian past.

Reference: Buchan (Rev. John Pratt).

Region	GRAMPIAN
District	GORDON

Address:	23–25 Gordon Street, Huntly
Category:	B, in Huntly Conservation Area
Occupier:	Department of Health and Social Security
Use:	Offices
Holding:	Crown

The development and growth of Huntly as a market centre was due to the Duke of Gordon, who drew up a development plan in 1776 based on a grid-iron pattern which is very much in evidence today. Gordon Street formed one of the later stages of this development, most of its buildings dating from early to mid-19th century.

No. 23–25 Gordon Street was built shortly after 1819 for a certain George Lawson, but the architect and the original purpose of the building are unknown. In 1870 it was sold to the Aberdeen Town & County Bank and altered for bank purposes in 1874. The alterations included comprehensive re-fronting. Its present use is a Job Centre and local Driving Test Centre.

The building is two storeys in height, constructed in squared granite ashlar. The street elevations of the building have different architectural treatments. The principal elevation to Gordon Street contains the two adjacent entrances. The seven-bay ground floor was given semi-circular headed openings and the cornice and parapet were raised when the Bank took over the property. At first floor, the windows are square-headed sash and case with astragals. The corner of the building takes the form of a single-bay shallow recessed curve. The skyline is broken above the roof parapet on the corner by a square panel supported by scrolls. The shorter two-bay elevation to Nelson Street has square-headed sash and case windows to both floors, symmetry being maintained by the introduction of blank windows in the bay next to the corner. A comparatively modest two-storey section, possibly belonging to the original development, completes the Nelson Street elevation. The rear elevation, with symmetrically placed stacks, indicates the probable general appearance of the original frontage, the piend roof of which is hidden behind the parapet. Originally a garden extended further along Nelson Street but this has now been surfaced to form a public car park.

The building was originally designed with self-contained offices on the ground floor and living accommodation above. When the building was adapted for banking purposes, alterations were made, the buildings were joined together and the two-storey extension to Nelson Street was added. Internal fittings such as wall safes and room safes were also constructed, all of which still remain.

The first-floor public room in the corner of the building possesses the best interior work. This room has an interesting plan shape incorporating the curved end wall. Within this is set a matching curved door-piece forming a cupboard, balanced by a window on the external wall to Gordon Street. Elsewhere the detailing is of little importance with the exception of an acanthus-pattern cornice to the public room in no. 23.

| Region | GRAMPIAN |
| District | KINCARDINE AND DEESIDE |

Name:	Victoria Barracks
Address:	Queens Road, Ballater
Category:	B
Occupier:	Ministry of Defence
Use:	Barracks
Holding:	Crown

The term 'barracks' conjures up a vision of acres of tarmac and vast ranges of grim institutional buildings. This is not so at Ballater, where these domestic-scale barracks, built in 1860, are set in the midst of granite Victorian villas, and softened by neat and trim gardens. The Barracks were built to house the Guard of Honour when the Court was in residence at Balmoral, which accounts for their appropriate scale. Only small numbers of troops need accommodation.

The Caretaker's house is a narrow building, stretched to the same length as the larger barrack blocks. Four identical barrack blocks open on to the parade ground. All the buildings are single-storey, using the same details throughout. Built of pinkish granite, with sandstone dressings, they have steeply-pitched slated roofs with heavy pierced bargeboards and ornamental white fireclay ridges which give them a prickly silhouette. The windows are mullioned and transomed at the larger openings. A water tank, raised on granite walls, is set rather arbitrarily between the buildings. Behind the blocks built for the 'other ranks' are small stores in an identical style, with the same steep roofs. Massive stone walls enclose roofless external latrines where, in the Victorian era, the private soldiers were expected to perform their ablutions in the open.

Things are different in the 1980's and the use of the main blocks has changed, affecting some internal detail.

Name:	Sheriff Court
Address:	Dunnottar Avenue, Stonehaven
Category:	B
Occupier:	Scottish Courts Administration
Use:	Court House
Holding:	Crown

Stonehaven Sheriff Court House grandly closes the vista at the south end of the town's main street. The front facade is sited symmetrically on the axis of the street, a device consciously planned to highlight the civic importance of the building.

Tenders were invited for the construction of a new Sheriff Court in Dunnottar Avenue in December 1862. Tenderers were advised to include costs for demolition works as 'the present Court buildings are to be taken down'. This referred to the 1797 Tolbooth which stood on the site, then to be replaced by the new Court facilities. The old County Jail, built behind the old Tolbooth in 1767, was to be retained and incorporated into the new Sheriff Court complex, having been previously altered and modernised by John Smith in 1822. The architect for the front pavilion and the new Court House, also described as the County Buildings, was J. C. Walker. Construction took place between 1863–65. The resulting building group therefore comprises Walker's classical front pavilion and Court Room, while to the south and linked to the main building is the earlier three-storey prison block and the Prison Superintendent's house. The wing at right-angles

to the frontage on the east contains the local Police Offices. The corresponding west wing which included Police houses is now disused. The high prison wall remains in part, as does the former flagstone exercise yard, a large portion of which, however, has been removed to make way for housing to the south. The Jail block is now redundant and a proposal has been made to demolish it and the former Superintendent's House for an extension to the Police Offices.

The frontage of the 1860's building is long, dignified and well-proportioned in a serious classical style already rather out of fashion in its day. It is two storeys in height, constructed in sandstone ashlar. The ground floor is faced with channelled stonework contrasting with the regular squared ashlar of the upper elevation. The facade is eleven bays wide, with advanced two-bay wings and single-bay centre-piece. The entrance is designed as a projecting porch with an arched doorway flanked by granite columns and capped by a balustraded parapet. At eaves level a similar balustraded parapet hides the piended roof in which are set chimney-stacks with pronounced cornices. Tall single chimney-stacks rise from pedestals in the balustrade on each side of the central bay, creating a necessary strong accent in the middle of the long facade. The windows are arched at the ground floor, and the larger, square-headed windows at the first floor have shouldered margins. The Court Room rises behind and parallel to the front block. It can be distinguished at the front by decorative iron cresting on the ridge and

from the rear by three tall, round-headed astragalled windows in pure Georgian style.

By contrast, the earlier Prison, with its small regular cell windows and steeply pitched slated roof, is built of local red sandstone, as is the rear elevation of the Court Room. The plan of the Prison is similar on each of the three floors. Five cells are arranged along one side of the corridor with washrooms opposite and a circulation stairway at one end. Iron gratings forming borrowed lights are inset in the corridor floors. The cells are barrel-vaulted in brick and are entered through original heavy timber doors with large iron locks and latch-type peepholes. Beside each door is a small glazed spy-light. The floors are flagstoned and natural light is provided through small high-level windows guarded by iron bars.

The interior of the Sheriff Court is symmetrically planned. The projecting central porch leads directly into the entrance hall which contains the main L-plan stairway. The Solicitors' Library and the offices of the Court officials behind the front facade, are entered off a corridor leading to the Sheriff Court which occupies the double-height volume behind. There is a secondary stairway at each end of the corridor. The Prison and jailer's flat are cleverly linked to the Court House by a mezzanine level which serves a corridor under the Court Room. This corridor is built over the vaulted basement and allows direct access between the dock in the well of the Court and the Prison. This access is now partially blocked up. The interiors are generally plain. Shutters and dado panelling are original, as are the door-pieces and four-panelled doors. The principal Court Room possesses the most important interior. It has an impressive coved ceiling supported on a series of heavy beams in a geometric pattern. A circular central ventilator is framed by a plaster garland. The ceiling is raised over a projecting egg-and-dart cornice with corbelled brackets. The Court Room is lit by three round-headed astragalled windows in the south wall. A smaller window occurs in the north wall, opposite the bench. The door-pieces are pedimented, as is the Judicial Bench. The original furnishings of the Court have all been retained, including the central oak table. The front of the bench is panelled, and the Witness Box, positioned in the well of the Court, is raised on a plinth and designed as an open lectern with handrails.

References: *Aberdeen Journal*, 17 December 1862
          Views in Stonehaven (A. Gibbs, 1840)—for pre-1862 appearance

Cell Block behind Sheriff Court

Name:	Christian's House
Address:	28–32 High Street, Stonehaven
Category:	B
Occupier:	Department of Transport
Use:	Offices
Holding:	Leased

This tall merchant's house survived the general rebuilding of the High Street in the 1950's, but remained in a very tattered condition until 1973, when it was somewhat drastically reconstructed as local authority flats.

The house dates originally from 1712, and the very thick gable walls may well be that old, but c. 1745 the house was reconstructed as a three-storey and attic house with a regular five-window ashlar frontage and two two-storey rear wings to form a U-plan block. The north-eastern wing links to a long two-storey warehouse which also formed part of the complex. The house takes its name from the Christian family, which probably occupied it in 1826, the year in which Peter Christian, the Chief Magistrate, laid the foundation stone for the south harbour in Stonehaven. James, perhaps his son, was Sheriff Clerk of Kincardineshire in the 1850's but after that its history is obscure. The ground floor later housed a cobbler and the upper floors were sub-divided into small flats. One of the bedrooms is reputed to have been used for illegal Episcopalian services in the middle of the 18th century. Another house in the street, where such services were certainly held, has been demolished.

The front elevation has deeply-splayed, margined windows with flush key-blocks in the courses above the lintels and a steeply-pitched roof with crow-stepped gables and end stacks. The south-eastern stack has been demolished. The building now has a somewhat more Georgian appearance than it had originally, since, in the course of the 1973 repairs, the ashlar face was cut back to leave raised quoins at the angles. The door-piece is artisan late Georgian, asymmetrically enlarged on the left to achieve a tripartite side-light arrangement. It is framed by anta pilasters bearing a cornice slab hood which rests directly on the capitals. At some time after Gibb drew the house in 1840, elegant cast-iron standards with an overthrow wrought-iron lampholder were added. The ground floor has shops on either side of the entrance hall, probably formed around 1800. The Driving Examiner's Office occupies the left-hand shop unit.

Inside, the house formerly had simple rooms with plain dadoes and a rather tight half-turn geometrical stair with an elegant rail and tall stair window of the typical Angus and Mearns 18th century type, but these details were all removed in the 1973 reconstruction.

62

Region	GRAMPIAN
District	MORAY

Name:	Sheriff Court
Address:	High Street, Elgin
Category:	B, in Elgin High Street
	Conservation Area
Occupier:	Scottish Courts Administration
Use:	Court House
Holding:	Crown

Situated on the south side of Elgin High Street and now linked to the 20th century Police Office, Elgin Sheriff Court was designed by A. & W. Reid and built in 1864–66. It has a two-storey five-bay facade to High Street and is set back from the roadway, lending a powerful civic quality to this part of the town centre. It fully maintains Elgin's strong tradition of fine classical building. The Court House is L-shaped on plan with a double-volume Court behind the frontage, allowing clerestory lighting to the circulation corridor along the internal wall and enabling the Court Room to have windows on three sides. It is constructed in polished ashlar sandstone, channelled at ground floor with projecting vermiculated quoins at first floor. Externally the classical detail is extremely consistent, down to the raised anthemion ornament of the rainwater heads, and the design of the ground-level ventilators, incorporating a sunflower motif.

The centre three bays of the High Street elevation are advanced, with an entablature supported by paired engaged Ionic columns in the centre and by pilasters at each end. A high projecting panelled parapet rises above the eaves while the entablature and cornice act as a lower parapet above the single end bays, concealing the

pitched slated roof behind. The ground-floor windows are four-pane square-headed sash and case. At first floor the windows are architraved with consoled cornices and pretty balustraded aprons below a thin string course. The design is returned as two similar bays to Glover Street where a wide wallhead chimney gives emphasis to the centre. This frontage is completed as a recessed three-bay two-storey ancillary office block faced in ashlar. The windows line through with those on the front block but a lower eaves cornice reveals the pitched roof behind. A single-storey outbuilding is attached to its south gable.

The interior of the building has remained remarkably unaltered. The central High Street entrance leads to an enclosed vestibule and thence into the main corridor through a pair of three-panel doors in a round arched doorway. A dog-leg stairway, lit by a full-height window with splayed reveals, rises at the east end of the corridor. The pen-checked stairs have an open stringer. The handrail is mahogany and the spiral wrought-iron balustrade terminates on square columns. Beside the stairway a second corridor, which runs behind the rooms in the east wing, gives access to the Sheriff Court. The corridor ceiling is ribbed and barrel-vaulted. The Sheriff Court Room, by far the most important interior in the building, is lit by high-level clerestory windows on three sides and an ornate four-light window in the south wall. The other walls contain single-arched windows with astragals. The Court Room has a raked floor with public benches in the southern part. Unusually, there is no balcony. The front of the varnished pine bench is panelled. An elliptical-arched ingo forms the back of the bench, over which hangs a projecting canopy with a pediment ornamented with carved fruit and foliage. The pine entrance doors are four-panelled with moulded architraves, a detail continued in the design of the dado. The ceiling is coffered and the projecting frieze and cornice are supported on corbelled brackets. The beam soffits are decorated with interlacing plasterwork and there is a geometric centrepiece in plaster. The only other interesting room is the Solicitor's Library, situated on the ground floor west of the main entrance. This room is finished with two levels of fitted polished timber bookcases on each wall, separated by a timber cornice.

Region	HIGHLAND
District	CAITHNESS

Name:	Sheriff Court
Address:	Bridge Street, Wick
Category:	Proposed for Listing
Occupier:	Scottish Courts Administration
Use:	Court House
Holding:	Crown

The Town Hall and adjacent Sheriff Court are the most dominant buildings beside the approach to Wick town centre from the south, which otherwise largely consists of domestic-scaled buildings of the mid-19th century.

The Town House and Jail were erected in 1828 at a cost of £2,000, the greater part of which was paid for by the Burgh although the Jail was large enough for the needs of the Burgh and County alike. The adjacent Sheriff Court occupies the site of a previous Courthouse and was built in 1862–66 to the design of David Rhind. Its dominant central tower complements the dome of the neighbouring Town Hall. The three-bay street frontage is built mainly of tooled ashlar, polished ashlar being used for the bold, giant channelled angle pilasters, base course and entablature.

The building is two principal storeys in height with an attic floor above a bold, projecting cornice. A blind balustrade separates the ground floor from the first-floor elevation, which contains three round-arched keystoned windows. Each window contains tracery of Dutch Renaissance derivation. A slender central colonnette divides the opening into two circular-headed lights with a rosette filling the arch-head. The ground-floor elevation comprises a central door-piece flanked by single round-arched windows. The entrance archway is also circular-headed, and is framed by twin pilasters supporting a corniced pediment.

Above the entablature, the central tower is linked by short, blind balustrades to segmental-pedimented dormers. The outer angles are marked by tall, ornately modelled pedestals. The central tower is capped by a mansard roof slightly set back behind a pierced parapet. The circular-headed dormer windows and the traceried window in the central tower echo, respectively, the detailing of those at ground and first floor.

The central doorway opens into a vestibule and thence into the stairhall which contains a dog-leg cantilevered stone stair, with a spiral iron balustrade. The stairhall is lit by a plain lantern-light set in a coffered ceiling and by a tripartite window. The double-volume Court Room occupies the full width of the building at the rear. Leading from it are the Sheriff's chambers and a Jury Room, both of which retain white marble chimney-pieces. The Court Room interior remains largely unaltered. The layout is traditional, with raked public benches. The front of the Sheriff's bench is panelled and the witness box has a curved timber sounding board. The ceiling is coved, with a lattice of plastered beams springing from a projecting corbelled cornice. The room is lit by a lantern-light and by high-level mullioned windows. A second stairway, of domestic proportions, rises from the first floor to ancillary rooms and a caretaker's flat within the attic space and the mansard roof of the tower.

V.   Kirkcaldy Custom House.

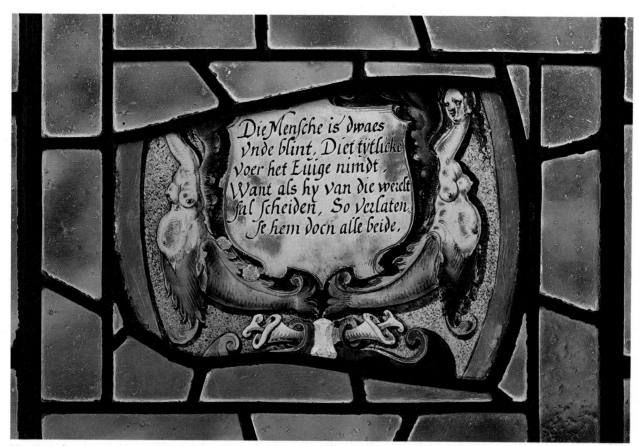

VI.   St. Luke's Viewfield, Aberdeen. Stained glass detail.

65

VII.   Kirkwall Custom House, Orkney.

VIII.   Fort George, Inverness.

| Region | HIGHLAND |
| District | INVERNESS |

Name:	Fort George
Category:	A, Scheduled Monument
Occupier:	Ministry of Defence
Use:	Barracks and Museum
Holding:	Crown

Garrison Church.   *SDD Ancient Monuments Division*

Fort George was planned in 1747 as an impregnable northern base for George II's army after the weakness of General Wade's small Highland forts had been exposed in the latter stages of the 1745–6 rebellion. The new stronghold was designed to the highest European standards of bastioned artillery fortification, in the classic forms perfected by generations of engineers, of whom the best known are Vauban and Cormontaigne. The construction of the fort was supervised throughout by the engineer William Skinner who, largely thanks to the reputation which Fort George gained for him, rose to be chief engineer of Great Britain with the rank of Lieutenant-General. Within the sophisticated defences Skinner designed comprehensive ranges of internal buildings on a monumental scale to accommodate the Governor and other officers of the fortress, the artillery detachment and the garrison of sixteen hundred infantry, with a magazine, ordnance and provision stores, a bakehouse, a brewhouse and a chapel. Works continued until 1769, the brickwork and masonwork contract being held by John Adam and occasioning frequent visits by his brothers Robert and James.

Although the Jacobite threat had evaporated by its completion date, the fort continued in use. Very little alteration or addition was made either to the

defences or to the internal buildings, even when the fortifications were clearly no longer needed after the place came into exclusive use as the depot of the Seaforth Highlanders in 1881. The superlative distinction of Fort George today is that there survive intact not only the bastioned defences with all their outworks but also the whole of the interior ranges. These are outstanding in their own right as Board of Ordnance buildings, many of them retaining their original internal planning. The P.S.A. is about to begin a major rehabilitation scheme for the barrack buildings, firmly respecting their historic character both in mass and detail, so that the fort may continue to be used by the British Army of the late 20th century.

Reference: Fort George guide (H.M.S.O.).
Footnote: Fort George was formerly in the care of P.S.A. as an ancient monument but since 1978 it has been in the care of the Secretary of State for Scotland and is maintained on his behalf by the Ancient Monuments Division of the Scottish Development Department. P.S.A. however, retains a responsibility for the areas used by the Army.

SDD Ancient Monuments Division

Address:	9 Ardross Terrace, Inverness
Category:	B, in Conservation Area 1
Occupier:	Property Services Agency
Use:	Office
Holding:	Crown

Ardross Terrace was designed by Alexander Ross, in the mid-1870's. It forms a continuous late Victorian riverside frontage, built as part of the westward expansion of the town across the River Ness in a style which may be loosely described as Gothic-inspired Scottish Baronial. The Terrace consists of a series of two-storey and attic town houses. Each house differs in detail, yet is similar in plan, unified by the common architectural vocabulary. The turrets, stepped parapets, gables and projecting bay windows ring the changes within the elevation and create an interesting overall rhythm. This is seen particularly well across the broad expanse of the River Ness.

No. 9, built in 1881, is typical of the houses in the Terrace, being a mirror image of its neighbour, no. 10. It is occupied by the PSA's Area Works organisation, and is approached up a short flight of steps through the retaining wall of the front garden. The ground falls naturally to the rear, where the backland was originally occupied by a single-storey domestic outbuilding. This has been heightened to three storeys to provide extra office accommodation. Its harling contrasts with the stonework of the main building. The long, narrow garden at the rear has been partly hard-surfaced to provide additional parking. The main walling of snecked pink sandstone rubble contrasts with the dressed stonework of the architectural features. The outer Gothic arch of the front doorway is supported on squat columns with foliate capitals. Above the entrance is a square-headed bipartite window with chamfered reveals, a detail common to all the other windows. At attic level there are two prominent gabled wallhead dormers above a curious double roll-moulded zigzag string course. Other notable details of the front facade include lead rainwater heads displaying the construction date 1881, and circular cast-iron downpipes which pass through the projecting string courses and are fixed by decorative iron straps. The rear elevation of the building is symmetrical with square-headed windows and dormers set into the roof. The timber back door is half-glazed, beneath a leaded glass fanlight.

The ground-floor interior has been much altered. The chimney-pieces and original four-panel doors have been removed. The entrance hall has a modern entrance screen and the stairway is sub-divided by a central spine wall. The stairway was originally of varnished pitch pine with square newel posts, having ball finials, and turned balustrades. The wall dado of embossed paper capped by a moulded timber rail remains. The only surviving interior of importance is the first-floor drawing room which retains its original oak chimney-piece with an inset brass surround. It is decorated with carved foliage and the monogram "DMcR", presumably for the original owner. At each side of the fireplace are arched wall niches. The cornice and frieze with naturalistic decoration of swags, shells and flowers, survive intact. The bay window has panel shutters with a matching dado below.

Name:	Sheriff Court
Address:	Castle Wynd, Inverness
Category:	A, in Conservation Area 1
Occupier:	Scottish Courts Administration
Use:	Court House
Holding:	Crown

The Sheriff Court complex is set on the most prominent site in Inverness, high above the east bank of the River Ness and overlooking most of the town centre. Occupying a strategic position, the site was fortified in Cromwellian times, when it was named Fort George. It was slighted by the Jacobites during the 1745 Rebellion and demolished some years later in favour of the present Fort George (q.v.) built on a new site near Ardersier, some 14 miles east of Inverness. Today, nothing of the original fortification survives except a contemporary plan produced by the Board of Ordnance, which indicates something of its layout and scale. The present group of buildings is in essence two substantial castellated blocks linked by a series of bastions and perimeter walls. Within the north block is the former County Hall and Police Department. The south block contains the Sheriff Court and Police garages. The Sheriff Court was designed by William Burn and built between 1833–36. The County Hall, originally the Prison, was the work of Thomas Brown, 1846–48. It is linked to Burn's building by a wall enlivened by towers and bartizans designed by Joseph Mitchell and built in 1839. Alterations, designed by Ross and Macbeth, were made at the beginning of the 20th century.

The castellated Sheriff Court is constructed in red sandstone ashlar and is two storeys in height with an advanced centre bay linked by narrow bays to outer square and circular towers with crenellated parapets. The projecting porch contains a round-arched doorpiece set into a gabled and buttressed surround. The Sheriff Court is approached past a bronze statue of Flora MacDonald raised on a granite pedestal, the work of Andrew Davidson in 1896–99.

Behind the Sheriff Court lies Brown's north block, now converted for use as a second Court. This three-storey castellated block is constructed in snecked red sandstone rubble with dressed ashlar margins to windows, doors and parapets. It is designed as a varied series of towers, hexagonal and square on plan, which also differ in height. An off-set circular stair turret rises boldly, like an index finger, above the main building. The window arrangement follows the same random pattern. Paired and tripled, round-arched and segment-headed lights are asymmetrically placed in the elevations. The towers have machicolated corbelled parapets.

The Castle theme continues inside William Burn's south block. Three areas are noteworthy; the entrance and stairway, the Faculty Library and the main Court Room. Pressure for increased court space has caused a number of alterations to the plan arrangement. The original entrance has been blocked and access is now from a side doorway. The entrance hall is approached under a colonnade opening into the grand central T-plan stairway. At ground and first floors, groined and barrel-vaulted colonnades spring from heavy twin pilasters supporting semi-circular arches. Over the stairway is an elliptical coffered barrel vault and relieving panels. The stairway is lit by a square-headed tripartite window with splayed reveals. The Faculty Library, next to the entrance hall on the ground-floor west side, is cruciform in plan. Its fine bay window is an important feature of the west elevation. The ceiling is groin-vaulted. The original furnishings include a break-front bookcase, library table and contemporary paintings. The centre Court Room is situated behind the entrance hall and extends through two

Graphic magazine, 4 February 1882

INVERNESS FROM THE RIVER SIDE

storeys, with a semi-circular gallery at one end. The room is lit by a series of round-arched tripartite windows. A castellated sounding board over the Sheriff's bench continues the theme of the exterior. The rather spartan panelling and seating within the Court is of stained and varnished pine.

The north block has a large civic hall on the first floor. A series of smaller anterooms are entered from the timber-lined stairway and adjacent corridor. This part of the building has recently been modernised for Sheriff Court purposes, but the original heavily-decorated plaster ceiling has survived the alterations, together with two castellated marble and sandstone chimney-pieces.

Name:	Custom House
Address:	58 High Street, Inverness
Category:	A, in Conservation Area 1
Occupier:	Customs and Excise
Use:	Offices
Holding:	Crown

This was formerly the town's General Post Office, constructed between 1841–4 on the site of demolished Meal and Fish Markets and incorporating two shops in the wings. The design is uncertainly attributed to Archibald Simpson of Aberdeen. By 1888 the Post Office had outgrown their premises, which were subsequently purchased and used by the Customs and Excise. The building is situated midway along the south side of High Street, directly opposite Inglis Street which provides an excellent view of the severe classical elevation. Built in sandstone ashlar, the three-storey frontage is dominated by the three-bay central block, which is framed by giant pilasters and a bold entablature and cornice. Above the arcaded ground-floor opening, the first and second storeys are recessed with engaged Ionic columns in antis dividing the bays. The projecting end bays are linked by narrow recessed single bays incorporating modern shops at ground level, whose frontages have obliterated the original arcaded openings. The windows are sash and case. The main first-floor sash-and-case windows are set in architraves with aprons and cornices, which are consoled in the outer bays. The Royal Coat of Arms, Scottish Quartering, is set in front of the central first-floor window. The rear elevation, built in local red sandstone rubble, has been altered at ground level by an extension. Some original twelve-paned windows remain. These have projecting margins with dressed quoins.

Only the central block, now self-contained, is used by the Customs and Excise. It has its own offset entrance at ground floor with panelled doors leading into a narrow vestibule. This opens into a stairhall serving the first and second-floor rooms. A large public office, lit by the circular-headed windows of the front facade, opens off the ground-floor corridor. This was originally the public counter of the Post Office, now much altered by a large slapping linking it with the room immediately behind. Many alterations have taken place at this level. In recent years subdivisions have been made to meet the Fire Regulations and the majority of the original panelled doors and architraves have been removed. The only original interior feature of the ground floor is a ribbed and corbelled plaster cornice. The straight-flight timber stairway has wrought-iron spiral balusters capped by a mahogany handrail.

On the first floor, the public rooms behind the main facade occupy the full width of the building. They are pleasantly proportioned and retain many of their original features including window shutters, four-panel beaded doors, moulded architraves and skirtings. Several simple marble chimney-pieces also remain. The second floor is simply detailed, and of no special interest.

References: Old Buildings of Inverness (William Glashan)
History and Description of the Town of Inverness (Douglas, Smith and Fraser)
The Heart of the Highlands (Inverness Field Club)

Name:	Cameron Barracks
Address:	Perth Road, Inverness
Category:	B
Occupier:	Ministry of Defence
Use:	Barracks
Holding:	Crown

Cameron Barracks is a large complex of military buildings, occupying a fine level site on the south side of Inverness with access from the Perth Road. It was built over a period of six years, between 1876 and 1884, and was designed in a restrained Scots Baronial manner by the Royal Engineers' office in Edinburgh. There are four main two-storey blocks, enclosing three sides of the parade ground, and a number of smaller buildings. The whole ensemble is constructed of bull-faced, coursed pink sandstone rubble with polished dressings. All the roofs are steeply pitched and slated.

Entrance
The site is entered at the north-east corner between heavy stone piers with iron gates. Beside this entrance is a massive, four-storey stone tower with a battered lower stage and a corbelled parapet at roof level. The masonwork is of coursed pink sandstone rubble with dressed angles and contrasting string courses in grey sandstone. The tower is pierced by a number of small narrow windows suggestive of ancient gun-loops.

Barrack Blocks
The east block is eighteen bays wide. The two end bays and the four centre bays are slightly

North-West Barrack Block

advanced, each having a crow-stepped gable. Those at the centre are paired. The roof above is pitched and slated with prominent stone chimney-stacks.

The north-west and west blocks are identical, each nineteen bays wide with twin, very French-looking conical-roofed drum towers at the centre of the elevation toward the barrack square which are linked at first-floor level by a balcony over the arched entrance. There are small angle turrets at the outer corners, each with a conical stone cap. Alternate first-floor windows have crow-stepped wallhead gablets. Two shouldered chimney-stacks rise from the ground at the front of each building, neatly articulating the long barrack wings.

Other Buildings
The Piping School is a small single-storey building fronted by a triple arcade of neo-Gothic design with a continuous, linking hood-moulding. The tall windows behind the arcade are multi-pane sash and case. The eaves are corbelled and the roof above is pitched, piended and slated, with terracotta ridges.

The former stable block, now used for vehicles and general storage, is single-storey, in character with the rest of the complex, as are a number of houses for the use of permanent staff.

Internally, all the blocks are very plainly detailed although there are shallow plaster cornices in most rooms. All former fireplaces have been removed but panelled doors and their moulded architraves have generally been retained.

All the buildings are in an excellent state of preservation and the grounds are well maintained.

References: *Inverness Courier* November 9th and 30th, 1876.
Guide to Inverness, 1903 (Alexander Mackenzie)

Address:	1 Young Street, Inverness
Category:	B, in Conservation Area 1
Occupier:	Inland Revenue Office
Use:	Offices
Holding:	Leased

This property forms the picturesque corner block of a single development which embraces nos. 1–3 Young Street and nos. 1–5 Ness Walk. The Ness Walk elevation faces towards the river and the complete building groups well with those to the west, which in turn play the part of a precinct to Alexander Ross's imposing Episcopal Cathedral.

The block dates from 1884 and was designed by Alexander Ross in a Scots Baronial style. Built of snecked rubble with polished dressings, it is three storeys in height with an additional attic storey to the corner block. There are modernised shop fronts at ground-floor level, which have not improved the overall character. Only one of the original shop fronts remains, that at no. 3 Ness Walk.

The asymmetrical elevation to Ness Walk is six bays wide. The corner block has a common entrance at ground-floor level with a two-window frontage above. A double string course at second-floor level continues across the canted angle on both elevations. The rounded angle is corbelled to square at this level, above which is a granite column set in front of an angled window— altogether a weirdly wilful detail. The two attic windows have elaborate pedimented heads and the gable facing Young Street contains a tiny oriel. The roof above is steeply pitched and slated, with crow-stepped gables incorporating corniced chimney stacks. The remaining bays of the Ness Walk elevation are asymmetrical with a variety of window and gable-head designs, all consistently part of the whole picturesque composition. The windows were originally timber sash and case but some have recently been unfortunately replaced with aluminium pivot-hung windows with hopper sashes. The office accommodation above ground-floor level was originally domestic. The Inland Revenue occupies the upper floors of the corner block, which contain no features of particular interest.

Region	HIGHLAND
District	NAIRN

Address:	79–79A High Street, Nairn
Category:	B, in Nairn Conservation Area
Occupier:	Manpower Services Commission
Use:	Offices
Holding:	Leased

Nos. 79 and 79A are adjoining two-storey properties in the historic part of Nairn High Street, on the corner of Castle Lane South. The buildings form an L-shaped group enclosed by front garden walls bordering the street. No. 79A is gable-ended to the pavement edge and no. 79 is set back from the street, parallel to it. Little is known of the origins or history of these buildings, but a date-stone incorporated in the pediment over the projecting re-entrant porch inscribed "vive ut vivas" (live that you may live) is dated 1867. It is known that this relates to one of the earlier owners of the property, a Sheriff Falcon. From the appearance of the buildings it can be assumed that they date from c. 1800, and that they were built as separate dwelling houses. No. 79A was probably originally single-storey. By 1880 it had been altered to form a two-storey dwelling with a shop below and was then occupied by Mr. Rae, the local chemist. He purchased no. 79 and joined both buildings together, living in no. 79 and further extending no. 79A to create a larger shop. The property passed through Mr. Rae's family and in 1972 it came into the Government Estate. It presently functions as a Job Centre.

The street elevation of no. 79A is a good example of a fancy Victorian commercial shop front. Its heavy Italianate character contrasts with the remainder of the building both in materials and design, being built in sandstone ashlar to regular courses while the remainder of the building is harled. Above the modern shop front a projecting cornice and frieze is supported on a carved console. At first floor a pair of semi-circular headed windows with opening timber casements is framed by stubby twin pilasters which support a fancifully-detailed segmental pediment. The shop may originally have had a curved side window abutting the doorway. The north elevation, facing the garden, has a random window pattern with exposed stone margins, and a later wall head dormer. The windows are sash and case, those near the street having been modernised as single-pane. The west elevation of no. 79 is also harled, with exposed stone margins, and a later wallhead windows. The porch with a shaped parapet and a shouldered lintel above the doorway, seems to date from c. 1867. An arched gateway with stepped parapet adjoins the north gable, incorporating a keystone with monogram also dated 1867. This marriage stone was originally sited in the entrance gate to the street frontage. Early photographs show iron railings on the low wall enclosing the garden.

The interior of no. 79A has been much altered. Inside the shop the enriched plaster cornice is the only vestige remaining of the original fabric. The upper floors have also been altered. No. 79 has a traditional floor arrangement and remains largely unaltered. The main public room on the ground floor contains a marble chimney-piece with a balancing niche on either side. A dog-leg stairway of simple design, with heavy timber stringers and plain square balustrades, rises to the first floor. The drawing room, at the rear, has a curved end wall, an impressive plaster cornice and a timber chimney-piece. Six-panelled doors with moulded architraves skirtings and original fixed panelled shutters remain throughout the interior.

Region	HIGHLAND
District	ROSS AND CROMARTY

Name:	Sheriff Court
Address:	Ferry Road, Dingwall
Category:	Proposed for Listing
Occupier:	Scottish Courts Administration
Use:	Court House
Holding:	Crown

This is one of a number of similar 19th century buildings erected in former Scottish county towns to serve the combined functions of prison, police quarters and Sheriff Court.

The prison at the rear was the first section to be built, from 1842–45. The design by Thomas Brown, Architect to the Prison Board of Scotland, is typical of his standard schemes (e.g. Dornoch, Stonehaven). It is a two-storey building, substantially built in squared rubble with ashlar dressings to the doors and windows. It consists of two wings with identical gables to the rear, linked by a five-bay recessed section. A moulded string course runs round the block at first-floor level. The roof is pitched and slated. Windows are set in chamfered reveals and some have retained the original astragals. The cells are indicated externally by the small horizontal barred windows. A large exercise yard adjoins the building at the rear. The cell block has been disused for many years but some of the ancillary accommodation has been converted to office space by the Local Authority.

The second stage incorporating the Sheriff Court was built in 1864, also to Brown's design. It partly follows a Baronial style, but is mainly Tudor Gothic. The central section consists of three parallel two-storey rectangular blocks, each with a gable towards the street, the two outer ones being slightly lower. Both are slightly advanced from the centre block and are linked together by a string course at first-floor level. A large tripartite window in the centre block incorporates a shallow balcony and gives light to the Courtroom. Each of the outer blocks has a canted bay window with a crenellated parapet. The side walls also have crenellated parapets and steeply-pitched slated roofs. All these gables have dressed skews terminating in sculptured finials at the apexes. The centre block incorporates flanking stone chimneys. The masonwork is of evenly-cut tooled sandstone blocks with ashlar dressings. The central entrance doorway is four-centred with a hood-mould. Set back from the gabled central section is a pair of symmetrical flanking three-storey stair towers with tall narrow hood-moulded windows and crenellated parapets. This neo-Tudor design is extended to the west by an ashlar faced two-storey wing, three bays wide with two-pane sash and case windows, terminating in an almost identical square three-storey tower.

Internally, the Courtroom on the first floor is well-proportioned and spacious with a high ribbed ceiling featuring panelled braces and decorative plasterwork around the ventilators. The Court is lit by three tall round-headed windows at each end. These are flanked by round-arched niches in the wall behind the original panelled bench. The raked floor supports curved rows of public benches. Certain upper rooms have been sub-divided to provide necessary additional accommodation but this has been carried out without adversely affecting the character of the interior. The stone stair has a cast-iron balustrade and hardwood handrail. Certain ground-floor accommodation has been retained for the use of the Court but other space is used by the Local Authority departments which share the use of the building.

The site is surrounded by a low stone wall, with massive gateposts and an iron railing, to a height of approximately six feet. The front area is now laid out for car parking.

Name:	Sheriff Court
Address:	20 High Street, Tain
Category:	A, in Tain Conservation Area
Occupier:	Scottish Courts Administration
Use:	Court House
Holding:	Crown

The building now operating as Tain Sheriff Court combines the Tolbooth with a purpose-built Court House of 1848–49. This replaced an earlier building of 1825, which burned down in 1833.

The Tolbooth is an excellent example of its type. It replaces the Tolbooth of 1631, which collapsed in 1703. Rebuilding began in 1706 under the control of the contractor, Alexander Stronach. By 1708, the tower and a two-storey Council House were finished. The bartizan was added in 1733. Solidly built in Tain freestone, the Tolbooth is a massive square tower crowned by a conical-spired stone turret with four smaller angle turrets of similar design. Near the wallhead, on the south and west elevations, are clockfaces. This 1877 clock replaced one installed in 1750. Some earlier stonework is built in to the present building, including one stone inscribed 'THIS WARK— BIGIT 1631 JOHN MACKULLOCH BEING PROVOST'. The date is confirmed by the inscription on the large bell inside the turret stating that it was made in 1630 for the original tower by the Flemish master founder Michael Burgerhuys. The present tower contains a stone

turnpike stair giving access to the bell chamber, with a connection to a small gallery in the adjacent Court House. Two stone string courses link through with those on the Court House. The arched entrance at the base of the tower, on the High Street elevation, is contemporary with the Court House, and originally served as its principal access.

The Court House of 1848–49 is the work of the architect Thomas Brown. It is a wide rectangular two-storey building, ashlar-built in the Baronial style, with turrets and crenellations at the eaves which echo the skyline of the Tolbooth. The centre and end bays facing the High Street have gables with sculptured stone finials. At ground- floor level, the windows and the entrance door are round-headed, linked by a continuous wavy moulded string course. At first floor the neo-Tudor windows are grouped in units of two, with linked hood-moulds. In 1873 the four-bay block facing Castle Brae was added to the design of Andrew Maitland.

Internally, the Courtroom has a coved and ribbed panelled ceiling with bosses. There are moulded surrounds to the ventilators and a large centre-piece. The room is lit by two high-level bipartite windows. There is a plaster cornice some distance below the barrel vault and the wall space above is divided into panels in a simple Perpendicular Gothic style. The joinerwork and courtroom furniture are equally simple. There are two niches in the wall behind the bench. Doors are panelled with heavy moulded architraves. The former Town Council accommodation has been adapted without extensive alteration, to provide space for the Witnesses, Jury Rooms and the Advocates' Room. These rooms have semi-barrel ceilings similar to the Courtroom. The stair is constructed of stone and has an iron balustrade and hardwood handrail. All the windows are sash and case and the panelled ingo shutters are also original.

References: Tain through the Centuries (R. W. & J. Munro)
Tain Town Council—Official Guide

Region	HIGHLAND
District	SKYE AND LOCHALSH

Name:	Sheriff Court
Address:	Somerled Square, Portree
Category:	B, In Portree Conservation Area
Occupier:	Scottish Courts Administration
Holding:	Crown

This two-storey building stands on a prominent corner site in Portree's main square and is linked to the public library behind it.

It was completed between 1865 and 1877, to the design of Matthews and Lawrie, architects, Inverness, in a simple classical style. It has three bays to the principal north elevation, which is constructed in tooled ashlar. The pedimented centre bay is slightly advanced, with long and short quoins at the angles. The elevation is framed by channelled pilasters and a blocking course. Urn terminals provide the only light touch to this somewhat austere facade.

The plain central entrance has a door-piece supported on brackets. Windows are sash and case with moulded architraves and plain aprons on the north elevation only. A band course at first-floor level extends around the whole structure. The other three elevations are extremely plain. A new fire stair, linked to the library building, is attached to the rear elevation. The piended, platformed slate roof completely lacks chimney-heads, adding to the stark simplicity of the building's appearance.

Internally, the building has been completely modernised. The few remaining original features include the open-well stair with its elaborate cast-iron balustrade and Victorian mahogany handrail. An original doorway, which has a three-pane arched fanlight and heavy moulded surrounds, leads from the first-floor landing. No other internal fitments are noteworthy.

The police formerly occupied part of the ground floor but they are now located in custom-built accommodation beside the court building.

Region	HIGHLAND
District	SUTHERLAND

Name:	Sheriff Court
Address:	Castle Street, Dornoch
Category:	B, in Dornoch Conservation Area
Occupier:	Scottish Courts Administration
Use:	Court House
Holding:	Crown

This building occupies part of the site of the former Bishop's Palace on the south side of Castle Street, facing obliquely across to the Cathedral. Adjoining on the west is the Castle Hotel, incorporating a 16th century tower house which also formed part of the Bishop's property. In 1813, the tower house was restored as the Court House, Jail and School. This use, in turn was superseded by the present complex, which was constructed in two stages to the design of Thomas Brown, architect to the Prison Board of Scotland.

The prison, to the east, which is not in the care of the P.S.A., commenced building in 1842 and was used as such until 1879, after which it was sold to a Volunteer Company. A Drill Hall was added at the west end in 1896–7. The prison is a substantial three-storey building in a simple Scots Baronial style, sturdily constructed with vaulted cells and passages. The masonwork is stugged ashlar with smooth dressings. The roof is steeply pitched and slated. Decorative features include crow-stepped gables crowned with sculptured stone crosses (possibly reflecting the use of the building which originally occupied the site) and corbelled angle turrets with conical stone roofs and finials. The Drill Hall reflects the same character, but is much simpler. Much of the jail interior has been retained and restored as a museum.

The County Buildings, which include the Sheriff Court, were constructed as the second phase of the development in 1849–50. They consist of two parallel two-storey rectangular blocks, with pitched slated roofs. The symmetrical Castle Street elevation is three bays wide with a central gable containing a triple-arched window which lights the first-floor Courtroom. The side bays each have a tall first-floor window, crowned with a stone wall-head pediment. Entrance is through the centre bay of an arcade of three widely-spaced round-headed arches linked together by a moulded string course. Masonwork is stugged ashlar with smooth dressings. Single-bay, two-storey supporting wings are recessed behind the line of the arcade. These resemble the long south-facing rear block, though lower in height and of a more domestic character. The windows are astragalled sash-and-case with pedimented wallhead gables. The central bay of the rear block is wider, with a crow-stepped gable.

Internally, the most interesting space is the large, well-proportioned Courtroom. A central doorway gives access to the panel-fronted bench which incorporates a coat of arms in the pediment above. A shallow balcony at the opposite end has a front of delicately moulded fielded panels. The ceiling is supported by four-centred arched ribs, with bosses on the central ridge. The stair is constructed of stone with a cast-iron balustrade and hardwood handrail. The supporting rooms, which have been little altered, have no unusual ornamental features.

Reference: The Royal Burgh of Dornoch (D. Matheson)

Region	LOTHIAN
District	EAST LOTHIAN

Name:	Sheriff Court
Address:	Court Street, Haddington
Category:	B, in Haddington Conservation Area
Occupier:	Scottish Courts Administration
Use:	Courthouse
Holding:	Crown

Haddington County Buildings were erected in 1832-3 from a design by William Burn, at a construction cost of £5,500.

This two-storey structure is in a style derived from late perpendicular Gothic. The front block is finished in smooth ashlar, transported from a quarry in Fife, and the rear elevations are in local sandstone. The building has a symmetrical front elevation. A central projecting gabled bay has an arched and recessed doorway with a wide oriel above. There are tall, three-light mullioned and transomed windows with continuous hood moulds and panelled aprons. The plain parapets are punctuated by turrets at either side of the projecting gable.

Inside most rooms have been substantially altered, the main Court Room having been completely re-furbished in 1968. The most impressive internal feature of the building is the main entrance stair linking the ground and first floors. This open-well staircase is constructed in stone with heavy oak balusters and newel posts topped with a substantial handrail. The walls are hung with impressive paintings, one of which is a portrait of the 8th Marquis of Tweeddale by Sir John Watson Gordon.

The County Buildings were extended in 1931-2 by the acquisition of the adjoining building, designed in matching style by W. J. Walker Todd of Dick Peddie and Walter Todd, architects.

The old prison and police station, formerly located at the rear of the main building, have been demolished and new Council Buildings have been erected on the site.

The Scottish Courts Administration occupancy is limited to part of the first floor only and includes a Court Room, waiting areas and office accommodation.

Reference: Lothian (McWilliam)

Address:	15 Lodge Street, Haddington
Category:	B, in Haddington Conservation Area
Occupier:	Department of Health and Social Security and Department of Employment
Use:	Offices
Holding:	Crown

This building is situated at the west end of Haddington High Street, in a key position within this outstanding Conservation Area. It was built in 1870 for the City Bank and was one of the first such establishments in East Lothian. This bank was eventually taken over by the present Clydesdale Bank after the integrity of the City Bank directors had been brought into question. A solicitor's firm occupied the building for some time but it is presently occupied by two government departments.

The prominent west elevation is constructed in ashlar, channelled at ground floor with raised quoins at first-floor angles.

Ground-floor windows are two-pane sash with voussoired flat arches. First-floor windows are four-pane sash with shouldered architraves and circled aprons. Chimneys rising from the north and south wall heads are constructed in ashlar, with cornice and scroll brackets. The walls are finished by a cornice and blocking course.

The main entrance was originally on the north elevation but has since been infilled to form a window with a louvre above. Main entry is now by Lodge Street, but is rather restricted due to the later addition of an external fire-stair.

Internally, the building has been greatly altered, with unsympathetic sub-divisions to the main rooms. Few of the original features remain. Surviving cornices and centre-pieces provide the only evidence of its former usage and finishes.

CENTRAL EDINBURGH

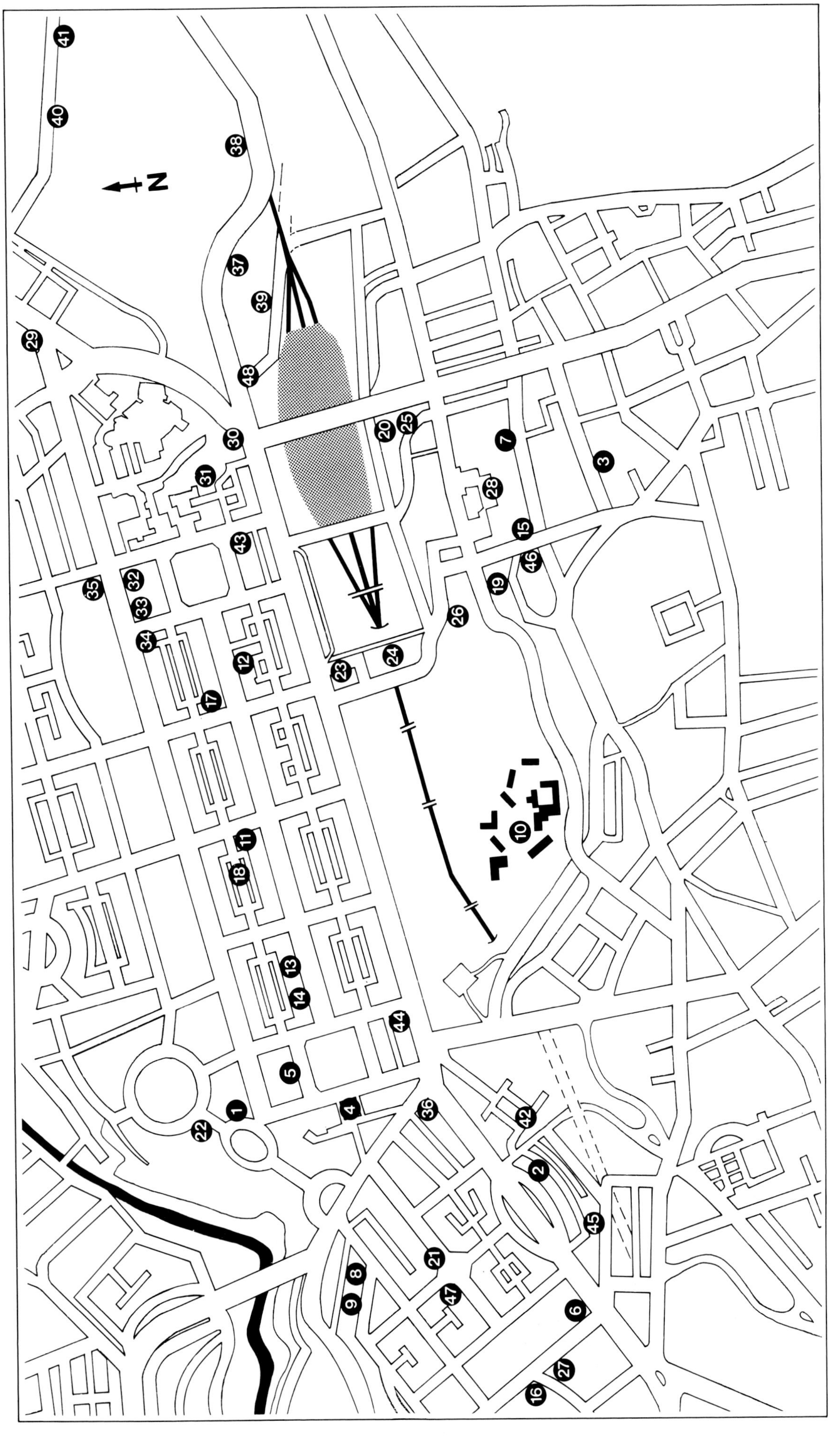

CENTRAL EDINBURGH

1. Ainslie Place
2. 9 Atholl Crescent
3. The Royal Scottish Museum, 44 Chambers Street
4. Register House, West Annexe, Charlotte Square
5. Bute House, 6 Charlotte Square
6. Coates Place
7. Solicitors' Building, 94–114 Cowgate
8. 25 Drumsheugh Gardens
9. 38–39 Drumsheugh Gardens
10. Edinburgh Castle
11. 50 Frederick Street/Hill Street
12. 22–24 George Street
13. 125 George Street
14. 127–129 George Street
15. National Library of Scotland, George IV Bridge
16. 1 Grosvenor Crescent
17. 73 Hanover Street

18. 18–20 Hill Street
19. National Library/Carnegie Library 312/320 Lawnmarket
20. 4 Market Street
21. Melville Street
22. Queen's House, 36 Moray Place
23. Royal Scottish Academy, The Mound, Princes Street
24. National Gallery of Scotland, The Mound
25. 28 North Bridge
26. 16 North Bank Street
27. 44 Palmerston Place
28. Supreme Courts of Scotland, 1–11 Parliament Square
29. 16 Picardy Place
30. General Register House, 1 Princes Street
31. New Register House, 1 West Register Street
32. National Museum of the Antiquities of Scotland/ Scottish National Portrait Gallery, 1 Queen Street

33. N.M.A.S. 2a Queen Street
34. 3 Queen Street
35. York Buildings, Queen Street
36. 3 Queensferry Street
37. St. Andrew's House, Regent Road
38. (Former) Royal High School, 5–7 Regent Road
39. Governor's House (Old Calton Jail) Regent Road
40. 16 Royal Terrace
41. 26–27 Royal Terrace
42. 29 Rutland Square
43. Prudential Building, 2 St. Andrew Square
44. Charlotte House, 2 South Charlotte Street
45. 25 Torphichen Street
46. India Buildings, 1 Victoria Street
47. 20 Walker Street
48. Waterloo Place

Region	LOTHIAN
District	CITY OF EDINBURGH
	Central Edinburgh

Address:	17 and 23 Ainslie Place, Edinburgh
Category:	A, in New Town Conservation Area
Occupier:	17 National Gallery of Scotland
	23 Vacant
Use:	17 Office and Restoration Unit
	23 Offices
Holding:	17 Crown 23 Leased

Ainslie Place holds a key position between Moray Place and Randolph Crescent in the dramatic layout of the Earl of Moray's estate. William Burn was involved at sketch plan stage, but James Gillespie Graham was responsible for the elevations. Elliptical in plan, Ainslie Place was designed in 1822. No. 17 stands on the south side, between Glenfinlas Street and the western section of Great Stuart Street. No. 23 forms part of the short eastern side, north of Glenfinlas Street.

The houses, built on a curve, are of three floors with basements and later attics. They are built of finely dressed ashlar, rusticated on the ground floor with tall, corniced, first-floor windows and moulded cornices at eaves level with plain parapets above.

Some of the sash and case windows at no. 17 have retained their astragals, and all the first-floor windows of the front elevation have cast-iron balconies. The inner glazed doors in the entrances are later insertions. Cast-iron spearhead railings protect the basement area.

Internally, both buildings have been altered, but most of their original character survives.

No. 17 has a Doric screen in the entrance hall. In both houses, fine plasterwork is visible in the major rooms as well as panelled doors with moulded architraves. At no. 23, both marble and timber chimney-pieces remain. In both properties, the staircases are cantilevered and are lit by lantern cupolas with moulded plasterwork below.

References: The Making of Classical Edinburgh (Youngson)
The Heritage of Greater Edinburgh (E. J. MacRae)

17 Ainslie Place.

Address:	9 Atholl Crescent, Edinburgh
Category:	A, in West End Conservation Area
Occupier:	Royal Fine Art Commission for Scotland
Use:	Offices
Holding:	Leased

Atholl Crescent was developed with Atholl Place by the Heriot Trust as part of the westward extension of the city in the early 19th century. Shandwick Place runs from the west end of Princes Street towards the Haymarket and is flanked on both sides by twin crescents, Coates and Atholl, which are separated by gardens from the main street. The development, designed by Thomas Bonnar, was complete by 1825.

Originally each property was an individual dwelling, three storeys high with attic and basement. The main elevation to the Crescent is of dressed ashlar with raised string courses at first and second-floor levels and a continuous moulded cornice. The ground floor is rusticated and the basement is rock-faced. The central nine bays are accentuated by Ionic pilasters at first and second-floors, with a moulded balustrade forming part of the parapet. The entrances are over flying stairs from the pavement under porticos supported on unfluted Ionic columns. A balustraded parapet is unique to this centre section, the rest of the facade being completed by a cornice and blocking course. The basements are flanked by railings, some renewed in plain modern ironwork, others retaining the original spearhead pattern. The first-floor sash and case windows are emphasised by moulded architraves. Many retain the original astragals. Original trellis-pattern balconies remain at first-floor level throughout, but only no. 10, in the centre, retains its original second-floor balconies.

On both ground and first floors of no. 9 there are curved walls at the end of the main rooms, incorporating curved panelled doors with richly moulded architrave and door-head features in hardwood.

References: An Edinburgh Journal (Edinburgh City Library, Edinburgh Room).
Making of Classical Edinburgh (Youngson).

Name:	The Royal Scottish Museum
Address:	Chambers Street, Edinburgh
Category:	A, in South Side Conservation Area
Occupier:	Royal Scottish Museum
Use:	Museum
Holding:	Crown

The Great Exhibition of 1851 stimulated an interest in education, and led to the building of many museums and art galleries during the second half of the 19th century.

The Industrial Museum of Scotland, the forerunner of the present building, was founded in 1854. Ten years later it was renamed the Museum of Science and Art. From the beginning it was a National Museum, administered first by the Department of Science and Art and from 1901 by the Scottish Education Department. It was renamed again in 1904 as the Royal Scottish Museum.

Prior to 1865 the industrial exhibits were housed in several old buildings on the south and west sides of the site. The present Museum building was begun in the spring of 1861, and on the 23rd of October of that year the Prince Consort laid the foundation stone. The official opening was performed on 19th May 1866 by Prince Alfred, who shortly afterwards became Duke of Edinburgh. At that date only the central entrance and the eastern half of the building had been completed. The western section of the original scheme was finished in two stages; 1871–74 and 1885–89.

The original building was designed in the Early Venetian Renaissance style by Captain Francis Fowke, R. E. (1823–65), engineer and architect to the Department of Science and Arts. He was assisted by Robert Matheson (1808–77) of H.M. Board of Works, a Scottish architect who supervised much of the construction.

By the early 20th century, the growth of the Museum's collections made further extensions necessary and in 1910, plans for these were prepared by W. T. Oldrieve, H.M. Principal Architect for Scotland. Between 1911 and 1937 an administrative block, a staircase and a series of galleries were erected on the south side of the Victorian building. The last major extension to the Museum was the construction of a Lecture Theatre, Library and Galleries on the Lothian Street frontage, built between 1959 and 1961. Since then, the north-west and the north-east wings have undergone a complete internal reconstruction. The north-east wing containing the Evolution

86

exhibition was opened by the Duke of Edinburgh on 25th November 1975.

The building displays a remarkable variety of architectural style and technique, including the use of cast-iron, plate glass and terra-cotta. The massive two and three-storey sandstone facade in the Venetian Renaissance style contrasts strongly with the graceful modernity of the interior, which was clearly influenced by Sir Joseph Paxton's Crystal Palace and earlier cast-iron glass structures. Semi-circular timber ribs support the roof. The lower parts of the cast-iron columns supporting the galleries of the main hall were replaced by steel in 1954. The present travertine marble floor was laid in 1970–1. The original floors of ornamental ceramic tiles were retained in the arcaded galleries on the left and right of the main entrance.

The fine sculpture above the north facade was executed by John Rhind, R.S.A., as part of Captain Fowke's original design. The large central figure represents Science, and the smaller groups on its east and west sides, Natural History and Applied Art respectively. The six heads in the spandrels above the doorways represent Queen Victoria and Prince Albert, James Watt, Charles Darwin, Michelangelo and Sir Isaac Newton.

References: *Builder* November 22 1862.
    Old and New Edinburgh II, p.274 (Grant)
    Plans S.R.O. (Fowke, Matheson, W. W. Robertson).

Name:	Register House West Annexe
	(formerly St. George's Church)
Address:	Charlotte Square, Edinburgh
Category:	A, in New Town Conservation Area
Occupier:	Scottish Records Office
Use:	Storage
Holding:	Leased

In his design for Charlotte Square, completing Craig's original plan for the New Town, Robert Adam included a large church in the centre of the west side, but his plans were abandoned after his death, and the present building was erected by Robert Reid between 1811 and 1814. He provided single columns in place of Adam's proposed coupled version, enlarged the dome and eventually omitted the flanking cupolas. The plan is square and the elevation to Charlotte Square consists of a large recessed Ionic portico with four large unfluted columns surmounted by a tall peristyled dome over the entrance hall. The dome is sheathed in copper and bears a small gilded cupola, with a cross finial about 150 feet above ground level. Reid's single Ionic columns are somewhat grandly scaled for the remainder of the Square, and must have been designed rather to provide an effective closure for the lengthy vista along George Street. In the context of the Square, it may be regretted that the Adam design was not used. Originally, the interior, which was smaller in area than the scale of the entrance portico might suggest, contained a noteworthy Spanish mahogany pulpit with sounding board, but the building had to be gutted because of extensive dry rot infestation and was reconstructed as the Register House Annexe in 1965–70.

The reconstructed building, which has been divided vertically into a number of floors and galleries by means of a framed structure within the old walls, is frequently used for exhibitions in addition to its primary use as record store and search room.

References: *Scots Magazine* April 1, 1814 Modern Athens (Shepherd) Georgian Edinburgh (Lindsay) The Making of Classical Edinburgh (Youngson) Post-Reformation Churches (Hay).

Photographs: One taken from the Square to show the complete elevation and the dome.
One showing a close-up of the Ionic capitals.

c. 1830

IX.   General Register House, Edinburgh.

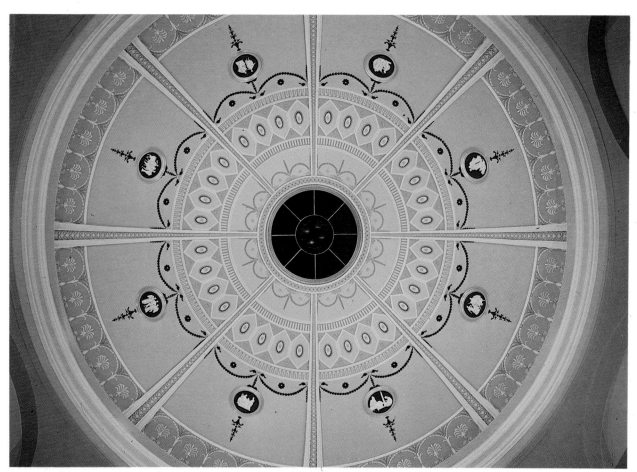

X.   General Register House, Dome interior.

89

XI.   Bute House, Charlotte Square, Edinburgh. Drawing room.

XII.   Parliament Hall, Edinburgh. South window.

Name:	Bute House
Address:	6 Charlotte Square, Edinburgh
Category:	A, in New Town Conservation Area
Occupier:	Secretary of State for Scotland
Use:	Official Residence
Holding:	Leased

Bute House forms the centre-piece of the terrace of dwellings on the north side of the square designed by Robert Adam in 1791, completing James Craig's plan for the New Town of Edinburgh of 1767. The house was built in 1792 as a property investment by a prosperous shoemaker, Orlando Hart.

No. 6, now the official residence of the Secretary of State for Scotland, first secured a place in history as the home of Sir John Sinclair, who masterminded the Statistical Account of Scotland and became the house's third owner in 1806.

The terrace elevation is of three storeys with attic and basement. The whole attic roof is free of any subsequent accretions such as dormer windows. This is due to the Sixth Marquess of Bute, who in 1924–27 removed the dormers and balconies throughout, restoring the cills of the first-floor windows to their original level, partly by acquisition and partly by persuasion. The

magnificent eight-bay centre piece makes up the frontage of three individual dwellings, and is articulated chiefly by a series of giant Corinthian columns at first and second-floor levels arranged in 2-2-2-2 rhythm. The three central bays which form the front of Bute House itself are pedimented at roof level, creating the central point of emphasis in the north elevation of the square. The masonry is of finely dressed ashlar, except at the ground floor, which has V-jointed rustication and at the basement which is boldly rock-faced. The basement area is enclosed with iron railings, designed with refinement to incorporate twin street lights at the entrance. The acanthus frieze in the entablature is not repeated elsewhere, except on the advanced bays of the adjacent houses at 5 and 7 Charlotte Square. The central pavilion is notable for ornamental detail as refined and beautifully executed as any in Robert Adam's career.

The interior contains all the best features of the classical idiom. Even the attic spaces each have classical cornices and good joinerwork and at least one marble chimney-piece. Only minor alterations have been made to fit Bute House for its present official purpose. These include the provision of a lift, additional cloakroom space and small sculleries to serve each floor. The alterations have

been sensitively executed, and in no way detract from the character of the house.

The entrance door, which is unusually wide, is in polished oak. The vestibule entrance has a patterned ceiling and a floor of polished Caithness flagstone in a pattern of large octagons and squares. This area is lit by a very fine semi-circular door-head fanlight. The staircase is constructed in stone, cantilevered from the surrounding stone walls, and has an iron balustrade and hardwood handrail. It is lit at roof level by a circular cupola with a finely moulded frieze and cornice below.

The drawing room and library are typical of the best domestic interior work of the period, including panelled dadoes and doors and elegantly patterned plasterwork ceilings. The white marble chimney-pieces are particularly notable for their Ionic detail. The mantelpieces follow the design of the Ionic entablature, with the characteristic egg-and-dart moulding and green marble inserts in the frieze.

References: Architecture of R. & J. Adam (Bolton)
The Making of Classical Edinburgh (Youngson)

Address:	4, 5, 5a, 6, 7 Coates Place, Edinburgh
Category:	B, in New Town Conservation Area
Occupiers:	5, 5a National Museum of Antiquities
	4, 6, 7 Royal Commission on the Ancient and Historical Monuments of Scotland
Use:	Offices
Holding:	Leased

Coates Place forms part of West Maitland Street, the thoroughfare which runs from Shandwick Place on the east to Haymarket on the west. It is part of the Walker Estate development designed by John Lessels in 1864 and built in 1868, extending Robert Brown's original scheme south-westwards. The design exemplifies a somewhat tentative phase between the assurance of the earlier Georgian New Town and the later Victorian development of the western part of the Walker Estate. The quality of the external detail is generally inferior to both.

The complete terrace consists of four storeys and basement. Originally, it was made up of main door dwellings with an individual access, and flats above with entrances from a common stair. Nos. 4, 5 and 6 are now interconnected at various levels and operate as one office property. The ground floor entrance to no. 6 has been altered to form a window. Access is now gained through a common stair shared with no. 7.

The eight-bay elevation to Coates Place is of dressed ashlar with rubble masonry at basement level. There is an emphatic string course at third-floor level. A shallow cornice at roof level, forming part of the parapet, screens the pitched and slated roof from view. The stone chimneys create a regular rhythm along the length of the terrace. The ground and first-floor windows have moulded architraves, those of the second and third-floor windows being plain. The second-floor windows have segment-headed lintels, marking a departure from the characteristic rectangular Georgian pattern. The entrance doors are approached from street level by flying steps over the basement, which is guarded by iron railings. The doors are arched, and incorporate console cornices at the door-heads, supporting individual balconies with cast-iron railings. All windows are two-pane sash and case. Both surviving entrances retain original panelled doors with semi-circular fanlights.

Internally, extensive alterations have been made to enable the three properties to function as one unit. A number of modern glazed screens flank the access corridors and some of the finely proportioned rooms have been sub-divided to form welfare facilities. A lift occupies the stairwell of no. 6. A number of individual features are, however, worthy of note. At no. 4, one room on the third floor retains polished pine joinery, including architraves and skirtings with panelled window shutters. This room also contains a very fine Corinthian chimney piece in oak. At ceiling level there is a plaster frieze with flowing floral ornament. Two polished white marble chimney-pieces survive in other rooms on this floor.

On the second floor there are two notable chimney-pieces; one in painted timber with classical mouldings, the other in oak incorporating small Ionic columns. A further chimney-piece is in black marble. There is also a rich variety of ceiling plasterwork.

No. 5 has an individual entrance at ground floor level, and retains a rich variety of ceiling plasterwork, mostly of heavy Victorian classical design.

Joinerwork throughout is painted, but is generally of good quality with panelled doors, architraves and skirtings.

Reference: Documents in possession of Walker Trust.

Name:	Solicitors' Building
Address:	94–114 Cowgate, Edinburgh
Category:	B, in Old Town Conservation Area
Occupier:	Scottish Courts Administration
Use:	Court Rooms and Offices (Fourth, Fifth and Sixth Floors only)
Holding:	Leased

Won by J. B. Dunn in a competition, this striking building was constructed in 1888–91 for the Solicitors to the Supreme Courts, to provide a Library Hall and other offices linked to the Parliament House at the same level. This involved substantial underbuilding, separately planned to house small shops on the ground floor (Cowgate) level and tenement flats on the next three floors.

Only the fifth and sixth floors were used by the Solicitors, with the lower part of the building constructed in fire-resistant materials to minimise the fire risk inherent in a separate usage. At present only the three top floors are occupied, the remainder being locked and shuttered and in poor

94

condition. Entry to the top floors is made from the Parliament Square Courts Buildings, with provision for a fire escape exit to the Cowgate.

The building style is Scottish Baronial, of mixed late Gothic and early Renaissance character, mainly constructed of snecked grey rubble with red sandstone dressings and quoins.

Dunn has cleverly taken advantage of the grander function of the Solicitors' rooms to provide rich top-floor and skyline embellishment above the humbler and plainer lower walls of the building. There are echoes in this of such classic Scottish tower houses as Glamis, Craigievar and, particularly, Huntly Castle. The top floor is of dressed red sandstone with oriel windows, crow-step gables and false gargoyles at eaves level, with a crocketted spirelet over the oriel at the south-western angle. The oriel corbelling is moulded, and wallhead chimney-stacks form an important part of the silhouette. Below the oriels, the centre facade is recessed between plain pilasters with corbel courses above. The side walls are decorated with simple plain cartouches and string courses. Window styles are varied with stained glass on the top floor, leaded glass on the fourth floor and Georgian sash and case on the three domestic floors. There are shop fronts on the Cowgate pavement level.

Entrance is through the Courts Buildings in Parliament Square into the staircase hall on the top floor, from which there is direct access to the very fine Solicitors' Library Hall. This room is a very good example of mixed Renaissance style interior design, rectangular in plan with an ornate coved ceiling. The vault ribs are decorated and the stained glass lights in the coves illuminate the centre of the hall. A richly ornamented entablature below the vaulting spans between composite fluted pilasters which rise from a panelled wood dado. On the end walls of the hall, heroic Atlantid figures support the longitudinal ceiling ribs. These walls also contain stained glass windows. The east window is large, with a semi-circular arched head and figures depicting Peace, Justice and Trust,

with the motto 'Pro Juri Pace et Fiducia'. The west, half-round window portrays Andrew Fletcher of Saltoun. The bookcase alcoves are contained within the oriel bays and are also lit with large stained glass windows, portraying legal figures from Scottish history in the lower panels. The gallery to the upper bookcases has a fine wrought iron balustrade with a thistle motif and scroll. The bronze chandeliers and brass door furniture are original.

Within the staircase hall there is a notable decorated panelled ceiling with bosses at the intersection of the mouldings. Doric pilasters articulate the walls and the doorways are panelled with wide architraves and pediments. All the windows contain stained glass with portraits of legal figures in Scottish history, complementing those in the Library.

Also on the top floor is a large room now used as a Court Room. This has a fine vaulted ceiling with plain glazing between the ribs and fine cornice and frieze ornament. The rib volutes are decorated with acanthus leaf mouldings.

On the fourth floor, a room at present used for Juries has a good cornice, a plain frieze and a Tudor-style stone chimneypiece. The windows are leaded, with panelled shutters to the ingoes.

The third floor has been converted from tenement flats into offices and contains nothing of architectural merit.

Reference: *British Architect* July 13, August 24 1888.

Solicitors' Library

Address:	25 Drumsheugh Gardens, Edinburgh
Category:	B, in New Town Conservation Area
Occupier:	Scottish Development Department, Historic Buildings Division
Use:	Offices
Holding:	Crown

This tall terrace house, originally the residence of a prosperous solicitor, forms part of a four-storey and basement astylar classic terrace of nearly identical houses on the north side of the Gardens. The terrace was designed by John Lessels for the Walker Estate in the early 1870's and no. 25, like most of the other houses in the Gardens, was built by John Watherston and Son, the interior being wholly to their designs. It was completed in 1879. The ashlar facade consists of a channelled ground floor with a canted bay rising through basement, ground and first floors, and a consoled doorpiece and single first-floor window on the left. There are three evenly spaced windows on the second floor, beneath the main cornice, with the attic storey above. Windows are single-pane sash and case.

The interior is in excellent condition, and has undergone very little alteration or adaptation, apart from the removal of the original bathrooms and subdivision of the main first-floor drawing room. The stair is of cantilevered stone, with turned timber balusters and a moulded handrail terminating at an octagonal newel post. The walls have dado panelling. At first and second floors the stairhall leads to access corridors which act as two tiers of galleries, with three-bay pilastrades of oblong piers. The stair is top-lit by a rectangular cupola with chain moulded plasterwork. The ground-floor dining room has a pine dado and a timber beamed ceiling with diagonally boarded compartments. A decorative timber chimney-piece frames the original cast-iron register and grate, ornamented with striped and chevroned tiles.

In 1893, a billiard room was built in the garden, its unusual shape being due to the awkwardness of the site. Designed by Sydney Mitchell, this room is wainscotted in stained pine. It has a canted and consoled timber ceiling with a rectangular rooflight. In one corner there is a semi-elliptically arched inglenook with a marble chimney-piece. On the north wall there is a broad oriel bay with leaded translucent glass. This bay is also semi-elliptically arched and has a raised floor.

References: Walker Trust
Descriptive leaflet obtainable from S.D.D. Historic Buildings Division.

Address:	38–39 Drumsheugh Gardens, Edinburgh
Category:	B, in New Town Conservation Area
Occupier:	Vacant
Use:	Offices
Holding:	Crown

This property, originally two separate houses but now linked, occupies the centre of the south-west section of the triangularly-arranged Drumsheugh Gardens. This was one of the later developments on the Walker Estate. It was designed by Peddie and Kinnear in 1874 and built in 1878 by John Watherston & Sons, who completed the northern end of the block to a modified design, using canted bays, in 1899.

Consisting of four storeys with a basement, the ashlar facade has doorways with consoled balustraded balconies over, and two-storey (over basement) rectangular window bays with Corinthian details at first floor. Otherwise the character is boldly Italianate, with a low-pitched slated roof over a bracketted cornice and an attic treated as an entablature with square windows and panels. The basement area has the usual cast-iron railings and steps to entrance platts. The internal linking of the two houses has resulted in the entrance doorway to no. 38 being built up to form a window opening. The rear elevation, of coursed and squared rubble, is mostly original. One top-floor window has been enlarged, with a roof-light formed above to light an operating theatre when the building was a nursing home.

Internally, minor alterations have been made at all levels due to the linking of the two properties. A lift has been inserted in the stair-well of no. 39 and some principal rooms have been partitioned, but these changes have done little damage to the original features. The major ground and first-floor rooms have retained their plasterwork and joinery features intact and in good condition. These include an elaborate timber chimney-piece with a triple mirrored panel over the mantle, and stained panelling above and below dado rails. Both staircases are of pen-checked stone in straight flights with quarter landings and with iron balusters surmounted by moulded timber handrails. They are naturally-lit by large rectangular cupolas with decorated plasterwork to the upstands and ceilings.

Reference: Walker Trust.

Name:	Edinburgh Castle
Category:	A, Scheduled Monument, in Old Town Conservation Area
Occupiers:	Ministry of Defence, Scottish United Services Museum
Uses:	Banqueting Hall, Museum, War Memorial, etc.
Holding:	Crown

SDD Ancient Monuments Division

A tribal stronghold on the rock existed in 600 AD. When the Kingdom of the Scots took in the Lothians, the site developed through the Middle Ages from the end of the 11th century as one of the most important royal castles in Scotland. As a fortress, palace, treasury, arsenal, gun foundry and repository of the national records it reached its summit of prestige from the reigns of James III to James V (1460–1542). The palace was reconstructed for James VI in 1615, but by then royal use was almost at an end and there followed a gradual shift towards purely military occupation. In the 18th century, its exclusive use as a fortified barracks was marked by the progressive spread of buildings over the whole summit of the rock. A dawning awareness of the importance of the Castle as a great national symbol led to Victorian attempts to make the place look more picturesque with restorations and new buildings. The final essay in reconstruction was Sir Robert Lorimer's Scottish National War Memorial, completed in 1927.

All save the very earliest part of this long and

SDD Ancient Monuments Division

complex history, reflecting much of the general history of Scotland, is illustrated by surviving buildings and defences. Among these should be noted the early 12th century St Margaret's Chapel, James IV's Great Hall, which may have been ordained for his 1503 marriage with Margaret Tudor, the Half Moon Battery (wrapped round David II's Tower ruined by siege in 1573), the Palace with its major external alteration by William Wallace in 1615, the remodelled north and west defences of 1730–38 designed by the engineer John Romer and built by William Adam, the 1742 Governor's House and the 1796 New Barracks, Hippolyte Blanc's 1886 Argyle Tower restoration which owes a great deal to Viollet-le-Duc, and Ingress Bell's 1896 Baronial conversion of Ordnance Stores into the Hospital. The supreme distinction of this spectacular site does not, however, lie in the long list of important individual structures, but in the collective value of the whole ensemble in the striking evidence that it provides of continuity of use through great patterns of change.

Reference: Edinburgh Castle guidebook (H.M.S.O.)

Footnote: Edinburgh Castle was formerly in the care of P.S.A. as an ancient monument but since 1978 it has been in the care of the Secretary of State for Scotland and is maintained on his behalf by the Ancient Monuments Division of the Scottish Development Department. P.S.A. however, retains a responsibility for the areas used by the Army and the Scottish United Services Museum.

Address:	50 Frederick Street/Hill Street, Edinburgh
Category:	B, in New Town Conservation Area
Occupiers:	Inland Revenue Office, Scottish Home and Health Department
Use:	Offices
Holding:	Leased

The Frederick Street/Hill Street development forms part of the original scheme prepared for the New Town of Edinburgh by James Craig. It was built between 1786 and 1795 in a simple Georgian style, and originally consisted entirely of three-storey, basement and attic flatted blocks. It is now largely of a mixed office and commercial character, with many later shops protruding over the basement area.

No. 50 was originally a ten-window frontage but the northern half has since been demolished and replaced by a new building on the corner of Frederick Street and Hill Street. Only six bays of the original frontage now remain. The front wall is of ashlar, with a lightly tooled finish but no decorative dressings. The roof above is pitched and slated, with one original chimney in stone. There are three shops at ground-floor level and one entrance to an adjacent property. The windows have lost their astragals at the front, but these have been retained in the rear windows facing west. The new development, which approximately reflects the original character, has a flat roof on the Hill Street frontage.

Few noteworthy features remain inside the building. On the second floor, one former drawing room retains its original character with a curved wall on the short side, a panelled dado and a simple plaster cornice. The rear room at second-floor level is lit by a fine tripartite window. Its original panelled shutters remain unaltered.

Reference: R.C.A.H.M.S. Inventory, City of Edinburgh.

Address:	22–24 George Street, Edinburgh
Category:	B, in New Town Conservation Area
Occupier:	Royal Society of Edinburgh
Use:	Archives, Library and Lectures
Holding:	Crown

Built in 1843 to designs by William Burn and David Bryce for the Edinburgh Life Assurance Company, incorporating rooms for the Edinburgh Subscription Library and the Faculty of Actuaries, this building was converted for the use of the Royal Society by W. T. Oldrieve in 1909, the Society having previously been housed in the R.S.A. building at the Mound (q.v.). Internal reconstruction designed by Robert Hurd and Partners was carried out in 1982.

The building consists of three floors and basement with a ground-floor lecture room at the rear adjoining the main building. The front is symmetrical Italian Renaissance, five windows wide, in ashlar stonework with advanced Roman Doric porch entrances at the ends and a balustraded basement area. Pedimented first-floor windows are set between fluted Corinthian columns. An ornamented string course below lines through with the porch entablature.

All the windows are cross-mullioned sash and case with moulded margins. On the ground floor there is a continuous string course at cill level with moulded and bracketted panels below the windows. The slated roof is hidden behind a bold balustraded parapet. Entrance doors are panelled with semi-circular fanlights above.

The interior displays a wealth of fine plaster and joinery work, with excellent examples of cabinet makers' skill in the hardwood bookcases. Fine original chimney-pieces remain in all the main rooms. On the ground floor the reception area has decorated ceiling beams, a deep cornice and two fine hardwood fluted Ionic columns on panelled pedestals. A corridor with patterned mosaic floor leads to the ground-floor lecture room, which is top-lit by three circular dome lights between the ceiling beams.

The Council Room on the first floor has ornate plaster decoration to the ceiling beams with bosses at intersections, a fine cornice and frieze and bolection moulded wall panels. In this room there is an excellent marble chimney-piece with original tile insets and a brass hood. The windows are double sash and case with shuttered ingoes.

A large seminar room on the first floor to the rear of the building has a fine plaster ceiling with bosses at the inter-sections of the beams.

The main staircase at the east end of the building is particularly fine, with an exceptional oval ribbed dome, on moulded pendentives. Its convex drum displays laurel leaf festoons above a projecting cornice and frieze. The stone stairs are cantilevered and the balusters are of ornamented wrought-iron with a hardwood handrail.

The main stair gives access to the first and second floors only. Access to the third floor is by a plain secondary stair at the west end of the building.

The basement contains book storage, kitchen and cloakrooms, and has modern finishes.

Reference: *Builder* May 27 1876.

Address:	125 George Street, Edinburgh
Category:	B, in New Town Conservation Area
Occupier:	Ordnance Survey/
	National Gallery
Use:	Offices
Holding	Crown

This property is part of the original terrace of Georgian houses built between 1780 and 1790, few of which now remain unaltered. It retains its full original elevation to George Street, although the properties on its west side have been extensively altered and partly restored again, while that on the east side was rebuilt in 1880.

No. 125 consists of three storeys, four bays wide with attic and basement. Some alterations were made in 1856 to designs by Robert Matheson, including an extension to the rear. Nevertheless, most of the original character has been preserved, and the extension reflects the internal character of the original building. The only outstanding feature of the otherwise plain street elevation is the handsome doorpiece, now one of the finest in George Street. Its arched tripartite opening includes a delicate semi-circular fanlight and is framed by Roman Doric pilasters and a shallow entablature. The masonry is varied according to usual New Town classical principles—rock-faced in the basement, rusticated at ground floor level and droved ashlar above. There are string courses at first and second floors and beneath the ground-floor cills. The four-pane windows are of typical Georgian proportion. The roof above is pitched and slated.

The original portion has retained features common to a building of the period such as plaster friezes and cornices, panelled ceilings, richly moulded architraves and door-pieces complete with shallow frieze and cornice detail. Certain panelled doors have retained the original brass ironmongery. There are a number of polished marble chimney-pieces of varying design. In the first-floor drawing room the original ceiling with plaster centre-piece and cornice has been preserved above a modern suspended ceiling. The stair is lit by a plain rectangular rooflight, and there are small moulded plaster representations of the arts of Peace and War on each stairhead wall.

In the rear extension, the most notable feature is at first-floor level, where one large top-lit room has a plastered barrel vault. The attic floor has been adapted for office use with dormer windows inserted to the north. The character of the joinery is similar to that on other floors, but more restrained. The basement is used for storage of records and is floored in polished flagstone.

Address:	127–129 George Street, Edinburgh
Category:	B, in New Town Conservation Area
Occupiers:	Department of Employment, Manpower Services Commission
Use:	Offices
Holding:	Leased

This three-storey attic and basement double frontage, originally two houses, was built between 1780 and 1790 as part of Craig's original New Town plan. The six-bay elevation to George Street and the rooms immediately behind are virtually the only original parts of the building to have been restored to their former character. The rest of the building to the rear is entirely modern and incorporates car parking space with access from the rear lane. The restoration work, carried out in 1975 as part of a larger reconstruction scheme, has been sensitively executed, and received a Civic Trust Award in European Architectural Heritage Year 1975. The architects for the restoration were Robert Hurd and Partners. In addition to the usual office space, the modern section includes lecture rooms and small halls suitable for staff training seminars and conferences. This section also includes a new stair and lift.

The George Street frontage has a variety of masonry finishes—rock-faced at the basement, rusticated at the ground floor and droved ashlar above. The roof is pitched and slated, and incorporates six semi-recessed hipped dormers. All the windows are sash and case with astragals. The first-floor windows have moulded architraves with a shallow frieze and cornice. Originally, the centre window of each group of three had a cornice supported by consoles, but only those over the eastern window now survive. There is a continuous string course at first floor and a simple cornice and blocking course. A platform oversailing the basement area leads to the handsome arched pilastered door-piece which has a delicate semi-circular fanlight and narrow flanking side lights. The iron railing to the basement area incorporates an ornamental lantern at each side of the entrance.

The restored interior has the usual decorative plaster cornices, panelled shutters and doors. Two timber chimney-pieces in the Adam style have been retained.

102

Name:	National Library of Scotland
Address:	George IV Bridge, Edinburgh
Category:	B, in Old Town Conservation Area
Occupier:	National Library of Scotland
Use:	Library
Holding:	Crown

The Library was founded as the Library of the Faculty of Advocates in 1682, largely through the efforts of Sir George Mackenzie of Rosehaugh, the King's Advocate. Originally it was intended solely as a legal library, but it soon became apparent that its efficient working required possession of books in other disciplines. The Copyright Act of 1710 conferred on the Library the right to claim a copy of every work published in Great Britain, and the sheer volume of material published made it inevitable that the Library would grow considerably in the heyday of the Scottish Enlightenment. Such notable figures as James Boswell, Walter Scott and David Hume served as Keepers of the Library, making it one of the intellectual centres of the country. Later, the Writers to the Signet, one of the two bodies of Scottish solicitors and closely associated with the Faculty of Advocates, became interested in the development of the Library and in 1922, a Scottish benefactor, Sir Alexander Grant of Forres, offered to give £100,000 as a permanent endowment. The present Library therefore derives from three sources, commemorated in the memorial window lighting the main stair, which portrays the Coats of Arms of the Faculty of Advocates, the Writers to the Signet and Sir Alexander Grant.

The present building, designed by the architect Dr. Reginald Fairlie, was begun in 1937. Work ceased during the second world war, and the building was not completed until July 1956, when it was officially opened by Her Majesty the Queen.

It consists of two main floors above George IV Bridge level with seven basements below, which are used almost exclusively for the stacking of books and records. The two lower floors facing the Cowgate contain administrative offices and canteen. A separate access for the use of the lower floors is provided from the Cowgate. The building is steel-framed and faced with dressed Blaxter sandstone with a polished granite base at pavement level. The heavy monumental main elevation to George IV Bridge consists of one large central block of nine bays with a lower block of three bays on either side. The style is classical modern with restrained detail in the form of pilasters, string courses and cornices. The ground floor, containing the central entrance, incorporates eight small Georgian pattern windows giving light direct into the entrance hall. A deep string course at first-floor level provides a seating for giant Roman Doric pilasters. These enclose seven figures by the sculptor Hew Lorimer, depicting the arts of civilisation—Medicine, Science, History, Imaginative Writing, Law, Theology and Music. The pilasters of the two lower blocks enclose three large Georgian windows with carved rectangular panels above. This austere monumentality is repeated on the two end walls facing the Signet Library and the Cowgate. The rear of the building is of rendered brick.

Internally, polished Westmoreland slate is used for skirtings and stair linings and for facing the four giant columns in the entrance hall. There is also lavish use of hardwood joinery.

The most interesting interior belongs to the top-lit Music Room, formerly the Map Room. A large glazed panel, hung below the roof-light, is engraved with a map of the world and the surrounding plaster frieze displays the signs of the Zodiac.

The Board Room is of pleasing proportions with astragalled sash and case windows at high level facing George IV Bridge. The opposite wall is sub-divided by a pattern of pilasters and high quality joinerwork. The floor is hardwood, of a parquet pattern. This room connects by a corridor to the Advocate's Lounge, and is used regularly by the Faculty. It is a spacious room, its walls lined in hardwood panelling. The ceiling has a large recessed circular centrepiece in plaster with concealed lighting. There is a surrounding plaster frieze and ceiling cornice.

The Exhibition Gallery, occupying the south wing, has four Roman Doric columns on separate dadoes.

The main Reading Room, running the full length of the centre block at first floor level, has a cupola light over each bay, but is also lit by windows from the east elevation. It has a mezzanine floor inserted at a later date to provide extra space both for books and users of the Library. There is a tinted glass baluster rail surrounding the mezzanine area from which it is possible to view the lower floor.

Reference: Reginald Fairlie (Patrick Nuttgens).

Address:	1 Grosvenor Crescent, Edinburgh
Category:	B, in New Town Conservation Area
Occupier:	Scottish Courts Administration (Scottish Land Court)
Use:	Offices and Court
Holding:	Crown

No. 1 Grosvenor Crescent is the corner pavilion of a three-storey, basement and attic terraced crescent designed by John Chesser for the Heriot Trust in 1868. Built in 1871, under the supervision of Peddie and Kinnear, who designed the interior, no. 1 has straight frontages to both Grosvenor Crescent and Palmerston Place. These are three and five bays wide respectively.

It is constructed of Craigleith ashlar stone with a central ground and first-floor canted bay to the front and a ground-floor bay window to Palmerston Place. The rear elevation is of coursed rubble. The entrance is by flyover steps to the ground-floor bay, which has a modern glazed door. All the windows are sash and case without glazing bars, the windows being plate glass from the start. Except for the basement, all the windows have moulded architrave surrounds with consoled cornices at first floor on the Grosvenor Crescent elevation. The stone surround to the front door has recently been painted. String courses link the windows at cill level on first and second floors.

A balustraded parapet conceals the slated roof and a series of attic windows with arched heads. A symmetrical pair of tall chimney stacks rise behind the parapet on each flank elevation. The basement area is protected by original cast-iron railings. The Palmerston Place frontage has been extended by a later addition of two storeys and basement, in keeping with the main building except for its flat roof.

Peddie and Kinnear's interior contains fine cornices and joinery, especially in the main front room on the first floor, presently used as the Courtroom, which has an ornate cornice, frieze and central rose, bolection-moulded wall panelling and a very fine door-piece. All chimney-pieces have been removed.

Address:	73 Hanover Street, Edinburgh
Category:	B, in New Town Conservation Area
Occupier:	Ministry of Defence
Use:	Office/Recruiting Centre (ground floor only)
Holding:	Crown

This property, forming part of a block containing nos. 75 and 77, was part of the original plan for the New Town of Edinburgh prepared by James Craig circa 1767. Feuing did not begin until 1784, but Hanover Street was almost complete by 1790.

Hanover Street slopes steeply towards the north, admitting reasonable natural light into semi-basement rooms. No. 73 is typical of the plainer New Town buildings of its date, three bays wide and three storeys high, with attic and basement. All the windows above ground floor level have astragals. The shop front is almost certainly an early alteration, probably c.1815. The access doors to nos. 73 and 77 are pilastered with patterned fanlights. An entablature runs the full width of the building with a central bow window lighting the ground-floor office. Unusually long flights of steps rise to the entrances, with wrought-iron railings on both sides. Above first-floor level the ashlar is lightly tooled. There are no architraves to the windows but the stone cills project slightly. There are rusticated quoins at the north corner. The roof is pitched and slated and the two dormer windows have pitched roofs. There is no cornice or parapet at roof level.

Internally, little of the original character remains, apart from the plaster cornices to the outer vestibule and the inner hall. These are typical of the period, including mutules and egg-and-dart mouldings. The vestibule is panelled in oak to lintel level and the inner door is glazed, with small fielded panels. A recent suspended acoustic tile ceiling in the main office obscures the original.

The accommodation above ground-floor level is a separate holding with entrance from no. 77.

Reference: R.C.A.H.M.S. Inventory, City of Edinburgh.

Address:	18 and 20 Hill Street, Edinburgh
Category:	B, in New Town Conservation Area
Occupiers:	Gaming Board, Ministry of Defence, Department of the Registers of Scotland
Use:	Offices
Holding:	Leased

A pair of terraced houses, forming part of a row built in 1788–94 by James Hill, mason, and financed by Robert Belshes of Greenyeards. This section was described as part of Thistle Street in James Craig's plan of 1767, but the Town Council gave Hill approval to change its name in 1788.

The houses at nos. 18 and 20 consist of three storeys, attic and semi-basement, in unembellished droved ashlar with slated pitched roofs and slated cheeks to the dormers. These are original, and nicely curved at the angles. The windows throughout are of Georgian sash and case pattern, with plain flush architrave surrounds. The front windows are modern replacements. The door-pieces are tripartite, consisting of a doorway and narrow side lights divided by pilasters and set within a moulded architrave, with fluted frieze and rosettes over. The door to no. 18 is not now in use.

Both houses are used as offices. Mainly because of a recent fire, the interior has been completely refurbished on all floors. Very few of the original fittings remain, but most windows retain original shutter ingoes. The original stone stairs with cantilevered steps and plain square cast-iron balusters remain between ground and second floors.

106

Name:	National Library/Carnegie Library
Address:	312/320 Lawnmarket, Edinburgh
Category:	A, in Old Town Conservation Area
Occupier:	National Library
Use:	Offices, Conference Room
Holding:	Crown

This building forms part of the south facade of the Lawnmarket, near the top of the Royal Mile which runs down the crest of the rock from the Castle to the Palace of Holyroodhouse. The front building was built in 1752 by Thomas Fisher, an Edinburgh merchant of the period. His name is commemorated in Fisher's Close, alongside, where an older wing dated 1699 has been incorporated. The frontage was restored in 1950–53 as the Carnegie Library, by James Shearer, a Dunfermline architect who worked substantially for the Carnegie Trust, and who completely reconstructed the building behind the facade.

The five-storey and attic building originally consisted of well-to-do flats and still appears basically domestic in character. The attic elevation to the Lawnmarket has three curvilinear gables containing the windows, and in both form and detail shows the same Netherlandish influence as the similar block to the west, built by Captain George Riddell in 1726. The front is eight windows wide grouped 1–3–3–1. The main entrance is Shearer's work and is modern Scots Revival in character, finely moulded with a broken pediment enclosing the Coat of Arms of the Library. The detail of the curvilinear gables to the attic windows is also of high quality.

The interior is completely new with some fine joinerwork.

References: Royal Mile (E. J. Macrae)
James Shearer QJ. R.I.A.S. No.95, 1954.

Name:	'Scotsman' Buildings
Address:	4 Market Street, Edinburgh
Category:	B, in Old Town Conservation Area
Occupier:	Inland Revenue (part of 5th and 6th floors only)
Use:	File Storage
Holding:	Leased

The impressive block at nos. 1–6 Market Street was built in 1899 to 1902 to the design of Dunn and Findlay, as part of John Ritchie Findlay's "Scotsman" development beside the North Bridge. (See also 28 North Bridge). It replaced a Victorian building demolished to make way for the North Bridge development.

The lower part of the building was designed as fruit market units for wholesalers. This section, which extends below to the level of Waverley Station, has recently been adapted by Edinburgh District Council as the City Art Centre. The upper floors remain in their former use as offices and storage.

The frontage is five arcaded bays wide, with segmental arches to the ground floor and recessed segmental-arched panels fronting the first, second and third floors, all constructed in fine ashlar masonry.

The fourth floor is designed as an attic storey above a delicate string course. Tripartite windows, with Gibbs mullions, light the principal storeys above ground floor. The attic dormers have alternating straight and segmented pediments. The east gable wall accentuates the fourth (attic) storey treatment and the gable chimney stack is cleverly detailed with intersecting vertical and skew mouldings. The south gable has recently been rendered.

Internally, the Inland Revenue accommodation is used for file storage and is purely functional, without decoration of any kind.

Reference: R.S.A. 1899.

Address:	Melville Street, Edinburgh
Category:	A, in New Town Conservation Area
Occupiers:	Nos. 3–11 Scottish Development Department, Ancient Monuments Branch
	Nos. 18–22 Council on Tribunals and Mental Welfare Commission
	No. 23 Social Security Commissioners
	Nos. 52–56 Royal Commission for Ancient and Historic Monuments of Scotland
Uses:	Offices
Holding:	3–11 and 23 Crown
	18–22 and 52–56 Leased

52–56 Melville Street.

The complete Melville Street Development was part of the Walker Estate section of the western New Town, purchased by William Walker in 1813 for his son, Sir Patrick, and immediately developed. The plan appears to follow a scheme drawn up by James Gillespie Graham, embracing the interests of several proprietors, but the Walker Trust's architect was Robert Brown, who designed Melville Street in 1814. The development was carried out between 1820 and 1862.

Melville Street has admirable qualities; in particular, its splendid breadth and spaciousness, the wide and handsome intersection with Walker Street and the fine architectural centre-piece in the north elevation of the terrace, on the Stafford Street axis.

All the properties are approached from the pavement by flying stairs. Iron railings flank the basement areas.

Numbers 3–11

This property, on the north side of the street, consisted originally of five separate dwellings. It now operates as one office unit, having functioned for several decades as a boys' school, Melville College, until 1976, when it was acquired by a commercial development company. A later porch was removed and doors and windows were restored to their original design. Many internal alterations have been made over the years, including the provision of interconnecting corridors at all levels, screens to corridors and removal of individual staircases. Some attempt, however, has been made to reflect the original character by fitting coved mouldings to partitions and by arching new openings in the party walls.

The main elevation to Melville Street retains the original impression of a terrace of domestic dwellings, although some doorways now operate only as fire exits and other lobbies have been converted into small storage spaces. The terrace generally is of three storeys with basement but

there are tall attic storeys to nos. 3 and 5. Each former house is three bays wide, the windows being Georgian sash and case with astragals except on the third floor of nos. 3 and 5. The ground floor is rusticated ashlar masonwork, with rusticated voussoirs over the entrance doors and windows. Doorways in the left-hand bay of each unit are flanked by narrow glazed panels on either side and astragalled fanlights above. There is a string course at first-floor level and an ornamental cast-iron balcony runs across the full width of each three-window bay. The stonework above the string course is of lightly tooled ashlar. At second-floor level a heavy moulded string course/cornice runs the full length of the terrace. A small cornice at roof level carries through at the attic floor of nos. 1 and 3. The roof above is pitched and slated. An arched, wrought-iron lampholder is a standard feature of each entrance.

Internally, only two original stairs remain. A lift has been built into one former stairwell. One of the remaining stairs is worthy of note, being semi-oval in plan with a full oval rooflight above, which has a delicately designed frieze and cornice. There are plaster festoons above the doors at landing level. The former entrance to no. 11 retains a Roman Doric columned screen. All the former vestibules have richly patterned plaster ceilings.

Some of the principal rear rooms have rich architraves and plaster cornices and bowed exterior walls containing Venetian windows. Two original polished marble chimney-pieces remain at second-floor level.

Numbers 18–22

This property forms part of the continuous terrace on the south side of Melville Street and originally comprised three separate dwellings. It now operates as two office units, the ground and first floors being used by the Automobile Association and the upper two floors by the Council on Tribunals. Only the facade towards Melville Street survives from the original fabric, everything behind having been demolished and rebuilt.

The frontage design is similar to nos. 3–11. The main elevation retains most of the original character, although the entrances to nos. 18 and 20 have been built up to form windows, and the door to no. 20 has been moved to the centre of the nine-bay block. The A.A. retains this separate entrance, direct from the pavement.

The new building which has been erected behind the old facade is typical office accommodation with patent partitioning, doors, and suspended ceilings.

Number 23

This is the right-hand flanking section of the majestic Ionic centre-piece on the north side of the terrace, on the Stafford Street axis. No. 23 consists of three bays, three storeys and basement. The east bay is slightly advanced and the ground-floor stonework is rusticated. The entrance doorway is tripartite with an arched fanlight above which, like all the windows, has lost its original astragals. The window over the entrance is emphasised by a moulded surround with a thin entablature supported on console brackets. The heavy blocking course over this bay becomes a balustraded parapet over the remainder of the elevation.

Internally, the former ground and first-floor living rooms are almost perfectly preserved. The main ground-floor room facing south towards Melville Street contains much rich plasterwork, and there is a simple black polished marble chimney-piece. Both north-facing rooms have bowed window alcoves. The full width main room at first-floor level is well-proportioned and is linked to the rear room by a double door with architraves. Its door-head incorporates a shallow cornice. The ceiling plasterwork displays a rich repertoire of the usual classical features such as dentil and egg-and-dart mouldings. The second floor, consisting of smaller rooms, has simpler detail but the overall character is similar. The cantilevered stone staircase has a notable oval roof-light with simple frieze and cornice.

The entrance vestibule has Roman Doric pilasters to the walls and a panelled ceiling with restrained plaster detail. The inner screen is a later insertion. The basement, which has a flagstone floor, is used exclusively for storage.

Numbers 52–56

The three original dwellings of nos. 52, 54 and 56 now form one interconnected office unit. The entrance doors to nos. 52 and 56 have been altered to form windows, the only access being by the original no. 54. This has involved considerable internal alterations, especially to no. 54 which was adapted for his own use as a residence in 1912 by the noted Scottish architect, Sir Robert Lorimer.

Each dwelling is three bays wide. At first-floor level, a full-width cast-iron balcony formerly existed, but Lorimer removed this feature at no. 54 and adapted the centre window to form a French door with an individual stone balcony and wrought-iron rail. The attic space at no. 54 was extended by Lorimer as a mansard roof with three dormer windows. The usual Melville Street design of arched lampholder forms part of the front railing. There are no astragals to the windows of no. 52 but these have been retained in no. 56. At no. 54, the astragals were replaced by Lorimer to a somewhat thicker early Georgian section enclosing smaller panes.

Internally, all three cantilevered stone staircases have been retained with their ornamental iron balustrades and hardwood handrails but a lift has been built into the stairwell at no. 54, serving all upper levels. Each stair is top-lit from an oval-shaped rooflight, with a rich surrounding frieze and a shallow cornice below.

At ground-floor level in no. 54, the south-facing library was extensively altered by Lorimer as a dining room. The rear window was lowered to floor level and widened to form a bay window. This has a surrounding architrave suggestive of perpendicular Gothic with a low four-centred pointed arch, and the ceiling is now divided into panels with carved bosses at the intersections. The cornice has been retained but adapted. The chimney-piece is of simple design with Dutch-type tiles. At first-floor level the former full-width drawing room is largely Lorimer's work including the central window which was lowered to floor level to form a French window. The stone balcony to the outside has a decorated wrought-iron balustrade. This room also has painted wood panels, built-in bookcases of delicate design and a finely designed doorpiece with architrave frieze and shallow cornice. One upper room in no. 54 contains a chimney-piece in dressed oak with carved sides and mantelpiece, and a room on the attic floor has a polished marble chimney-piece.

Name:	Queen's House
Address:	36 Moray Place, Edinburgh
Category:	A, in New Town Conservation Area
Occupier:	Grace and Favour Residence
Use:	Domestic
Holding:	Crown

Moray Place forms part of the Moray Estate Development designed by James Gillespie Graham in 1822 on the garden ground of the Earl of Moray's town house at Drumsheugh, since demolished. William Burn was consulted, but the extent of his contribution is uncertain. The elevations are typical of Gillespie Graham's classical manner. Moray Place forms the major element of the layout. This part of the development was rapidly built, being completed by 1827, the Earl himself taking a new house here. The plan of Moray Place is duodecagonal and its well-landscaped private gardens, in the centre, are among the best in the New Town.

Queen's House forms part of the four-storey and basement block at the north-west corner of Moray Place and Great Stuart Street. The ground floor has arched openings, two of which are blind. The first and second-floor windows are divided by giant Roman Doric pilasters. A deep entablature and main cornice divides the frontage of the principal

floors from the fourth-floor attic storey above. The windows are typically Georgian in character, retaining their astragals at the third and fourth floors. There are cast-iron balconies to the first-floor windows.

Queen's House comprises the ground floor and basement flat. The elevation is built of V-jointed ashlar, with arched windows recessed in round-headed panels. The original astragals have been replaced by two-pane sashes. The fanlight above the entrance door follows the radial pattern originally adopted throughout the estate. The stone lintel over the entrance door bears the words "Queen's House" engraved in classical Trajan lettering. This was executed when the property became a Grace and Favour Residence in the early 1950's. Twin ornamental lampholders form an integral part of the railing design.

The house itself has all the usual features of a town house of the period although some alterations have been carried out to provide more modern facilities. The two main rooms are of pleasant proportions, retaining moulded plaster cornices to the ceilings, panelled doors and moulded architraves. An oak chimney-piece survives in one room and the other main room has a notable plaster ceiling. The entrance corridor is unusually wide.

Reference: The Making of Classical Edinburgh (Youngson)

Name:	National Gallery of Scotland
Address:	The Mound, Edinburgh
Category:	A, in New Town Conservation Area
Occupier:	National Gallery of Scotland
Use:	Art Gallery
Holding:	Crown

Designed by W. H. Playfair, the National Gallery was begun in 1850 but not completed until 1857, the year in which Playfair died. It was the result of concerted action by the Treasury, a Board of Trustees and the city of Edinburgh which provided the site, and originally was divided longitudinally into the National Gallery and the exhibition galleries of the Royal Scottish Academy.

In this design, Playfair returned to the classical idiom in a pure and simplified form. The main galleries are single-storey, long and low, with a simple anta order, divided by a higher transverse block with hexastyle Greek Ionic porticos on both the east and west flanks. The entrance porticos on both end elevations are distyle in antis flanked by tetrastyle pedimented screens at each end. The building is crowned by a balustraded parapet. The columns are unfluted and there is no sculpture in any of the four pediments. The severe classical detailing is finely executed and the integration of the various parts of the exterior into one unified whole is outstandingly successful.

Inside, the Gallery is ingeniously divided into top-lit lozenge-shaped and octagonal rooms to provide maximum hanging space. The fine Corinthian columned screens between the galleries are later insertions.

Some internal alterations were made to the east section by W. T. Oldrieve in 1911–12 and further alterations were made in 1970, including the sensitive and well-concealed provision of basement galleries beneath the east flank of the gallery. The removal of the former cast-iron railing along the "Playfair Walk", which runs adjacent to the building, connecting Princes Street and the top of the Mound, has considerably improved the setting of the building.

References: Old and New Edinburgh (Grant)
Plans, Edinburgh University Library.
The Making of Classical Edinburgh (Youngson)
The Greek Revival (Crook)

Name:	Royal Scottish Academy
Address:	The Mound/Princes Street, Edinburgh
Category:	A, in New Town Conservation Area
Occupier	Royal Scottish Academy
Use:	Art Exhibitions and Offices
Holding:	Crown

The majestic Greek Revival Royal Scottish Academy was originally built as the Royal Institution, to house the Royal Society of Edinburgh, the Society of Antiquaries and the Society for the Encouragement of the Fine Arts in Scotland. Designed by W. H. Playfair in 1822 it was then only two-thirds of its present length and had a shallow portico to Princes Street. Its extensive reconstruction and further embellishment by Playfair in 1832–35 was a major exercise which turned a good building into a great one.

Modelled on Greek temple design, it is rectangular in plan with Doric colonnades along both flanks ending in distyle pedimented projections. There are central octostyle porticos on the south and north elevations with superb scroll sculpture in the pediments. The Doric order is elaborated by triglyph and wreath details in the entablature. The bold parapet was further embellished in 1844 by the addition of a statue of Queen Victoria, executed by Sir John Steell. The building is particularly impressive viewed from East Princes Street Gardens, the fluted Doric columns appearing to frame the windows of the east elevation. Internally, the building was reconstructed in 1911–12 by W. T. Oldrieve in a ponderous classical manner. A grand staircase leads to a series of inter-related galleries.

References: Georgian Edinburgh (Lindsay)
The Making of Classical Edinburgh (Youngson)
Plans SRO and Edinburgh University Library
Modern Athens (Shepherd)
Letter Book (Playfair) Edinburgh University Library
The Greek Revival (Crook)

Address:	16 North Bank Street, Edinburgh
Category:	A, in Old Town Conservation Area
Occupier:	Scottish Courts Administration
Use:	Offices
Holding:	Leased

This office was originally built for the Edinburgh Savings Bank, which took a ground and first-floor section of a large new building constructed jointly with the Free Church of Scotland in 1858–60. The architect was David Cousin. It was built on the site of the western section of James Court, which had been partly destroyed by fire, and incorporates part of it at its eastern end. Ground and first floors only are used by the SCA, the remainder of the building always having been occupied by the Free Church of Scotland.

The block is sited in a most imposing position at the head of the Mound, and is visible from most of Princes Street. It consists of five floors and double attics with a tower set back in the roof at the west end. In style it is Scots Jacobean, built of snecked rubble with richly ornamented strapwork window heads. The dormers have broken triangular and segmental pedimented heads set in an intricate roofline of towers, oriels, turrets and an upper, set-back tier of dormers. The window-head ornamentation is varied at the western section, but had to be replaced to a standard pattern when recent repairs were made to the eastern section.

The entrance to the Scottish Court section is set in a slim central entrance tower, slightly advanced from the main facade, and has an ornate door-piece of Doric pilasters on moulded pedestals framing an arched doorway with sculptured keyblock. Over the door is a cartouche with the motif ESB and the date 1860 carved in relief. In front of the building is a fine balustraded forecourt with strapwork obelisk lamp-standards.

In the Scottish Courts Office some fine original fittings remain, though most of the interior has been modernised at both levels. The vestibule and hall have fine barrel-vaulted ceilings with Doric pilasters and coffered coves. A bold, ornate moulded cornice and frieze, with centre-pieces on vault ribs incorporating the ESB motif, make a rich entrance to the building. The recent doors and fanlight are in keeping with the period. On the ground floor, the large room has a beamed ceiling, Doric pilasters and original panelled shutters.

Two small north-facing rooms on the first floor retain original detailing. The large conference room retains a beamed ceiling with cornice mouldings and plain frieze. Other fittings are much more recent.

References: Old and New Edinburgh (Grant)
Builder, October 30 1858 (ii)
Building News, March 27 1863

Address:	28 North Bridge, Edinburgh
Category:	B, in Old Town Conservation Area
Occupier:	Scottish Courts Administration
Use:	Offices
Holding:	Leased

No. 28 forms part of large complex (nos. 20–56) built between 1899 and 1902 to designs by James Bow Dunn and James Leslie Findlay, in Scots Renaissance style. The commission was by Findlay's father, John Ritchie Findlay, proprietor of *The Scotsman*. When completed, it was the largest single commercial development then erected in Scotland. (See also 4 Market Street).

The section at no. 28 consists of four floors, attic and garret with the ground floor giving access only to stairs and lift. There are also extensive basements below bridge level.

Constructed in ashlar with a three-bay frontage, the building has bipartite windows on all floors. The window bays are set in recessed corniced panels extending through first and second floors. A similar cornice separates third floor and attic. The bipartite windows on first, second and third floors have Gibbs surrounds and mullions, with stone transomes at first and second floors. The three pilastered dormers are bipartite with stone mullions and have alternating segmental and straight pediments. The entrance has been refaced and modernised, as have the flanking ground-floor shops.

The steeply pitched roof is slated, and there are prominent stone chimney-stacks with moulded cornices.

The staircase has a white glazed brick dado with stone stairs, plain cast-iron balusters and hardwood handrail. Stair landings have arched openings to circulation areas. Rooms on all floors lack ornament, apart from simple cornices. Panelled doors and architraves are of good quality, with varied mouldings. A mezzanine floor, between ground and first floor, contains a conference room with a beamed ceiling and a good mahogany chimney-piece. Some rooms have leaded glass partitions to circulation areas.

The Scottish Courts Administration uses the whole of no. 28, but private firms occupy the mezzanine floor.

Address:	44 Palmerston Place, Edinburgh
Category:	B, in New Town Conservation Area
Occupier:	Customs and Excise
Use:	Offices
Holding:	Crown

A three-storey and basement terrace house, in a row designed by John Chesser and built in 1877 in the fashionable residential area west of Melville Street and north of Atholl Place.

It is constructed of Craigleith ashlar, with three-window canted bays on all floors which establish its mid-Victorian character. Its front is well proportioned, with string courses at first and second-floor levels and a deeper dentilled cornice. The door-piece is identical with the rest of the block, having an elliptical-arched doorway surmounted by a consoled cornice lining with the first-floor string course.

The interior retains much plasterwork and joinery of its period, none of it exceptional. The main room on the ground floor has a beamed ceiling with decorated bays, cornice and frieze. On the first floor, the main room to the front has an ornate cornice with plain frieze. The alcove beam is decorated with a cornice and plaster brackets.

Reference: Heriot Trust

Name:	Supreme Courts of Scotland
Address:	1–11 Parliament Square, Edinburgh
Category:	A, in Old Town Conservation Area
Occupiers:	Scottish Courts Administration
	National Library of Scotland
Use:	Court Sittings and Administration
Holding:	Crown

Despite their continuous late Georgian neo-classical facades, the buildings on the south side of Parliament Square occupy one of the most historic sites in Scotland and are the result of some ten major building operations. Although now built up level to the Square, the site slopes steeply down to the Cowgate on the south. It originally formed the burial ground of the High Kirk of St Giles, then surrounded by the residences of the prebendaries which were jointly used by the Law Courts and the Scottish Parliament. Some of these buildings were demolished in 1631 to make way for the new Parliament House, built under the direction of Sir James Murray and completed in 1640. Its Parliament Hall, where the Scottish Parliament sat as one chamber (like the States-General in France) until the Union of the Parliaments in 1707, still survives as the nucleus of the complex, as does the

recently restored Laigh Hall beneath it. In 1680–81 this building was extended eastwards by an Exchange, built by Sir William Bruce for Thomas Robertson. It was burned in 1700 and internally rebuilt. Under Acts of Parliament of 1806 and 1808, these buildings were remodelled and recased in 1807–10 by Robert Reid, with classical elevations in a style derived from Robert Adam's Edinburgh University quadrangle. This complex was extended westwards by a new building to house the Libraries of the Writers to the Signet and the Faculty of Advocates, the latter now the Upper Signet Library. The impressive classical interiors of these libraries, which are not a PSA responsibility, were designed by William Stark and completed by Robert Reid following Stark's death in 1813. These extensive works, however, succeeded only in improving the courtroom accommodation without significantly extending it, Outer House cases still being heard in the Parliament Hall. In response to complaints from the Faculty of Advocates, new courts were built on to the south end of the Parliament Hall for the Lords Ordinary, to designs by Archibald Elliot, in 1818–19. The opportunity to improve the cramped quarters of the Inner House came in 1824 when a major fire burned the south side of the High Street from the Tron Kirk to the eastern half of Parliament Square. This allowed the extension of the original

L-plan complex eastwards as a symmetrical U-plan scheme. It was designed by Robert Reid and built in 1825–36. The original 1807–10 section of the central block was now completely rebuilt behind the facade, as new First and Second Division Courtrooms, while the new eastern section provided a Robing Room and a High Court, all built up from Cowgate level on a massive underbuilding of cell accommodation.

To the east, new Exchequer Chambers, completed by Reid in 1831, answered his facade which already screened the east flank of the Parliament Hall and the Signet Library staircase on the west. These developments left a vacant site at the south-east corner, between the Inner House and the Exchequer Chambers. On this plot, entering off the quadrant arcade at the eastern angle of the square, William Burn erected in 1827 a large plain fireproof building of whinstone for Sir William Forbes's Bank (latterly the Union Bank). By now, the growth of the Advocates' and Signet Libraries was such that the Advocates built a new Library to the south-west of the Parliament Hall to designs by William Henry Playfair in 1829–30, and sold their Upper Library to the Writers to the Signet. Further improvements came in 1849, when William Nixon was commissioned to rebuild Elliot's Outer House as four identical courts, probably re-using much of his furniture, and again in 1885 when the Forbes bank building was absorbed into the complex, the telling room being remodelled as Court No 4, to designs by W. W. Robertson.

The next major change came in 1888–91, when the Solicitors to the Supreme Courts built a library block on Cowgate to designs by James Bow Dunn, raised up on top of a tenement to enter off the south end of the Box Corridor. This building is now leased by PSA (see p. 94). Finally, in 1908–09, W. T. Oldrieve remodelled the main entrance Lobby in the western angle of the Square and the Box Corridor and reconstructed Nixon's four courts as three, to provide a passage to his new Oak Court at the south-western angle. Since then, there have been few changes, except for the remodelling of some of the ancillary accommodation to provide additional courts.

Parliament Hall
Parliament Hall is now used as an assembly point for counsel and litigants, and operates as part of the overall complex of Court buildings. It is rectangular in area and of fine proportions, some 120ft. long × 40ft. wide. The most notable feature is the roof, constructed by John Scott between 1631 and 1640. It is of dark oak with cross-braces and hammer-beams springing from carved corbels on the walls. This structure supports a flat roof, about 40ft. above floor level. Tudor gothic windows were inserted in the west and south walls by 1845, with stained glass added in the 1860's under the direction of Robert Matheson. The large south

c. 1830

Parliament Hall

Illustrated London News 1871

window, which depicts the institution of the Court of Session by King James V of Scotland in 1532, is the work of Wilhelm von Kaulbach and the Chevalier Ainmuller of Munich, 1868. The richly carved timber chimney-pieces, one of them incorporating high quality Italian Renaissance panels, were inserted at the same period, and are the work of an Edinburgh cabinet maker, wood carver and antique dealer, William Adams. A number of statues of historic figures are placed along the walls, the most notable being that of Duncan Forbes of Culloden by Roubiliac, 1752. Beneath the Parliament Hall is the Laigh Hall, which has a two-aisle plan with a central arcade, recently partly restored in conjunction with the provision of two modern courtrooms.

High Court of Justiciary
The High Court of Justiciary is the central element of the Parliament Square complex, and although built in two stages, 1807–10 and 1825–34, is of unified design. It is three storeys high to the square and fifteen bays long, with a rusticated V-jointed ground floor, which breaks boldly forward at the central five bays to carry a hexastyle Ionic portico with a pediment. This is recessed to a two-bay depth at the central three bays. The end bays are slightly advanced and emphasised by pedimented first-floor windows and festooned parapet panels surmounted by sphinxes. Three-bay quadrant links, with distyle in antis porticos, link to the

Exchequer Chambers and to the frontage screening the eastern flank of the Parliament Hall and the Signet Library stairs on the west. These are both five-bay facades with recessed distyle in antis porticos, continuously treated with the main High Court facade. To the rear, a tall, plain L-plan whinstone Georgian facade, its roofline punctuated by the clerestories of the Inner House courts, towers over the back yard area to Cowgate.

The interior has changed very little since early Victorian times, and accommodates a large number of Courts with the necessary service areas. Reid's three Inner House Courts, the High Court and the First and Second Division, are essentially similar. They are rectangular in plan with concave gallery fronts carried on console cantilever brackets, arcaded clerestories, and flat compartmented ceilings with rich classical or mildly Jacobethan details, still equipped with all the original apparatus of late Georgian justice. The corridors surrounding them are segmentally vaulted with impressive iron security gates in the area of the High Court. Court No 4 to the east at Reid's Courts is the former telling room of Sir William Forbes's Bank, remodelled by W. W. Robertson in 1885. It has coupled Corinthian columns with gilded capitals flanking the judicial bench, a rich entablature and a coved ceiling with pendants at the angles.

The original Outer House Courts west of the Box Corridor, the north-south division between the

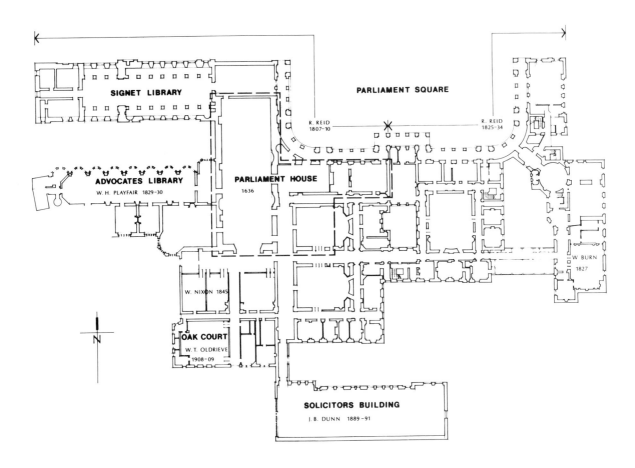

SIGNET LIBRARY

PARLIAMENT SQUARE

R. REID
1807-10

R. REID
1825-34

ADVOCATES LIBRARY
W. H. PLAYFAIR 1829-30

PARLIAMENT HOUSE
1636

W BURN
1827

N

W. NIXON 1845

OAK COURT
W. T. OLDRIEVE
1908-09

SOLICITORS BUILDING
J. B. DUNN 1889-91

PLAN OF PARLIAMENT HOUSE AND THE LAW COURTS

houses, are simple rectangles with grained neo-classical woodwork, but W. T. Oldrieve's Oak Court of 1908–09 is comparable in grandeur with the Inner House Courts. It is panelled in oak with a rich Doric entablature from which springs a cove bearing a ribbed and pendentived dome with lunette windows.

A number of additional courts have been provided at lower levels in recent years. These are unmistakably modern in character with suspended acoustic ceilings but many of the walls have been lined in good quality hardwood boarding to reflect the character of the older courts.

References: Georgian Edinburgh (Lindsay) The Making of Classical Edinburgh (Youngson) Modern Athens (Shepherd), Playfair Drawings (Edinburgh University Library) Building Chronicle v. 11, p. 212 (June 1857).

Address:	16 Picardy Place, Edinburgh
Category:	B, in New Town Conservation Area
Occupier:	Inland Revenue Office
Use:	Offices
Holding:	Leased

Picardy Place was designed by Robert Burn in 1800 for the Commissioners for Improvement of Manufactures in Scotland, and built speculatively, partly by Burn himself. As first constructed, the north side (nos. 2–22) was a symmetrical palace-fronted block with a tetrastyle pedimented centre-piece of Ionic pilasters, but some of the ground floors were later built out as shops. The south side of the street was demolished for road works in 1969, making the surviving north side one of the most prominent frontages in the city. No. 16 now comprises the whole of the eastern third of the terrace.

In 1973–75, the interiors of nos. 16–22 were demolished and the facade was partly restored and cleaned, the later shop additions being removed. Modern offices were built behind, retaining the original storeys to the front but incorporating further storeys to the rear. Attic rooms no longer remain. A modern slate roof has been constructed to the original pitch but the skews and chimneys were regrettably omitted, giving a dead and featureless appearance to the skyline. None of the original fittings were incorporated in the rebuilding.

The facade has V-jointed ashlar rustication on the ground floor, and a tooled finish to the upper floor and basement. The pilasters and other details of the upper facade are of polished ashlar. Ground-floor windows are now semi-circular arched with a fluted impost band. These arches were originally recesses for smaller square-headed windows, but these now survive only in the two right-hand bays. Modern windows have been fitted to these openings but the upper floors retain the original astragalled sash pattern. Basement windows have been converted to single large panes, sash and case. The surviving door-pieces to no. 16 and 18 consist of composite Doric columns set within the arched openings, with fanlights over the entablatures. Wrought-iron balconies at first-floor level span over the doorways.

At first-floor level, the windows are architraved with cornices. These are shallow-pedimented over the door-pieces at nos. 16 and 18. A moulded overhanging cornice at eaves level completes the facade.

References: Old Edinburgh Club. Vol. 25 p30.

Name:	General Register House
Address:	1 Princes Street, Edinburgh
Category:	A, in New Town Conservation Area
Occupier:	Public Records of Scotland
Use:	Offices and Records
Holding:	Crown

This building was commissioned in 1772 to house the National Records of Scotland, which up to that time had been kept 'in two laigh rooms' under the Inner Session House in somewhat precarious conditions. It was designed by Robert Adam, and was largely built between 1774 and 1788. The unusually long construction period was due to the intermittent supply of funds. The work was supervised by his brother, John, and by James Salisbury, Clerk of Works. It was still not complete in 1792 when Robert Adam died, but construction was resumed in 1822 by Robert Reid, who made some radical changes to the original design of the north wing. These changes did not greatly affect the Adam concept, and it is generally agreed that General Register House remains one of Robert Adam's finest works.

The building is square on plan, thirteen bays wide by nine bays deep with four corner pavilions and a large dome covering the centre court. It is two storeys in height above Princes Street with basements below. The main front consists of a central, tetrastyle, pedimented advanced three-bay section with attached Corinthian columns. Each angle pavilion is balustraded at roof level with a Venetian window at first-floor level and is surmounted by a square clock turret and cupola. The clock and wind vane were made by Justin Vulliamy of London in 1790. The ground floor is of heavily rusticated masonry with windows in arched recesses.

The original horse-shoe stairs were rebuilt in their present straight-flight form and the area wall was set back when the street was widened in 1890–91.

Inside, the building has been much altered, and the only major Adam interiors in anything like their original state are the large circular apartment under the dome and the Lord Clerk Registers. The most characteristic internal feature is the dome over the central area, the plasterwork of which was executed by Thomas Clayton. It is segmented with delicate raised ribs and decorated by a circle of large medallions with a fine frieze over the framing cornices at ceiling level.

Although not executed in the high style indicated in Adam's original design, General Register House is nevertheless a splendid and ingenious building. (See also New Register House, West Register Street.)

References: Architecture of R. & J. Adam (Bolton)
      Modern Athens (Shepherd)
      The Making of Classical Edinburgh (Youngson)

Name:	York Buildings
Address:	Queen Street, Edinburgh
Category:	B, in New Town Conservation Area
Occupier:	National Museum of Antiquities
Use:	Museum
Holding:	Crown

York Buildings is a large three-storey and basement block, on the garden ground of the house at the corner of Queen Street and Dublin Street.

The main block towards Queen Street was erected in 1878 as stockbrokers' chambers by John Boyd, an upholsterer, to designs by Robert Raeburn. It is three storeys high, with two basement storeys which cannot be seen from York Place. In 1919, Herbert Ryle of the Office of Works converted the buildings into government offices, adding the single-storey entrance wing which overlays the earlier building. Masonwork is dressed ashlar. The main elevation is symmetrical apart from the entrance wing, and consists of two end pavilions, each of five-window width and slightly advanced, framing a ten-window elevation between them. The style is restrained Victorian Renaissance. Each floor is marked by a string course with a cornice at the eaves, modillioned at the end pavilions. The pavilions have French mansard roofs rising into higher pavilion roofs at the centre, with round-headed

dormer windows and platforms crested by ornamental ironwork. At ground-floor level there are round-headed key-blocked windows which fronted small shops prior to 1919. First-floor windows have shouldered architraves with shallow pediments. At second-floor level, the pediments are segment-headed in the pavilion wings. All the lights are single-pane sash and case. The entrance through the single-storey bay consists of a tripartite Venetian feature with the outer arch designed as part of the rusticated masonwork. In the parapet is a panel containing recent applied lettering 'National Museum of Antiquities of Scotland'. The windows on the plain, rear elevation are astragalled.

The building has recently been reconstructed internally, a steel-framed structure having been inserted within the existing outer walls. Internal partitions have been removed to provide large open exhibition areas which are entirely modern in character, including suspended acoustic ceilings. Some original detail has been retained, such as window shutters and cornice plasterwork but the effect is very much that of a modern building. The office accommodation is mainly unaltered and polished marble chimney-pieces have been retained, although the fireplaces are no longer in use. Large areas of the top floor are intended to be used for storage and these are largely unaltered, as are two original stone stairs complete with iron balusters and hardwood handrails.

Name:	The National Museum of Antiquities of Scotland/Scottish National Portrait Gallery
Address:	1 Queen Street, Edinburgh
Category:	A, in New Town Conservation Area
Occupiers:	The National Museum of Antiquities of Scotland/Scottish National Portrait Gallery
Use:	Museum and Art Gallery
Holding:	Crown

The National Portrait Gallery was founded in 1882 on the initiative of Mr. J. R. Findlay of *The Scotsman*, who provided half the endowment fund of £20,000 and subsequently paid for the building, which cost over £50,000. Before its completion and the hanging of the pictures there in 1889, the collection was housed in a temporary building close to the site of the present gallery. It was decided, early in the planning stage, to include space for the National Museum of Antiquities. Work started on the building in 1885 and was finally completed in 1890. In July 1889, at the formal opening, the Marquess of Lothian, then Scottish Secretary, dramatically disclosed Findlay's generosity. Sir R. Rowand Anderson's

design, in Franco-Italian Gothic style, was awarded a Gold Medal at the Munich Exhibition of 1890. The lavish sculptural work is by W. Birnie Rhind. The interior murals are by William Hole.

The building is constructed in red Corsehill sandstone rubble with ashlar dressings and octagonal angle turrets. Three storeys high, with a basement, it is rectangular in plan, with galleries opening off a central hall and mezzanine floors at each end. The eastern end of building contains the National Museum of Antiquities and the Scottish National Portrait Gallery is at the west.

The elevation design recalls that of the Doge's Palace, Venice. A continuous first-floor band of traceried windows and sculptural decoration contrasts strongly with the high, blind frontage of the top-lit second-floor galleries. The ground floor, on the Queen Street side presents yet another contrast. Four wide, plainly-detailed Gothic windows symmetrically flank the highly sculptured central doorway. Octagonal corner turrets are corbelled out at mid ground floor. Each face contains figure sculpture under a tall, canopied niche, a device repeated between each pair of windows at the same first-floor level. The decorative scheme is based on selected figures from Scottish history and tradition, including

124

numerous representatives of royalty. The balustrading and the tall corner pinnacles have been removed for repair, with severe effect on the building's silhouette, but they are to be reinstated by the end of this decade.

Inside, the square, arcaded central hall rises through the full height of the building. It has a staircase on each side leading to the upper floors. The east stair serves the upper levels of the Museum, the west stair the Portrait Gallery. The hall is richly decorated. On each side, a triple arcade in the Decorated style, with gilded foliage capitals, supports the galleries on the upper floor. William Hole's fine painted frieze surrounds the hall on all four sides, depicting themes from Scottish history. Other decorations in the hall include armorial stained glass windows representing historic versions of the Scottish insignia. The ground and first-floor galleries have beamed ceilings with small plain cornices and are lit by side windows. Windows vary from floor to floor, and mostly have small-paned leaded lights. The walls are generally of painted brick with pine dadoes. The top-floor galleries have similar wall surfaces, but are lit by overhead lanterns in the barrel-ribbed ceilings. The lanterns are rectangular, with coffered coves and cornices. Offices in the mezzanine floors are domestic in scale, but retain arched windows with external tracery. Doors are panelled with wood architraves and skirtings. Smaller office rooms in the mezzanine floors at each end of the building are comparatively plain, as are the rooms in the basement used for storage and as offices. These have a structure of cast-iron columns supporting arched brick ceilings.

References: *Builder*, January 3 1885
            British Architect, January 11 1889
            The Scottish National Portrait Gallery 1891
            (J. M. Gray)

Address:	2a Queen Street, (formerly 9a North St. David Street), Edinburgh
Category:	A, in New Town Conservation Area
Occupier:	National Museum of Antiquities of Scotland
Use:	Offices
Holding:	Leased

Queen Street and North St. David Street were part of the original layout for the New Town of Edinburgh by James Craig, built between 1770 and 1780. The block containing 2a Queen Street is stepped to follow the steep slope of North St. David Street and finishes in a pitched gable facing Queen Street. 9 North St. David Street retains the original entrance from the street, across a fly-over with iron railings, and the former 9a has now become 2a Queen Street. The area of the building now occupied by the Design Section of the National Museum of Antiquities comprises the two former basements and is independent of the rest of the property.

The five-bay elevation to North St. David Street is three storeys high with attic and basement, built of coursed rubble with a lightly tooled finish. The entrance door has a plain architrave with frieze and cornice. This has been sensitively renewed. The two-window wallhead gable, relatively unusual in the New Town, is more characteristic of Edinburgh's South Side. All the windows are sash and case with astragals. There is no further embellishment to the elevation, apart from the plain string course at ground-floor level and bold quoins at the Queen Street corner.

The four-bay gable elevation to Queen Street is of three floors, with attic and basement. There are two small windows at attic level. All the windows are sash and case, retaining astragals. The former area to the lower basement has been roofed over in concrete with pavement slabs as a finish but the access from the pavement to the lower basement is still intact—an iron railing with access gate and steps.

Internally, none of the original character remains in the former basements comprising 2a Queen Street but the property above (no. 9 North St. David Street) retains much of the restrained classical detail typical of the period.

Reference: R.C.A.H.M.S. Inventory, City of Edinburgh.

Address:	3 Queen Street, Edinburgh
Category:	A, in New Town Conservation Area
Occupier:	Manpower Services Commission
Use:	Offices
Holding:	Leased

This section of Queen Street formed part of the original scheme prepared for the New Town of Edinburgh by James Craig and built *circa* 1780. The pair of flatted Georgian domestic buildings comprising nos. 2 and 3 were demolished, for structural reasons, in 1969, permission having been given on condition that the reconstruction would follow the original design.

The building is now four storeys high with a basement and has a five-window frontage. Originally it was of three storeys, with a two-window wallhead gable, similar to that at 2a Queen Street and 7, 9 North St. Andrew Street, in a 2-3 arrangement. The main elevation above the ground-floor string course is of coursed sandstone with a lightly tooled finish and the basement is of snecked rubble. The windows have dressed surrounds.

Wrought-iron lampholders, one on each side of the entrance, form part of the area railing design. The entrance has a moulded stone architrave with a plain frieze above and a shallow cornice. There is a fanlight above the new fielded panel doors. All the windows in the elevation have astragals. At roof level there is a stone cornice forming part of the parapet. The roof above is pitched and slated.

Internally, the building has been completely rebuilt and nothing of the original character remains.

This is a good example of rebuilding in the spirit, if not the letter, of the original. The elevation to Queen Street faithfully reflects the character of the rest of the terrace.

Reference: R.C.A.H.M.S. Inventory, City of Edinburgh.

Address:	3 Queensferry Street, Edinburgh
Category:	B, in New Town Conservation Area
Occupier:	Crown Office
Use:	Offices
Holding:	Leased

This four-storey and attic building occupies a prominent site at the west end of Princes Street, at the corner of Shandwick Place and Queensferry Street. It was designed in 1901, by the architects Sydney Mitchell, and Wilson, in a highly individual free Renaissance style. The ground floor, apart from the entrance doorway, accommodates a building society (formerly a bank), a public house and a general merchandise store. Entrance to the offices is from Queensferry Street. The building was designed originally as a private club and operated for many years as the United Services Club. Some alterations were made to the ground-floor bank frontage in 1938–40 when the original arched bays were faced in polished pink granite, to the design of Tarbolton & Ochterlony. The public house elevation displays the original treatment.

The elevation to Shandwick Place has a broad three-window feature rising the full height of the building with a wide curvilinear wallhead gable capped by a shell-head and with appropriate mouldings. There are three double windows at attic level and a moulded cartouche in the garret wall surrounding a small oculus window. The elevation to Queensferry Street has three identical bays above first-floor level each with two windows and a curvilinear wallhead gable with a square chimney block above. On both elevations, the first, second and third-floor windows have "Gibbs" type surrounds. At the first floor, alternate voussoirs project and are linked with bands of scrolls. The second and third-floor windows have quintuple key blocks, and those at second-floor have a thin continuous apron with classical guttae moulding. At the corner, there is a slightly recessed quadrant rising the full height with single windows at each floor level and an armorial cartouche over quintuple key-blocked lintels at the first floor. There are key-blocked architraved windows with cornices at the second and third-floor levels. A pilastered rotunda at attic level rises to a concave set-off with a cartouche, bearing a peristyle cupola with a distyle treatment between buttresses and capped by an ogee-shaped leaded roof with a small lantern at the top. The roof over the main building is semi-mansard in slate, visible only from Queensferry Street.

Apart from some internal partitioning to provide convenient office space, the interior of the building is unspoilt, containing good quality wood panelling in the entrance hall and the former lounge. Doors from the corridors are painted and have classical entablatures with low-pitched pediments. The former lounge has a patterned plaster ceiling. Throughout the building there is a variety of plaster cornices and friezes.

The main stair is in timber with balusters and newel posts richly carved. The wood panelling to the walls is in the form of a dado. The soffits below are also panelled. The stair is lit from above by a square roof-light with plaster frieze and cornice. There are a number of timber chimney-pieces, some in natural wood and some painted, well designed in the Georgian idiom. In the former lounge the chimney-piece is in oak with a polished marble mantelpiece. The oak-panelled hall includes a similar chimney-piece. Some smaller rooms have been fitted out with hung ceilings of acoustic tiles.

Name:	Crown Office Buildings (Former Royal High School)
Address:	Regent Road, Edinburgh
Category:	A, in New Town Conservation Area
Occupier:	Crown Office
Uses:	Offices and Debating Chamber
Holding:	Crown

Described in Crook's *The Greek Revival* as "the grandest monument in the Athens of the North," the Royal High School is one of the finest neo-classical public buildings in northern Europe.

The original High School of Edinburgh was founded in 1128 and is one of the oldest educational establishments of its kind in Britain. The school was rebuilt in the Cowgate in 1717, but by the early 19th century it had become inadequate for the needs of the boys of the town. Protracted negotiations followed and, as this was also the time of the massive Georgian northward extension of the city, considerable argument followed concerning the precise requirements for new building. The original idea, put forward in 1822 by a Committee of Subscribers, was for "a Seminary separate from, and altogether independent of, the High School of the City". Two new schools were ultimately built; the one by the original subscribers, which became the Edinburgh Academy, and the other by the Town Council, which became the Royal High School.

Thomas Hamilton was appointed architect, and the foundation stone was laid in 1825. The building occupies a commanding site on the south side of Calton Hill, above the valley which runs between it and the Canongate. The external design of the central hall is based on the Temple of Theseus, in Athens. This is the most prominent feature, with a hexastyle Greek Doric portico rising over two tiers of screen walls contained by massive footgates, the upper pair being boldly advanced and linked by cast-iron railings. Colonnaded wings link the main hall to two pilastered pavilions to the east and the west. At a lower level, retaining walls, railings and gateways terminate in two tetrastyle temple blocks. The whole composition forms an extremely impressive group, with the delicately detailed Doric portico being seen in profile from both the east and west ends of Regent Road.

The plan form is symmetrical around the central axis of the main hall. There is a considerable amount of fine internal work, notably in the main hall which has a finely detailed semi-elliptical arched ceiling with coffered panels and excellent plasterwork. The delicate capitals of the cast-iron columns supporting the gallery are of highly original design, prophetic of later 19th century taste.

The most impressive spaces in the wings are two large rectangular rooms with octagonal lanterns and circular cupolas, symmetrically planned about the central hall. One of these was formerly the School Library. The detailing is characteristically late Georgian.

The building has subsequently been altered internally, the most recent adaptations having been carried out to provide accommodation for the proposed Scottish Assembly. Since the suspension of this project, further adaptations have been made to provide accommodation for the Crown Office. These alterations have preserved the best original work and have treated the character of the building sympathetically.

The Royal High School now occupies a new site on the west side of the City and functions as a modern secondary school.

References: Georgian Edinburgh (Lindsay) The Making of Classical Edinburgh (Youngson) Modern Athens (Shepherd) The Greek Revival (Crook).

Name:	Governor's House, Old Calton Jail
Address:	Regent Road, Edinburgh
Category:	A, in New Town Conservation Area
Occupier:	Vacant
Use:	Storage
Holding:	Crown

This building is the only remaining part of the Old Calton Jail, which was demolished in the 1930's to make way for St. Andrew's House (q.v.). The site, on the southern slope of Calton Hill, is one of the noblest in Edinburgh, having a magnificent prospect over the valley between Calton Hill and the Canongate with Arthur's Seat and the Salisbury Crags beyond.

An Act of 1782 made provision for both the building of a prison and a Bridewell, or 'House of Correction', on the site. At first, only the Bridewell was built, to a design by Robert Adam, between 1791 and 1795. Semi-circular in plan, with a rectangular tower, it was later demolished. The prison was not constructed until 1815.

The whole prison complex, including the Governor's House, was built to a design by Archibald Elliot in a romantic castellated style with a towered curtain wall. In this composition the Governor's House assumed a donjon-like role, standing higher on a projecting spur of rock. The greater part of the curtain has been cut down to a massive bastioned retaining wall, but the Governor's House has survived complete. It comprises a rectangular block of fairly heavy masonwork dominated by a bold circular tower with a small, slightly higher octagonal turret attached. The circular tower is of three storeys with rather small round-headed windows and a crenellated parapet above, which is reflected in the parapet to the adjacent turret. The whole composition is strikingly picturesque in the view from Calton Road.

Internally, the building has been gutted and is unused, although it is maintained in a wind and water-tight condition. The only feature which remains is a stone spiral stair with iron balustrade and hardwood handrail, rising the full height of the building.

References: Georgian Edinburgh (Lindsay)
Modern Athens (Shepherd)
The Making of Classical Edinburgh (Youngson)

c. 1830

Name:	(Old) St. Andrew's House
Address:	Regent Road, Edinburgh
Category:	B, in New Town Conservation Area
Occupier:	Scottish Home and Health Department,
	Scottish Education Department,
	Scottish Development Department,
	Scottish Office Central Services
Use:	Offices
Holding:	Crown

Thomas S. Tait of Burnet, Tait and Lorne designed this monumental administration building, which was constructed between 1936 and 1939 to house the Departments of the Secretary of State for Scotland. It occupies the site of the former Calton Jail, of which the Governor's House (q.v.) is the only remaining building. The curtain wall of the Jail also partially survives, reduced in height, as a retaining wall.

The design is in a bold, if unadventurous international modern manner, influenced in some respects by the Palace of the League of Nations in Geneva. The elevation to Regent Road is symmetrical with a large central block of monumental character and scale. The building has been carefully designed in relation to its difficult site on the southern slope of Calton Hill. Viewed from the south, the component parts of the building group outstandingly well. The walls are of finely dressed masonry in polished granite and sandstone. The copper roof is low-pitched and is concealed by low parapets. The powerful centre block carries large representations of the Scottish Saints—Andrew, Ninian, Columba, Kentigern and Magnus—sculptured by Sir W. Reid Dick. The Royal Coat of Arms with Scottish quartering, above the main entrance, was carved by Alexander Carrick.

Internally, there is much use of polished marble facings to columns and walls. The former office of the Secretary of State is panelled in Scottish walnut from a tree taken from Balmerino in Fife, said to have been planted by Mary Queen of Scots.

The headquarters of the Scottish Office is now housed in New St. Andrew's House in St. James Square but the original building continues to provide office accommodation for other staff.

Address:	Royal Terrace, Edinburgh
Category:	A, in New Town Conservation Area
Occupiers:	No. 16 Ministry of Defence
	Nos. 26/27 Vacant
Use:	No. 16 Army Instruction Unit
	Nos. 26/27 Offices
Holding:	Both properties leased

These properties form part of the great symmetrical terrace, forty houses long, designed by W. H. Playfair between 1821 and 1824 as the major element of a large scheme which embraced the Calton Hill and Hillside Estates. The terrace runs east-west on the lower portion of Calton Hill, with the facade facing north and the gardens rising steeply to the south. On the north, further landscaped gardens stretch down to Hillside Crescent, also part of the Playfair scheme. The majestic frontage is symmetrical about an advanced nine-bay centre block divided by a giant Corinthian order at first and second storeys. Six similar, but narrower, sections articulate the wings of this enormously long composition, three on each side of the central block, divided by lower seven-bay and nine-bay sections without colonnades.

No. 16
This property occupies the eastern half of the four-storey and basement six-bay colonnaded section closest, on the west, to the central block. The ground-floor facade is rusticated, with semi-circular arched windows and doorways. It acts as the base for the giant engaged Corinthian colonnade which supports the deep entablature between second storey and attic. The notable cast-ironwork includes elegant bowed balconies to the first-floor windows and a lampholder integrated with the railings to the entrance platt and basement area.

Internally there have been few alterations. The interior is rich in high quality joinery and plasterwork, including ornately-panelled doors and enriched Greek-key banding in the stairhall. Beside the stairhead are three plaster relief panels depicting cherubs at play.

The building is now used as a study centre. The large well-proportioned ground and first-floor rooms are well suited for holding seminars and tutorials, the smaller rooms being used for individual study.

Nos. 26 and 27
These houses occupy the first six-bay section to the east of the central block. External details correspond with no. 16.

The interior has been extensively altered to provide office accommodation. In the principal rooms, only the window shutters and panels and the cornices remain untouched. Some doors and architraves, mainly on the ground and first floors, are original but their positions have been altered. All chimney-pieces have been removed and the openings built up. The stone stair to no. 27 rises in straight flights with quarter landings and wall niches. Cast-iron balusters remain and the stair-well is lit from an oval cupola with decorative plasterwork. The stair to no. 26 has been entirely removed.

References: Plans in Edinburgh University Library (1824).
The Making of Classical Edinburgh (Youngson).

Address:	29 Rutland Square, Edinburgh
Category:	A, in New Town Conservation Area
Occupier:	Ministry of Defence
Use:	Army Careers and Information Office
Holding:	Crown

Rutland Square formed part of the Learmonth Estate, and was originally designed by Archibald Elliot in 1819. It was not developed immediately, but was built between 1830 and 1840 with detail alterations by the architect John Tait.

Nos. 23–29 form a symmetrical block on the north side of the square. No. 29 is the east end house of this terrace, with a three-window front consisting of three storeys and basement. It is built of ashlar stone with an advanced portico of fluted Ionic columns in antis with a moulded entablature. Bold moulded stone window surrounds with cornices emphasise the first-floor windows. This

end block is distinguished by an open balustrade above the moulded cornice.

There is a continuous light wrought-iron balcony at first-floor level, and original iron railings guard the basement area.

The windows are sash and case with ground and first-floor front windows converted to single pane. All others are Georgian small-pane originals, except for the centre top-floor dummy window, since built up.

The roof is slated with stone chimney-stacks at the gable wallhead, one of which has lately been rendered.

The entrance door is panelled, but the top panels have recently been glazed and the fanlight blocked out.

The interior is largely unaltered, retaining most of the original plasterwork and joinery but all fireplaces have been removed and the first-floor front main room has been divided.

All three floors and basement are in use as offices.

Name:	Prudential Building
Address:	2 St. Andrew Square, Edinburgh
Category:	B, in New Town Conservation Area
Occupier:	Inland Revenue Office/ Rent Tribunal
Use:	Office
Holding:	Leased

This building, occupying a prominent site at the corner of South St. Andrew Street and St. Andrew Square, is a notable exercise in the Early Renaissance style popular in the latter part of the 19th century. It consists of four bays to each street frontage, and is four storeys high with an attic incorporating dormer windows. Both elevations are similar in treatment and are linked at the corner by a complex, spired, semi-octagonal tower which includes the main entrance at its base. This feature is an excellent example of effective design for a highly important city centre corner site.

The building was designed in 1890 by the architect, Paul Waterhouse (Alfred Waterhouse & Son) and built between 1892 and 1895. This firm was responsible for most of the Prudential Assurance Company's major buildings of the late Victorian and Edwardian periods.

The stonework is red ashlar sandstone with restrained surface sculpture. The building was designed in red brick, with stone dressings but, no doubt fortunately, Edinburgh Corporation insisted on the use of red sandstone throughout. The ground floor is arcaded on both elevations and faced with polished pink granite, the three arcades to South St. Andrew Street each containing one shop. One bay on each elevation is emphasised by a higher and more elaborate Flemish Renaissance gable. These are placed asymmetrically, at the west end of the north front and off-centre northwards on the east elevation. The main mutule cornice is at third floor level on both elevations. The first and second-floor windows are sash and case with two bipartites to each bay divided by panelled pilasters. The third-floor tripartite windows, two to each bay, have arched heads. Above the main entrance to the public office is a canopied niche containing the effigy of 'Prudentia', uncannily resembling some Gothic Saint. An additional entrance from St. Andrew Square gives access to the office accommodation.

Internally, the most notable feature of the upstairs accommodation is the cantilevered main stair, top-lit by a rectangular pitched roof-light. The balustrade, with hardwood handrail, is wrought-iron of a highly individual design. There is a dado of green polished glazed tiles and the doors have moulded architraves and door-heads. Restrained plasterwork, in the form of ceiling cornices, is apparent throughout the building which also contains several chimney-pieces of delicate classical design. Some alterations have been made to sub-divide the office space and certain panelled doors have been given additional fire-proofing but the overall character of the building is unspoilt.

Although not part of the Inland Revenue holding, the Prudential Company's public office on the ground floor is very well worth inspection. A tiled octagonal vestibule leads into the main hall, which is a tour-de-force of rich late nineteenth century interior design in coloured, glazed tiling.

Reference: *Builder*, September 28, 1895.

Name:	Charlotte House
Address:	2 South Charlotte Street, Edinburgh
Category:	B, in New Town Conservation Area
Occupier:	Inland Revenue Office
Use:	Offices
Holding:	Leased

This building occupies a prominent site at the west corner of South Charlotte Street and Princes Street. It consisted originally of an L-plan site, with separate narrow-gabled frontages to both streets, developed in 1903 to designs by the sculptor-architect Sir T. Duncan Rhind. The block forming the corner between the two frontages was built in 1924 to the design of J. D. Cairns, who repeated Rhind's motif,at the splayed corner but designed the linking facades in a more contemporary style. The northern section was added by the same architect in 1935. The complete building is four storeys in height, with a steep slated roof containing a double attic with dormer windows.

The original narrow frontages are of neo-baroque design with a bold sculptural treatment, and consist of a continuous run of keyblocked segmentally-pedimented windows between Ionic columns of individual design. The second-floor windows are architraved. At third-floor level they have Gibbsian surrounds. Above, the facades rise into gables with lunettes, that on Princes Street having an aedicule niche and that on South Charlotte Street an obelisk finial. At the corner, Cairns built a canted variant of Rhind's Princes Street facade, but the sections between it and the original frontages are made up of bronze panels. similar in construction to modern curtain walling. The windows, which are large, are also metal-framed. The design is unified by a prominent dentil cornice common to all five sections. The ground floor elevation consists of a series of segmental arches in polished pink granite, and this feature encloses all three parts of the design. The broad entrance in the 1935 section has a plain square-headed architrave, and was formerly sheltered by a canopy. It leads to a fine art-deco staircase, but otherwise the building has been much modernised over the years and again recently.

Reference: *Builder*, January 10, 1903

Address:	25 Torphichen Street, Edinburgh
Category:	B, in West End Conservation Area
Occupier:	Department of Health and Social Security (Medical Appeals Tribunal) National Galleries
Use:	Offices
Holding:	Leased

Nos. 3–25, on the north side of Torphichen Street, were built between 1824 and 1831 to the designs of Thomas Bonnar, the Heriot Trust's Superintendent of Works. The design is continuous with Atholl Place, also laid out by the Heriot Trust. The buildings on the south side (nos. 2–24), although contemporary, are to a different design by James Haldane for the Morrison Estate.

The tenement block consists of four floors and basement, with main-door ground-floor and basement houses and flats above, all originally residential. Most of the upper-floor houses are still domestic but the main-door houses, including no. 25, are in use as small offices.

The frontage is severe late Georgian classical, constructed of ashlar with a tooled finish to the basement. A wide band course over the ground floor forms the cill to the first-floor windows. There is a similar, narrower band at second floor and a simple main cornice. All these details are swept upwards at the right-hand gable end.

All windows are sash and case, but those at ground and basement now have single plate-glass panes. The windows on ground and first floors have moulded architraves with apron panels under the ground-floor windows. The door-piece has a consoled cornice and moulded architraves, enclosing a four-panelled door with fanlight over. The roof is slated with stone chimney-stacks which have recently been rendered. Ornamental wrought-iron railings guard the basement area.

Internally, all main rooms on the ground floor have good plaster cornices. The window shutters are retained. No fireplaces remain within the building. Doors are original, six-panelled. The basement has been adapted for offices and stores and contains no features of interest.

Name:	India Buildings
Address:	1 Victoria Street, Edinburgh
Category:	B, in Old Town Conservation Area
Occupier:	Scottish Courts Administration
Use:	Courtroom
Holding:	Leased

Victoria Street was planned by Thomas Hamilton under the City Improvement Act of 1827. He resigned in 1834 before any building was done, George Smith taking over in the same year. The street forms a steep slope connecting the elevated George IV Bridge and the Grassmarket. Some of the ancient domestic buildings remain in the surviving section of the West Bow, at the lower end of the street.

India Buildings was designed by David Cousin for Charles Lawson in 1864. The commission was taken over from John Henderson, who had already built the matching corner building for the same client. At that time, Cousin, the City Superintendent of Works, was permitted to undertake private commissions in addition to his official duties.

Distinctive in design, with a marked Scots Jacobean or "Old Flemish" character as prescribed in the Act, it is the richest building in Victoria Street and groups picturesquely with St. Columba's Free Church and the elevated walkway of Victoria Terrace on the north side. It has a curved frontage divided by moulded string courses into four and five storeys of dressed ashlar with a slim six-storey bartizaned tower. The ground and first-floor windows are set deeply into moulded flat-arched recesses. The second-floor windows are markedly Jacobean in character with light strapwork ornament above their entablatures. The roof is semi-mansard with pedimented wallhead dormer windows towards Victoria Street. The entrance door-piece is set in heavy vermiculated masonry, bearing a sculptured blind parapet with miniature obelisks. The Jacobean style entablature of the second-floor window carries in Latin the motto "The Lord will provide".

The internal plan is interesting. A long right-angled corridor leads to a 'scala regia' stair rising inside a circular galleried well. This is covered by a semi-dome carrying a central oculus. The compartments of the dome are ornamented by a delicate trellis of diagonal plaster ribwork.

India Buildings has had a variety of occupants, including the Scottish Chamber of Agriculture, the Geological Survey of Scotland and the British Linen Bank. It was acquired in the 1960's by Messrs T. G. & T. C. Gray, and is now leased to the Department of the Environment for use as Sheriff Court premises.

Reference: *Building News*, December 19, 1864.

Address:	20 Walker Street, Edinburgh
Category:	A, in New Town Conservation Area
Occupier:	Civil Service Pensions Tribunal
Use:	Offices
Holding:	Leased

This property forms part of the intersection between Melville Street and Walker Street. This intersection, which takes the form of the octagon called Melville Crescent, is one of the most notable features of the Western New Town and appears to have been conceived in the original feuing plan by the architect, James Gillespie Graham. The Walker Estate section, on which Melville Street and Walker Street stand, was, however, designed by Robert Brown in 1813, although most of the intersection dates from 1855–56 when John Lessels simplified Brown's design, substituting an anta order for Brown's central attached porticos, to reduce costs and get the scheme completed.

The splay frontage forming nos. 1, 2 and 3 Melville Crescent connects with no. 20 Walker Street. The whole frontage to Walker Street, including no. 3 Melville Crescent, is of five bays. The two end bays advance slightly from the three-window centre and have panelled blocking courses contrasting with light stone balustrading in the centre.

The complete unit is three storeys in height plus basement. The ground floor is of rusticated ashlar with an arch over the central doorway and arched recesses containing square-headed windows in the two end bays. The upper stonework is finely dressed ashlar. The centre window above the entrance door has a narrow moulded architrave and a shallow consoled pediment. The single windows in the end bays are similar, but have shallow cornices instead of pediments. A cast-iron balcony runs the complete width of the three windows of no. 20. All windows are single-pane sash and case. The entrance doorway is tripartite with a narrow glazed panel on each side and a delicate semi-circular fanlight over.

Unlike its neighbour at no. 3 Melville Crescent, no. 20 Walker Street is internally a late Georgian house. The entrance vestibule has a richly patterned plaster ceiling divided into a series of panels with the usual classical mouldings and floral decoration on the soffit of the ceiling. The hall containing the stair has a flat arch with Roman Doric mouldings. The stair is of stone with an iron balustrade and hardwood handrail. There are plaster mouldings to the soffit. The main room on the ground floor is in excellent condition and completely unspoilt, with a panelled dado, moulded door joinery, rich plaster frieze and cornice. The original panelled shutters to the windows are intact. The former drawing room on the first floor has a particularly rich swag frieze. Doors are panelled and many have moulded door-pieces. There are polished marble chimney-pieces in both principal rooms.

The stair is lit from above by an oval roof-light, which has a shallow cornice at the top of the dome and a richly moulded frieze and cornice beneath the pendentives.

Reference: The Making of Classical Edinburgh (Youngson)

Name:	Estate Duty Office
Address:	6–14 Waterloo Place, Edinburgh
Category:	A, in New Town Conservation Area
Occupier:	National Museum of the Antiquities of Scotland
Use:	Storage
Holding:	Crown

Waterloo Place runs through the Calton Burial Ground from the Calton Hill to the east end of Princes Street. Two balanced blocks stand on each side, linked together by the Regent Arch, built as a memorial to those who fell in the Napoleonic Wars. The complete scheme was designed by Archibald Elliot, a Scot, practising from both Edinburgh and London, although the Post Office's Surveyor, Joseph Kay, was also involved with the design of nos. 16–22 in 1818–19.

This palace-fronted block rectangular in plan, consists of three and four storeys above Waterloo Place with substructure basements down to Calton Road. It has a symmetrical facade of Miletus anta order with a tetrastyle Ionic colonnade facing west towards Princes Street, a feature matched in the buildings on the north side of the street. There is a similar Ionic screen to the centre block of nos. 16–22. A finely detailed balustrade at roof level links the centre block and the four-storey end blocks. Due to the slight rise of Waterloo Place towards the east, there are two changes in level, well handled in the elevation design. The external walls are of Craigleith stone, and the masonwork is of particularly good quality.

Internally, the principal feature is an Ionic screen in the main hall entrance. The building is semi-derelict inside.

References: Georgian Edinburgh (Lindsay)
The Making of Classical Edinburgh (Youngson)
Modern Athens (Shepherd)
APSD

6–14 Waterloo Place.

Name:	Old Post Office
Address:	16–22 Waterloo Place, Edinburgh
Category:	A, in New Town Conservation Area
Occupier:	Scottish Office Central Services
Use:	Offices
Holding:	Crown

Nos. 16–22, the original Post Office, was superseded in 1865 by Robert Matheson's new building at the corner of North Bridge and was subsequently converted into an hotel. It became semi-derelict after a fire in 1935. The building was completely reconstructed in 1967, when a new structural frame was built behind the existing external walls and an extension was added to the south, forming one building for Crown use. It is nine bays wide and three storeys high above Waterloo Place, with an attic storey to each three-bay wing. A multi-storey basement extends down to Calton Road. The plan is rectangular, and the principal front and side facades are articulated by giant Miletus anta order pilasters. Distyle in antis Ionic columns emphasise the recessed centre of the front elevation to Waterloo Place, which is surmounted by a finely detailed balustrade with a solid raised centre section. This originally formed the podium for a sculptured group, which was removed for safety reasons after the fire in 1935. As in the adjacent section of the terrace, the architectural detail is of excellent quality, particularly the ashlar masonwork, the joints of which are barely visible.

References: Georgian Edinburgh (Lindsay)
The Making of Classical Edinburgh (Youngson)
Modern Athens (Shepherd)
APSD

16–22 Waterloo Place.

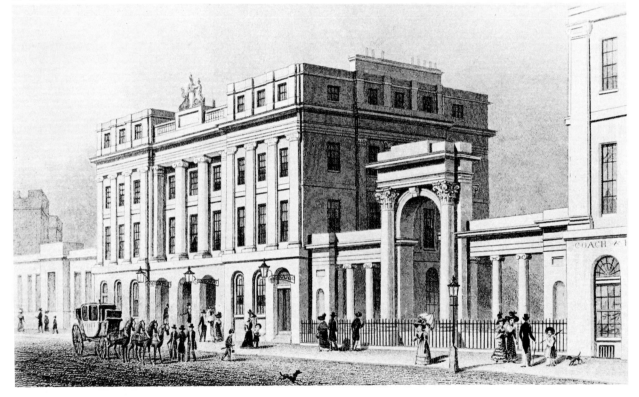

Name:	New Register House
Address:	West Register Street, Edinburgh
Category:	A, in New Town Conservation Area
Occupier:	Public Records of Scotland
Use:	Offices and Records
Holding:	Crown

By 1856, the accommodation in Robert Adam's General Register House was insufficient to house all the accumulated records and it became necessary to provide a new building. An adjacent site was obtained in what came to be called West Register Street with an open frontage towards Princes Street and a boundary somewhat to the north of the existing building. Construction began in 1857, to designs by Robert Matheson.

This grand mid-19th century version of a Renaissance palazzo makes an instructive contrast with the more delicate and restrained Classicism of Adam's building in front. The main nine-bay south elevation, only part of which can be seen from Princes Street, is arranged in three-window groups. The three central bays are slightly advanced, with paired Corinthian columns to the first storey supporting a pronounced entablature at second-floor level. The first-floor windows are architraved with balustraded aprons and alternating triangular and segmental pediments supported on consoles. The second-floor window architraves are lugged. All the windows are astragalled sash and case—behind the times for 1856 and perhaps provided with conscious respect for Adam's adjacent masterpiece. The bold channelled stonework of the ground floor is carried up to frame the end bays of this principal elevation and those of the seven-bay side elevations. These, too, are notable for their refinement and for the excellent condition of the sharp masonry detail. The return ten-bay north elevation is much plainer. The open area in front is surrounded by a tall railing with ornamental gates and gateposts, all in iron, which were set back to this position in 1891.

Internally, the most significant space is the domed central area, entered directly from the vestibule. It is overlooked by five tiers of galleries, excellent examples of Victorian cast-ironwork, which incorporate two spiral stairs. The ribbed dome above has a central oculus.

The domed rotunda to the south-east, designed to serve both General Register House and New Register House, was built in 1871 to plans by the same architect. It is fifty-five feet in diameter and sixty feet high and is connected to General Register House by a top-lit passage.

References: Old and New Edinburgh Vol. 1. (Grant).
Book of the Old Edinburgh Club Volume 17.

Region	LOTHIAN
District	CITY OF EDINBURGH
	Outer Edinburgh

Name:	John Watson's School
Address:	Belford Road, Edinburgh
Category:	A, in Dean Conservation Area
Occupier:	Vacant
Use:	Under conversion for Gallery of Modern Art
Holding:	Leased

Interior before conversion

This building resulted from a bequest in 1759 by Mr. John Watson, Writer to the Signet, for the endowment of a Foundling Hospital. The Society of Writers to the Signet considered this proposal problematical, and applied to Parliament for permission to use the fund for a Hospital for the Maintenance and Education of Destitute Children. A site was therefore procured to the west of the City, on the Estate of Dean, consisting of open pasture and woodland, and William Burn was appointed architect. Burn, a pupil of Sir Robert Smirke, based his design on his earlier unexecuted scheme for the rebuilding of George Watson's Hospital. The building was erected in 1825–28. It is now being modified to provide accommodation for the Scottish National Gallery of Modern Art.

The building is of two storeys and basement on the main east front and three full storeys on the rear elevation. It is long and low, twenty-one bays wide with a pedimented hexastyle Greek Doric central portico and tetrastyle anta order end pavilions. The design owes much to Smirke's Covent Garden Theatre in London and to Stark's Justiciary Courthouse in Glasgow (q.v.). It has been observed that the character is simple and severe, with so much window space as to seem almost modern. The main elevation and terminal bays are built of dressed Craigleith ashlar, with fine putty joints. Snecked Craigleith rubble, with ashlar dressings, is used for the remainder of the exterior.

A single-storey lodge, at the entrance to the estate, has a noteworthy Roman Doric porch in character with the main building.

A south-east extension was made in 1870/80 and a modern laboratory block has been added on the south-west. These extensions have not greatly affected the character of the main building, which retains its original severity, typical of William Burn's Greek Revival work.

The interior has changed little and the entrance vestibule and main hall, in particular, display fine joinerwork. In adapting the building for use as an exhibition gallery, every effort has been made to retain the best features of the original design.

References: Georgian Edinburgh (Lindsay)
Modern Athens (Shepherd)
The Making of Classical Edinburgh (Youngson)

Name:	Redford Barracks
Address:	Colinton Road, Edinburgh
Category:	B
Occupier:	Ministry of Defence
Use:	Barracks
Holding:	Crown

At the end of the last century, accommodation for troops in the Edinburgh area was very inadequate. The cavalry troopers were stationed in old, cramped barracks at Piershill and the infantrymen suffered equally over-crowded conditions in Edinburgh Castle. This, as well as the need for larger training grounds for a modern army, encouraged the War Department to provide better facilities.

This very extensive site at Redford, near Colinton village, was chosen for the erection of a new barracks for both cavalry and infantry battalions, a decision which raised strong opposition at the time from the residents in the Colinton area who believed that the peaceful amenity of the then rural setting would be disturbed. A modern barracks complex was designed by the Director of Barrack Construction, Harry B. Measures, which included indoor and open training facilities, and incorporated all the latest improvements in soldiers' accommodation. Redford was, in its day, the most advanced barracks in Britain and the first military establishment where living, dining, baths,

recreation, instruction, stores etc. for the other ranks were all included in one main barrack block. Nothing so impressive of its type had been constructed in Scotland since the completion of Fort George in the 1760's.

Construction occupied about six years from February 1911. The contract was of such magnitude that the builders, Colin Macandrew Ltd. of Edinburgh built their own railway to transport materials from the main line at Slateford. The stone used in the construction all came from the well-known Northumberland quarries at Blackpasture and Doddington.

The Cavalry Barracks have seen many changes since 1915 when as many as one thousand horses could be stabled at Redford. The stables are now used for other purposes, such as stores and garages. The riding school now belongs to the Local Authority and a large room intended for fencing instruction is used occasionally for military band practice. Many famous Scottish regiments, some now disbanded, have been stationed at Redford, including the Scots Guards, Cameronians, Royal Scots Greys and the Gordon Highlanders. The Cavalry Barracks is situated at the east side of the spacious site and the Infantry Barracks on the west, each with their own entrances and separate accommodation. All the buildings are in the late Victorian/Edwardian Imperial manner with predominately early Renaissance ornamental detailing.

Reference: *Edinburgh Evening News*, 13 July 1939.

Name:	Custom House
Address:	65 Commercial Street, Leith
Category:	A, in Old Leith Conservation Area
Occupiers:	National Museum of Antiquities of Scotland (Royal Scottish Museum)
Use:	Store and secondary display
Holding:	Crown

This heavily monumental classical building was designed as Customs and Excise Offices by Robert Reid and built in 1812. At that time it was situated on the north side of the entrance to the Old East Dock constructed by John Rennie in 1800–06 (now infilled). It then comprised only the two-storey and attic main building and cost about £12,600. In 1820, single-storey wings with segmental arcading were added and, since the original layout had proved unsatisfactory, William Burn was called in to add the perron to the portico and a new main stair in 1824. The detached blocks to the north of the main building were originally stables for use of the Customs and Excise men, whose duties involved visits to the harbours along the coast.

The front is eleven-windowed, Grecian Doric with an advanced central pedimented portico and single end bays. The stonework on the front and side walls is ashlar with two plain string courses. The rear wall is built of coursed rubble, linked to the front and sides by the continuous string courses. A strong moulded cornice with mutules completes the upper storey which is topped by a heavy parapet and balustrade, hiding the slated hipped roof. The portico is recessed distyle, flanked by ground-floor niches. A splendid Coat of Arms is carved in the central pediment and the raised entrance is reached by balustraded stone steps forming a perron. Ornamented iron railings denote the original front pavement line. Windows on all elevations are twelve-pane Georgian sash and case with shuttered ingoes internally.

Entry is by the perron, through a two-leaf panelled door into a raised entrance hall. Burn's geometric stairs give two-way access—down to the ground floor and up to a first-floor gallery. The gallery and stairwell are top-lit by an oval lantern light, with fine coffered plasterwork in the dome, ornate pendentives, cornice and frieze. The stone staircase is penchecked and cantilevered, with a wrought-iron balustrade having a lion rampant motif and a hardwood handrail.

Circulation lobbies on either side of the stair on ground and first floors give access to the principal rooms. The first-floor lobbies are top-lit by oval lanterns, similar to the stairwell but with plain

c. 1830

domes and cornices. Some of the original panelled doors and fireplaces remain, despite the modifications that have been made over the years. All the main rooms have simple cornices, friezes and dadoes. A fine oval room at the east end of the first floor retains its original superb decoration including an egg-and-dart cornice and frieze, a splendid six-panel door and door-head and a plain marble chimney-piece. It obviously belonged to a senior officer. Another fine coloured marble chimney-piece remains in an adjacent room.

Attic rooms are reached by an iron spiral stair at the east end of the building and a recent concrete stair at the west end. Interesting features of the attics are two arched dormers containing loading doors. They still retain the hoists used to raise contraband for safe storage in the attic. The single-storey east wing contains a room with a fine coffered moulded ceiling and cornice.

The old stables to the north are mainly single-storey with two-storey end bays, built in coursed rubble with a hipped and slated pitched roof and Georgian sash and case windows. They are presently used as stores by the Department of Agriculture and Fisheries.

Plans have now been drawn up by the PSA, to convert the Custom House into storage accommodation for the National Museum of Antiquities of Scotland, with access to the public for temporary exhibitions.

References: R.C.A.H.M.S. Inventory, City of Edinburgh
Modern Athens (Shepherd).
Views of Edinburgh (Storer).
Leith and its Antiquities (Irons)

Name:	Craigiehall
Categories:	A, Craigiehall House
	C, Steading (or Stable Yard)
	C, Dovecot
	C, Grotto
	B, Rustic Bridge
	B, Sundial
Occupier:	Ministry of Defence
Use:	Offices
Holding:	Crown

Craigiehall House

This major late 17th century house was built for William Johnston, second Earl of Annandale, who was created Marquis in 1701 and his wife Sophia, daughter and heiress of John Fairholm of Craigie. In 1710, on the death of the second Marquis, the estate passed to Charles Hope, third son of the first Earl of Hopetoun. It was purchased early in the present century by the Rosebery family, and was later acquired from them for use by the Ministry of Defence.

Built to a design by Sir William Bruce, the house formed the focal point of an extensive landscaped park which, by the end of the 18th century, included the ancillary buildings and ornamental features listed above. Completed in 1699, the house then consisted of two floors with basement and attic. This now appears as the six-bay by four-bay block at the south end of the building. Its symmetrical ashlar east facade features one of the earliest pedimented centre-pieces in Scotland.

The tympanum contains fine sculptured scroll-work, the building date and the initials of the Earl and Countess. The basement masonry is rusticated up to the ground-floor string course, with finely-dressed ashlar above. The ground-floor windows have moulded, straight-corniced architraves. There is a first-floor string course. The first-floor windows have plainer architraves. The central entrance is by means of a two-flight stair with iron railings. The door-piece is remarkably fine. Above the cornice it incorporates an unusual, perhaps unique, feature in the form of a deep circular recess containing a white marble urn. It is uncertain whether this was part of Bruce's original design or a later insertion.

Later alterations have devalued much of Craigiehall's outstanding interest as a Bruce mansionhouse. The first major extensions were made in 1828 to the design of William Burn, unbalancing the symmetry of the original layout.

from *Vitruvius Scoticus*

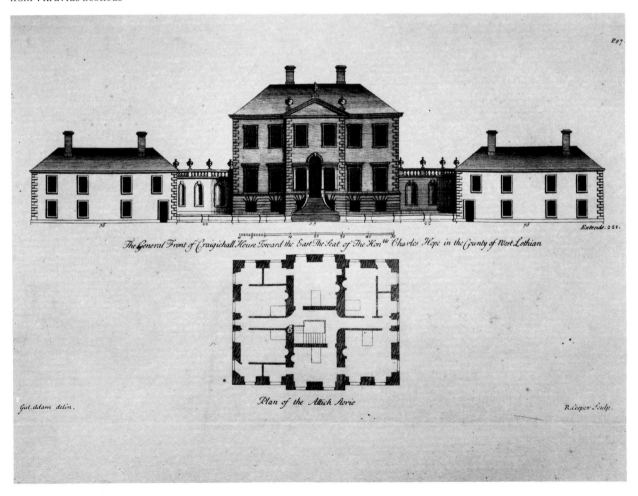

The General Front of Craigiehall House Toward the East The Seat of The Hon.ble Charles Hope in the County of West Lothian

Plan of the Attick Storie

These comprise the advanced, two-storey and basement three-bay block to the north of the Bruce house and the lower service wing beyond. Attached to the north-east corner of Burn's extension, beside the main approach, is a two-bay hipped-roof section. Now embedded in the present complex of buildings, this is almost certainly the northern pavilion of the single-storey pair designed by Bruce to balance the main block, to which it was originally attached by quadrant corridors. Its counterpart has disappeared. In 1852, David Bryce was called in to design minor additions to the service quarters and to remodel the principal south drawing room. Further changes took place in the 1920's, when Sir Robert Lorimer again remodelled parts of the interior and added an asymmetrical bay window to the south elevation. The most recent alterations, carried out for the Ministry of Defence in the 1950's, brutally simplified the outline of the 1699 block, removing the original hipped roof, the tall twin chimney-stacks, the pineapple finials on the pediment and the central lantern which lit the main staircase. The pitched roof and pedimented gable of Burn's extension were also removed and replaced by the present flat roof behind a plain parapet.

These adaptations have resulted in the loss of some original internal features such as decorated plasterwork and wood panelling, but most of the later work is of high quality. The intricate wrought-iron staircase balustrade, with intertwined rose and thistle motifs, is probably the finest of the original features remaining. There is original panelling in the entrance and inner halls, made of fine light oak with delicately designed architraves and door-pieces. Two major chimney-pieces of Bruce vintage also remain. The ceilings are entirely modern.

Steading (or Stable Yard)
Constructed in the mid-19th century to replace earlier outbuildings dating from the Hope-Weir period of ownership, the Steading encloses an open quadrangle. The main two-storey and attic elevation is five bays wide. The masonwork is random rubble and the roof is pitched and slated. The wallhead dormer windows have dressed stone pediments, except for one which has a swept slate roof. The central bay is advanced with a gable incorporating a clock and is surmounted by a small spired, octagonal bell turret with weathercock. The former cart sheds have segment-headed arches. The wings forming the sides of the square are single-storey with slated roofs. Windows are Georgian in character, with astragals. Entrance to the yard is through a low wall with decorated gate

Craigiehall House and Sundial

piers, retained from the first steading buildings. One pier is inscribed CAR H W POSUIT, for (Charles) Hope-Weir. The outer pier bears the inscription ANNO 1749, indicating the date of the original stable buildings.

Dovecot

This traditional structure is rectangular on plan, constructed of coursed split boulder rubble with a projecting ledge below roof level. Early drawings show a pyramidal slated roof which no longer exists. The entrance door is square-headed and checked. The building contains six hundred and seventeen nesting boxes constructed in stone. The west skew-putt bears the inscribed date 1672.

Grotto

The Grotto was constructed by Charles Hope-Weir towards the end of the eighteenth century, following his return from the Grand Tour. The design is uncertainly attributed to Robert Adam. It is sited on the north bank of the River Almond and is a two-storey building constructed of rough rocks, the lower floor being square on plan with a barrel-vaulted stone roof. This acted as the bathhouse, to serve which a lade was constructed to divert the waters of the river. The upper floor, circular on plan and complete with fireplace, is

Detail of main door-piece

known as the Saloon. The building is roofless and in a dilapidated state. Until recently it was used to house an emergency electrical generator. The vegetation along the river bank is overgrown and

Stable Yard

The Grotto

access to the building is difficult. It can, however, be clearly seen from the opposite bank.

Rustic Bridge

The bridge was constructed by Charles Hope-Weir to gain access to his other estate on the opposite bank of the River Almond. The design is attributed either to John or James Adam. It is built of very roughly hewn masonry and consists of a single segmented arch across the deep river valley. The parapets are roughly dressed. One bears a panel with the date 1757 and the other an initialled panel.

Sundial

The sundial, situated on the axis of the main building, on a stone paved area surrounded by a lawn, was restored to its present position by the Ancient Monuments Branch of the Ministry of Public Buildings and Works in the late 1960's. It dates from *circa* 1700 and consists of a tall red sandstone obelisk set on a sphere. The total height is approximately twelve feet. It is typical of large sundials of its period, having a square base shaft, a spherical capital and a tapering finial. The finial is divided on the faces into approximately twenty compartments decorated with carved impressions of the sun or moon. Repairs have been carried out in contrasting grey sandstone.

References: 'Craigiehall'—The Story of a fine Scots Country House (Major C. B. Innes, The Black Watch, 1982).
Vitruvius Scoticus
The Architectural Review Vol. 31 June 1912
'Old Doocots' III (Robertson)

Name:	Craigs House
Address:	East Craigs, Craigs Road, Edinburgh
Category:	C
Occupier:	Department of Agriculture & Fisheries
Use:	Unused
Holding:	Crown

Craigs House, originally the residence of the East Craigs Estate, was acquired for use as a research establishment operated by the Department of Agriculture and Fisheries. The site, between Corstorphine and Maybury Road, is occupied by a large complex of modern buildings. Craigs House is unused and semi-derelict, although it is maintained in a wind and watertight condition.

The house, which dates from 1768, was originally rectangular, three storeys in height with three-window symmetrical frontages, gables and a steep pitched and slated roof. The general character is unpretentiously domestic mid-Georgian, with straight skews and club skew putts. The walls throughout are roughcast, with stone margins at the corners. On the south front of this original section, a semi-octagonal canted central bay contains the stone stair which rises in a series of winder steps. This bay has an arched and key-blocked window at half-landing level.

The original three-storey building included a semi-basement, but extensive alterations in the early 19th century converted the building to two storeys and basement. The entrance, which has a wooden porch, is now approached by asymmetrical steps to the east of the centre axis. Two single-storey and basement canted bays were added on the east and west ends of the building, each with three tall astragalled windows.

Internally, the building is derelict and has suffered considerably from dilapidation, although a new slated roof was recently constructed and steps have been taken to eliminate dampness in the walls. Some of the original joinerwork, such as panelled doors and architraves, remain, together with simple plaster cornices on the ground floor. The basement floor is of flagstone.

It is intended to rehabilitate the building and to use the accommodation as extra operating space for the Research Centre.

Name:	H.M.S. Claverhouse
Address:	Granton Square, Edinburgh
Category:	B
Occupier:	Ministry of Defence
	Royal Naval Reserve
Use:	Headquarters and Training Centre
Holding:	Leased

In or about 1838, the Duke of Buccleuch commissioned William Burn to design this building as a hotel, for use by railway travellers before the Forth Rail Bridge was constructed.

At this time the journey north from Edinburgh was by train to Granton Station and then by ferry to Burntisland, in Fife, for further rail connection. The Granton Hotel was used as a staging post for these travellers. A second hotel, of similar size, was erected at the Burntisland terminus, to the design of John Henderson.

The Granton building was acquired for military use during the First World War, and is now used by the Royal Naval Reserve as a Headquarters and Training Centre. It consists of three floors and basement. The seven-windowed frontage, with a slightly recessed three-bay centre, is constructed in coursed rubble with corner quoins of V-jointed ashlar. There is an answering but smaller building of similar design on the west side of the square.

The Roman Doric entrance porch has recently been painted and now carries the sign 'H.M.S. CLAVERHOUSE' on the frieze. All the windows are original Georgian sash and case with architraved surrounds. The first-floor windows in the end bays also have cornices. Both gables are three-windowed. The north gable is more ornate, the centre windows at ground and first floor being tripartite with stone mullions. A shallow stone balcony projects at first-floor level, with moulded brackets and a Jacobean-style balustrade. The roof is pitched and slated, with hip extensions over the end bays.

Entrance is by fly-over stair to a panelled door with sidelights and an astragalled fanlight. The basement area is protected by a modern rendered wall.

Internally, all the main rooms are corniced with heavy mouldings. Though they retain the original character, they have generally been utilised as mess rooms with built-in fittings such as bars. The doors are mostly the original four-panelled pattern with architraves and the windows have shuttered ingoes. On the first floor, three plain marble chimney-pieces remain, with the fireplace openings blocked up.

A half-turn stair with landings, constructed of cantilevered, pen-checked stone with decorated wrought-iron balusters and hardwood handrail, gives access to all floors.

A large rear extension was erected in 1951. This is used for training purposes. The main building is used for messing and offices.

Reference: *Illustrated London News* vol. 1. no. 20.

Address:	20 Inverleith Row, Edinburgh
Category:	B, in Inverleith Conservation Area
Occupier:	Scottish Office
Use:	Training Office
Holding:	Crown

A detached house on a site feued from the Rocheid Estate, on condition that the building would comply with a plan and elevation of 1824 by Thomas Brown, Architect and Surveyor of Works for the City of Edinburgh. It was also stipulated that the house would cost not less than £500.

No. 20 Inverleith Row consists of two storeys and basement, rectangular in plan, with a central pedimented door-piece of fluted Ionic columns in antis between Roman Doric pilasters, framing a panelled door with a plain fanlight. The three-window east-facing front is constructed of ashlar with a heavy moulded cornice. Side and rear walls are constructed of rubble with ashlar quoins and all windows have dressed stone surrounds. The pitched, slated roof with hipped ends has tall wallhead chimney-stacks which have recently been rendered.

Front and side windows are twelve-pane sash and case, in contrast to the west-facing rear windows which are either single-pane or four-pane. A full-length iron balcony spans the west wall at first-floor level.

Internally, the house retains its original basic plan, despite some modifications required for office accommodation. The basement has been stripped to the stonework and is used for rough storage. Ground-floor rooms are intact, except that most chimney-pieces have been removed. Access to the first floor is by a pen-checked cantilevered stone stair with a simple wrought-iron balustrade with hardwood handrail. All rooms have cornices, panelled doors and architraves. The main room on the first floor has excellent plasterwork and wall-panelling. This room also has a fine marble chimney-piece with relief carving of female figures from Greek mythology.

References: R.C.A.H.M.S. Inventory, City of Edinburgh.

Name:	Inverleith House
Address:	Royal Botanic Garden, Inverleith Row, Edinburgh
Category:	B, in Inverleith Conservation Area
Occupier	Gallery of Modern Art
Use:	Art Gallery
Holding:	Crown

This Georgian country house was built in 1774 by David Henderson, mason, for James Rocheid of Inverleith and was purchased jointly by the City of Edinburgh and H.M. Government in 1877 to enlarge the Botanic Garden.

The entrance was then re-orientated from south to north, when the entrance porch at the base of the central semi-elliptical staircase bow was added by W. W. Robertson. There is a recent addition in stone to the west of the entrance.

The house is of three storeys with attic and basement, linked to pavilions on the north-west and north-east by diagonal screen walls, forming a most impressive setting for the modern art and sculptures on display.

It is constructed of rubble stonework with V-jointed dressed ashlar quoins and has a pitched slated roof with hipped ends.

All the windows are Georgian sash and case with dressed stone surrounds. The original boldly architraved door-piece on the south face is now a french window leading by a flyover stair to the ornamental garden.

The modest two-storey pavilions are of rubble stonework, in character with the main building.

Internally, the three floors of the main house have been adapted to form galleries for exhibition purposes. Some alterations have been made, including the bricking up of windows, but the overall character of the house generally survives.

Original cornices and architraves have been retained, together with two classical marble chimney-pieces on the ground floor.

The staircase follows the semi-elliptical form of its enclosure and is constructed of pen-checked cantilevered stone with a simple wrought-iron balustrade and hardwood handrail.

The attics are used for office accommodation and the basement for storage and the heating chamber.

Both pavilions have been utilised, one for storage. Most of its windows have been bricked up

internally. The other pavilion, greatly altered to form a restaurant for visitors, was originally the stables of the Rocheid house.

The Gallery of Modern Art is intended to be rehoused in the former John Watson's School (see page 142).

Reference: The Heritage of Greater Edinburgh (E. J. MacRae)

Name:	Large Palm House
Address:	Royal Botanic Garden, Inverleith Row, Edinburgh
Category:	A, in Inverleith Conservation Area
Occupier:	Royal Botanic Gardens
Use:	Environmental Glasshouse
Holding:	Crown

The Palm House was built in 1856–58 to designs prepared by Robert Matheson in 1854–55.

It is rectangular in plan with a smaller octagonal tropical Palm House to the rear. This was built in 1834 as the Palm Store, and was heightened by the addition of a dome in 1859–60. Its glazing, originally flush with the outer faces of the columns, has now been recessed behind them.

The Palm Houses now form part of an integrated group, with modern plant houses, making an exhibition area for public viewing.

The solid walling consists of Roman Doric pilasters of ashlar stone, flanking metal-framed windows with semi-circular arched heads and fine Georgian pattern glazing bars. A deep stone entablature supports the lower tier of the convex roof, which is an excellent example of Victorian iron and glass structural design.

Internally, cast-iron columns with simple bases and capitals support the second tier of glazing.

Access to a maintenance walkway at eaves level is reached by two fine cast-iron spiral staircases, which have balusters with rose motifs.

Edinburgh's sunshine is recorded on the southwest corner of the large Palm House, which also houses a specimen palm, Livistona Australis, 60 ft. in height.

References: *Transactions of Botanical Soc.* Vol. VI p. 133
Plans SRO 1854–5

Name:	Linnaeus Monument
Address:	Royal Botanic Garden,
	Inverleith Row, Edinburgh
Category:	A, in Inverleith Conservation Area
Occupier:	Royal Botanic Garden
Use:	Monument
Holding:	Crown

Professor John Hope became Regius Keeper of the Garden and King's Botanist in 1761, holding these posts until his death in 1786. He taught Materia Medicina in the University of Edinburgh in the winter and Botany in the summer. He held in very great esteem his contemporary Carl von Linne Linnaeus (Sir Charles Linnaeus), the Swedish doctor and scientist who became a most distinguished naturalist, and is now regarded as the founder of modern botany. Linnaeus' 'Systema Naturae' was published in 1735, and was the first to expound the true principles of defining genera and species. The Linnaean system of classification of plants was a major breakthrough in scientific botany.

Hope commissioned Robert Adam to design a monument in Linnaeus' memory. It was erected in 1779, the year after Linnaeus' death, in the presence of the students of the University Medical Faculty. It takes the form of an urn on a decorated pedestal, with an inset marble panel embellished by a carved mask and foliage swag. On the panel is the inscription 'LINNAEO POSUIT J. HOPE 1779'.

After several changes of site, the memorial is now appropriately located in the Botanic Gardens, in a patio to the north of the Exhibition Planthouses.

Address:	8 Leopold Place, Edinburgh
Category:	A, in New Town Conservation Area
Occupier:	Department of Health & Social Security
Use:	Medical Board
Holding:	Crown

This property was designed by W. H. Playfair in 1820 as part of a tenement block comprising nos. 1–11, with semi-circular corners to Elm Row and Windsor Street. With Montgomery Street and Hillside Crescent, it formed part of the Calton plan, which also embraced Royal Terrace and Blenheim Place opposite, the former extending into Carlton Terrace and Regent Terrace on the west. This vast development was promoted jointly by the City and Mr. Allan of Hillside. Leopold Place, begun in 1823, was on the Allan of Hillside section. The plans are preserved in the University Library.

The impressive corner block is of three and four storeys, with giant Ionic columns articulating the recessed circled corner bays. The frontage is constructed of rusticated ashlar stonework at ground floor and plain ashlar above, with a tooled finish to the basement.

No. 8 is a main door, ground floor and basement house situated in the four-storey, five-bay section of the block facing south towards Calton Hill. Windows are Georgian sash and case, except on the first floor, where single-pane sashes have been substituted. The first-floor windows are alternately pedimented.

A bold moulded string course, continuing round the block at third-floor level, defines the main part of the elevation from the lower attic storey.

The ground floor contains some fine features, notably in the large room to the left of the entrance which has a decorated ceiling and cornice and a plain frieze. A delicate white marble chimney-piece with free-standing, fluted Doric columns displays good relief sculpture, in particular the central motif depicting an animal sacrifice. Other ground-floor rooms also retain good original classical embellishment together with six-panelled doors. In the hall there is a fine panelled ceiling with moulded frieze, composite pilasters and dado rail.

References: The Making of Classical Edinburgh (Youngson)
Calton Estate Plans, Edinburgh University Library

156

Name:	Former Dreghorn Castle Estate properties
Address:	Redford Road, Edinburgh
Categories:	C(S): Farmhouse & Steading Dreghorn Mains
	C(S): Woodend Cottage Dreghorn Mains
	B: Old Bridge Redford Road
Occupier:	Ministry of Defence
Use:	Property Services Agency and Private Tenant
Holding:	Crown

Dreghorn Castle Estate lies at the mouth of Howden Glen, in the parish of Colinton. The Castle was probably built in the late 17th century by William Moray, Master of Works to King Charles II and the brother of Sir Robert Moray, founder of The Royal Society of London. He is known to have laid out the grounds with beech avenues. The Castle was reconstructed for Alexander Trotter, circa 1805. He enlarged and castellated the original house, with lavish use of neo-Norman detail, to designs by Archibald Elliot. The Castle was demolished in 1958 and nothing of Elliot's work now remains.

Farmhouse and Steading, Dreghorn Mains

The original two-storey farmhouse formed the east range of the farm court. Its walls are stuccoed and divided into a pattern of rectangles with plain rendered margins. This building was extended in the mid-19th century, becoming in effect the rear wing of a new two-storey, three-bay house built at right-angles in snecked rubble. The principal, south front is dominated by two broad, bargeboarded gables, enclosing two-storey canted bays built of ashlar with their own slated caps. Between them a linking gablet marks the central, entrance bay. The door-piece is also of ashlar with moulded architraves and a rather coarse open-pedimented hood on consoles, framing a good six-panelled door. Some of the original tall octagonal chimney cans survive. A long single-storey east wing features a jerkin-headed gable. A D-shaped walled garden to the south contains a variety of trees and shrubs. The house is unoccupied but is maintained in a wind and waterproof condition.

The steading buildings date from the late 18th and early 19th centuries. They are used in part by P.S.A. foresters, as a workshop and partly by the tenant farmer who leases adjoining grazing land. The north and west ranges of the square are two storeys in height, constructed of whitewashed rubble with red pantiled roofs. Particularly notable

Dreghorn mains steading

are the cartshed openings, with shouldered flat arches of finely-jointed dressed stonework. The south range is single-storey. A later, slated L-plan addition, attached at the south-west corner, incorporates a high pend entry to the court. The masonry is in fairly good condition but the pantiled roofs are in need of repair.

Woodend Cottage, Dreghorn Mains
Woodend Cottage is a small two-room and kitchen single-storey building. Built circa 1800, it is roughly square on plan with a piended slate roof. The masonwork is droved ashlar with raised quoins at the angles, a shallow cornice and a deep blocking course above. The west wall of the living room is bowed, with two single-pane sash and case windows. The kitchen area has a window to the north and the other apartment looks east. A combined central chimney-stack rises above the apex of the roof. The single-bay kitchen wing of stugged stonework was added in the mid-19th century at the north-east corner. Probably at the same time, a tall, arched and key-blocked pedimented porch, distinctly out of scale with the cottage, was inserted at the re-entrant angle.

Old Bridge, Redford Road
The Howden and Bonaly Burns, which run north from the Pentland Hills, meet within the Dreghorn Estate to form the Braid Burn, over which the Old Bridge was built in the early 19th century on the original line of Redford Road. The road has now been diverted about one hundred yards to the north.

The single-arch bridge, constructed of roughly-dressed stone, is reinforced on each side by semi-circular buttresses. These rise to form stepped parapets, the intervening spaces being filled with open iron railings. The remains of an artificial waterfall are still visible some distance to the north, between the bridge and the diverted Redford Road.

The northern entrance to the estate was situated beside the bridge. The square castellated lodge by Archibald Elliot, has been demolished.

References: Castles & Mansions of the Lothians (Small)
Parish of Colinton, Vol. 1, 1879–1964

Name:	Stenhouse Mansion
Address:	Stenhouse Mill Lane, Edinburgh
Category:	A
Occupier:	Scottish Development Department (Ancient Monuments)
Use:	Office/Working Studios
Holding:	Leased

Stenhouse Mansion (earlier, Stanhopemilne) is a good example of a sixteenth century laird's house and was restored for its present use in 1962 by the architect Ian G. Lindsay. It is owned by the National Trust for Scotland and leased by the P.S.A. for the use of the Ancient Monuments Branch of the Scottish Development Department. In the early sixteenth century it was a dependency of the Abbey of Holyrood. In 1511 its Abbot granted Saughton Mills in tack to the Stanhope family. In 1623 it was acquired by Patrick Ellis, an Edinburgh merchant, who added two side wings to the original rectangular building, to form an F-plan. His initials and arms are engraved over the lintel of the entrance door together with the words "BLISIT BE GOD FOR AL HIS GIFTIS".

The building consists of one main block three storeys high, and two slightly lower side blocks at right angles. The internal floor levels are served by two interconnecting spiral stone stairs in excellent condition. It would appear that one stair was part of the original house and that the other was erected when the side wings were added in order to connect the slightly varying floor levels.

The building is constructed of random rubble with roughly-dressed quoins and dressed window surrounds. The gables are crow-stepped and the pitched roof is covered with Caithness slates laid in diminishing courses, with a stone ridge. There are stone relieving arches over the window lintels.

The semi-dormers are in stone with pediments and individual finials, those on the lower of the two side wings having swept roofs. The restored windows are in two sections, the upper part being of leaded crown glass and the lower in dressed oak shutters, following sixteenth century practice. Some windows retain iron grilles across the lower part. There are no gutters but a stone channel at ground level drains rainwater away from the building.

The two entrance doors with bolection-moulded architraves open off a small courtyard paved in flagstone slabs. The courtyard is surrounded by a low wall. The arms of Patrick Ellis, picked out and gilded, are contained within a square consoled panel, dated 1623. There is a solid stone vault over the ground floor in the northern end of the main block. A doocot, with two triangular entry holes, is set into the north gable as is a beebole. A bake oven and two fireplaces survive on the ground floor (one of which retains the original iron 'swee') and two further fireplaces remain on the first floor. There are two ogee-headed aumbries built into the walls on the first floor. A Charles II period plaster ceiling with three Royal cyphers has been restored in a small room on the top floor. There are moulded plaster cornices in other rooms of the building. One ceiling with exposed timber joists has been restored. Two rooms in the side wings have also been restored.

Stenhouse Mansion now contains a stone preservation studio, chemical store and equipment store on the ground floor, a paintings restoration workshop and laboratory on the first floor, two small offices, storage and welfare facilities on the second floor and a small library on the lower first floor.

References: R.C.A.H.M.S. Inventory, Midlothian.
National Trust for Scotland.

Region	LOTHIAN
District	MIDLOTHIAN

Name:	The Clock Tower and The Keep
Address:	Glencorse Barracks, Midlothian
Category:	B
Occupier:	Ministry of Defence
Use:	Barracks
Holding:	Crown

The complex of buildings comprising Glencorse Barracks occupies the former estate of Greenlaw. Its history begins in 1803 when Greenlaw House was converted into a prison for French prisoners of war. It subsequently became a military prison, and finally a military barracks, when the name was changed to Glencorse. Greenlaw House no longer exists. The present buildings have been frequently altered and extended.

The Clock Tower

Entrance to the barracks is from the east side of the Edinburgh to Penicuik road. The Clock Tower is placed on the entrance axis and is the most prominent building on the site. It is probably the oldest building in the complex. Octagonal in plan, it is four storeys in height, built of roughly-dressed coursed masonry. Each face displays a tier of blind windows with projecting cills. Entrance doors occur on the east and west faces and plainly-figured clock faces are set into the north, south and west elevations below the cornice. This broad band, incorporating blind windows, is shaded by the oversailing slated pyramid roof. The rafter-ends are exposed at the eaves and there is a flagpole at the apex. Formerly a guard room but now used only for storage, the Clock Tower is the centre-piece of an open exhibition area which includes various artillery weapons.

The Keep

This building, formerly the Armoury and Quartermaster's Store, is sited on the same axis as the Clock Tower, slightly further east. It is of three storeys, castellated and approximately square, with higher engaged stair towers at the opposite north-west and south-east angles. The masonwork, of superior quality, is of snecked rubble and dressings to the doors and windows. The walls are battered over the height of the ground floor and there are pronounced string courses at first-floor level, and immediately below the castellated parapet. The towers are castellated and machicolated, with slit windows which, at first and second floors, follow the staircases behind. The windows to the main block are tall twelve-pane sashes constructed in iron.

Internally, the building has been extensively altered and adapted and the detail is very plain and unrefined.

Region	LOTHIAN
District	WEST LOTHIAN

Name:	Sheriff Court
Address:	High Street, Linlithgow
Category:	Recommended for Listing, in Linlithgow Conservation Area
Occupier:	Scottish Courts Administration
Use:	Court House
Holding:	Crown

Linlithgow Sheriff Court was built to designs of Wardrop and Reid between 1861 and 1863. The building is set back from the south side of the High Street, next to Dick Peddie, Todd and Jamieson's neo-Georgian County Buildings of 1936. To the west, public and commercial buildings give way to domestic scale in an assortment of Georgian terraced houses, while across the road a redevelopment of the late 1960s screens the Palace from view.

The two-storey Court building is a dignified neo-Tudor design with an almost symmetrical frontage to the High Street. This elevation is given interest by the massing of the bays rather than by elaborate architectural detail. The two central gabled bays project boldly forward and are linked by narrow bays to outer gabled wings which also project but less than those in the centre. The western wing has a canted window at ground floor. Snecked and squared rubble is used throughout with polished and tooled ashlar for the moulded window dressings, quoins, string courses, parapet, gable copings and finials, and for the distinctive octagonal-shafted stacks. These stacks are set in pairs or groups of three and five, except on the central gables of this main elevation and on one rear gable, where apex stacks replace finials.

Windows for the most part are two or three-light with mullions and transomes and square hood-moulds. The Courtroom windows, visible at the rear, are Tudor-arched with decorative glazing. The ground-floor hood-moulds continue as a string course, linking the windows. The Court is entered through the right-hand central bay by an arched doorway with panelled spandrels and a stepped hood-mould. Beside the doorway is a framed memorial plaque to the Regent Moray designed by Sir Noel Paton, executed by Mrs. D. O. Hill and erected in 1875. The inscription states that 'on the street opposite this tablet James Stuart Earl of Moray Regent of Scotland was shot by James Hamilton of Bothwellhaugh on 20 January 1570'. The only other decorative feature is a carved thistle above the central rainwater head, dated 1863.

Internally, the first-floor Courtroom remains relatively unaltered apart from modern light fittings. The timber-panelled Tudor-arched ceiling is supported by moulded and braced tie beams which spring from colonettes supported on corbels. Original courtroom fittings survive. The remaining rooms are simply detailed.

Reference: Buildings of Scotland, Lothian (McWilliam).

Islands Council	ORKNEY
Name:	Custom House
Address:	33 Albert Street, Kirkwall
Category:	B, in Kirkwall Conservation Area
Use:	Offices
Occupier:	Customs and Excise
Holding:	Crown

The Custom House is situated mid-way along Albert Street, one of several narrow stone-flagged thoroughfares in the town where the buildings are typically gable-ended to the street. Most of the nearby buildings are vernacular in character, built of traditional local materials but the Custom House is distinguished by its more sophisticated facade design and its white-painted, smooth-rendered finish. Originally a private house dating from approximately the last quarter of the 17th century, it was remodelled and extended in 1828 by Captain Balfour, R.N., sometime Provost of Kirkwall. Before this house was built it is known that the site was consecrated and dedicated to St. Barbara. The present house acquired the distinctive nickname of "Hell", for reasons now obscure, while the property on the other side of the narrow street was called "Purgatory".

The building has its short main frontage onto the public street and is contained behind a small front

plot by a low wall with iron railings. The name of the building is lettered on the entablature of the pilastered door-piece. The window spacing is regular. A single ground-floor window balances the door-piece, in line with a pair of windows above. A dormer window with a piended slate roof rises from the wall head. All the windows are six-pane sash and case, with plain raised margins. A tall, wall-mounted flag pole rises over the entrance. Between the first-floor windows and below the dormer is fixed a handsome gilded Royal Coat of Arms. The rear elevation, which faces onto a narrow garden, has a similar window arrangement. The side elevation beside the adjacent lane has a random arrangement of windows to the ground floor with, at first floor, a single large twelve-pane window which lights the internal stair.

The narrow frontage dictates the plan arrangement. The entrance opens onto a corridor through a semi-circular headed arch. The main public room is set to one side, with a circulation corridor leading to the rear rooms and to the stairway. It is likely that the ground floor originally contained a large public room entered direct from the street, since the party wall forming the corridor breaks the line of an earlier, continuous acanthus leaf cornice. The timber stairway to first floor and attic occupies the full depth of the building. It is of open-well design with plain square balustrading and a slender Regency-style veneered mahogany handrail which begins with a volute scroll at ground level. There are no landings on the upper floors, access being gained directly from the stair into each room. The room interiors are late Georgian in detail, typified by the classical decoration of the plaster ceilings. The first-floor public room which extends the full width of the front facade has an interesting Greek-key pattern cornice over an egg-and-dart frieze. The ceiling includes a leaf-pattern centre-piece contained within an oval garland. Three-panel window shutters have been retained, as have most of the original door-pieces. Their architraves, with ribbed and fluted moulding, terminate on square block bases. The doors are generally six-panelled with raised centres. Chimney-pieces have, however, been removed.

XIII. Greenock Custom House.

XIV. Fort George, Inverness.

163

XV.   Balhousie Castle, Perth

XVI.   Perth Sheriff Court. Chimney-piece.

164

Islands Council	**SHETLAND**

Name:	Fort Charlotte
Address:	Lerwick
Category:	B, Scheduled Monument in Lerwick Conservation Area
Occupier:	Highlands Territorial Army Volunteer Reserve
Use:	Territorial Army Centre
Holding:	Crown

Fort Charlotte, overlooking the harbour of Lerwick, is of great importance in Scotland as a complete example of a bastioned coastal defence work. Its present form is the result of two principal phases of construction. The basic pentagonal plan of the fort dates from the first phase of construction in 1665, when it was built to the designs of the King's Master Mason, John Mylne, to provide protection for shipping in the Bressay Sound at the time of the Dutch War. Its defences proved insufficiently strong to counter the Dutch attack on Lerwick on 13 August 1673, and the fort was burned with the rest of the town. The land it occupied subsequently passed into private ownership, although its walls were not demolished.

The second phase of the fort's history came with the American War of Independence, at a time when British shipping was much troubled by the action of privateers. The fort was purchased back from the owner by the Secretary of State for War in 1782, and its walls repaired and strengthened to the designs of Lt. Col. Frazer, Chief Engineer for North Britain. It was at this time that it was given its name, in honour of George III's Queen. Fraser reconstructed the battery on the seaward side, and repaired the breaches in the landward walls and bastions. Within the fort he provided the necessary accommodation for the garrison, along with the structures required for its defence. The Board of Ordnance drawings for this operation still survive.

In the early years of this century the fort was used by the navy. A variety of additional buildings were erected within its walls, with little sympathy for the seventeenth and eighteenth century structures, which were themselves considerably modified. In the 1920's responsibility for the maintenance of the perimeter walls passed to the Ministry of Works, along with a number of buildings in the fort used by the Coastguard Service; regular—if limited—works were sub-

National Library of Scotland

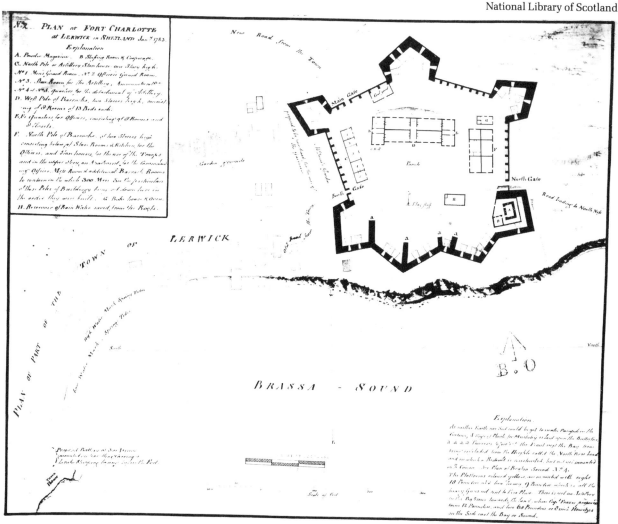

sequently undertaken to ensure the preservation of the walls. Growing appreciation of the fort's importance meant, however, that, from the early 1960's particular care began to be taken to safeguard the preservation of the walls in a historically authentic state. In 1971, as an extension of this policy, it was decided that the whole fort should be handed over to the Department of the Environment (the successor of the Ministry of Works). Since then the Ancient Monuments Division (now part of the Scottish Development Department) has undertaken an extended programme of restoration and improvement involving the removal of unsympathetic later structures within the fort, and general reinstatement of the eighteenth century buildings.

The fort was planned as a pentagon, with bastions to protect the four landward faces, whilst the wall on the seaward side was set out as two adjacent obtuse triangular projections in order to provide a wide range of firing angles across Bressay Sound. (The cliff beneath the seaward wall originally dropped down to the water line, obviating the need for flanking fire on that side.) Three gates into the fort were provided, the principal one being in the south-west face. Provision for artillery fire was made in the five bastions, and along the seaward face, whilst along the landward faces planked stages for musketry fire were constructed 'As neither Earth nor Sod could be got to make Parapets in the Curtains'.

The main barrack building is aligned with its eastern face overlooking the central parade ground. It was built as a two-storeyed double-pile structure of eleven bays, the terminal pair of bays at each end of the east front set in projecting pavilions to distinguish the Officers' Quarters. The structure has been extensively modified to form a drill hall with flanking blocks, but its facades are in course of restoration to their original, handsomely restrained classical form. A second barrack block to the north of the parade ground provided accommodation for the Commanding Officer on the first floor, along with stores and a kitchen. This also is a double-pile two-storeyed block, and is similarly in course of restoration. Along the south side of the parade ground is a single-storey range for the guard rooms and artillery stores. These, originally open towards the north, were later enclosed by a wall along that side.

Of the other principal buildings, the powder magazine and shifting room were placed within a separate enclosure in the north-east bastion. A water reservoir, with flanking lean-to additions, stands at the north-east corner of the parade ground, and a bakehouse was constructed to the west of the north barrack block.

Footnote: Fort Charlotte was formerly in the care of PSA as an ancient monument but since 1978 it has been in the care of the Secretary of State for Scotland and is maintained on his behalf by the Ancient Monuments Division of the Scottish Development Department. PSA, however, retains a responsibility for the areas used by the Territorial Army.

SDD Ancient Monuments Division

Name:	Sheriff Court
Address:	King Erik Street, Lerwick
Category:	C(S), in Lerwick Conservation Area
Occupier:	Scottish Courts Administration
Use:	Court House
Holding:	Crown

This group of buildings, designed by David Rhind of Edinburgh, was erected in 1875 as a Sheriff Court House and Prison for the Shetland Commissioners of Supply. The contractor, D. Outerson, also came from Edinburgh but he employed a mainly local workforce.

Situated on high ground to the north end of the town in a neat grassed area opposite the War Memorial and the Town Hall, the Sheriff Court House is one of the first urban landmarks visible from the sea approach to Lerwick. The building group is laid out to an irregular plan with the Sheriff Court House on the south facing King Erik Street, linked by the old County Hall to the Prison buildings at the rear. The County Hall is used as offices by the Shetland Islands Council and the Prison has been adapted by the police as their Divisional Headquarters.

The group is Scottish domestic in style, the Sheriff Court House being small in scale and less monumental than most contemporary mainland court houses. It is constructed in snecked freestone rubble with a tooled finish. Contrasting lighter coloured stone is used for the cills, lintels and window surrounds. The roofline is varied and the silhouette is made more picturesque by numerous crow-stepped gables.

The old Prison building is plain with small segment-headed small-pane windows, protected by heavy iron cross-bars. Facing King Erik Street, the Sheriff Court House frontage consists of three bays with a fourth, recessed bay formed by the gable of the east wing. On the ground floor the central entrance doorway is flanked by bipartite windows, with single windows lighting the semi-attic floor above. The frontage symmetry is nullified by the treatment at the wallhead. The west bay has a crow-stepped dormer while the other two bays feature wide gables, that on the east carrying a massive chimney-stack. All the gables are crow-stepped with skew-putts. They incorporate either tall central chimney-stacks with moulded cornices or are finished with iron or stone finials. The windows are sash and case with depressed, straight-arched heads and are mostly of four or two-pane pattern. They are domestic in scale except for the tall Courtroom windows. The entrance doorway is plain, with a panelled two-leaf door and fanlight. The building date is carved above it, on a stone panel enclosed by a straight hood-mould. A length of delicate iron railing is fitted as a skyline ornament to the ridge above the high Courtroom roof. Grass lawns around the building are surrounded by a low stone wall topped by ornamental iron railings and balusters. In front of the Court House, a pair of stone gate piers with flat pyramid caps support a decorative iron arch which formerly incorporated a central lamp fitting.

Internally, the building is plainly decorated, with simple cornices. The fine stone staircase with twisted iron balusters is lit by a tall window at the half-landing. The first-floor Courtroom is small but well-proportioned with a coved ceiling decorated with moulded cornices. It is well lit by tall windows on two sides. The Sheriff's bench and the pew seating have recently been cleaned and revarnished giving a crisp and attractive appearance to the room. The ceilings of the upstairs rooms are generally coved at the outer walls, with dormer or semi-dormer windows. A simple marble chimney-piece remains in the Sheriff's room.

References: Shetland Commissioners of Supply Minutes, 1873.
Lerwick During the Last Half Century (T. M. Y. Manson)

Region	STRATHCLYDE
District	ARGYLL AND BUTE

Name:	Inveraray Pier
Category:	B, in Inveraray Conservation Area
Occupier	Ministry of Defence
Use:	Pier
Holding:	Crown

Inveraray, the traditional home of the Dukes of Argyll and a Royal Burgh since 1648, is the site of the earliest large mansion built in the Gothic Revival style, and the earliest eighteenth-century planned town in Britain. The original village near the ancient castle was burnt by the Royalist Marquis of Montrose in 1644, but more than a hundred years passed before the 3rd Duke of Argyll conceived his plan to build a new town.

Work began on the pier in 1759 and was completed in 1762. Since 1758, thirty pounds annually had been allowed by the 3rd Duke towards its cost. When the Duke died before its completion, a further £30 was given by the 4th Duke. This first pier, a modest 100-foot jetty, was designed by John Adam for a fee of ten and sixpence and built by James Potter. It provided anchorage for only two small vessels. In 1765, it was raised in height, but by 1771 it was reported to be in a ruinous condition due to the violent storms. By 1795, the pier was totally inadequate in a port which now served a herring fleet of over 500 boats

and had to cope with the unloading of a growing amount of building materials, meat and grain, as well as the town's exports of wool and timber bark. The 5th Duke therefore ordered estimates for the pier's extension and repair. Eventually, after much difficulty, an estimate to restore and lengthen it was received from William Johns, a mason. Unfortunately, there were doubts about Johns' proposals and James Gillespie, better known as Gillespie Graham, "an Architect of Eminence" from Edinburgh who had occasionally visited Inveraray, was asked to inspect the pier. His recommendations were reluctantly carried out by Johns, and the work was completed in 1806. The building of the 116-foot extension had been so protracted and expensive that a proposal to erect an ornamental lighthouse designed by Alexander Naysmith never materialised. The final extension was completed in 1836 at a cost of £1,200 of which £800 was provided by the British Fishery Society and the remainder by the 7th Duke.

The size of the herring fleet dwindled gradually, until in 1937 the local fishermen had to appeal to the local Member of Parliament for action against the illegal use of the trawl net in Loch Fyne. Today, not a single boat sails to fish for herring from a burgh whose motto is 'May the herring always hang from thy nets'.

References: Inveraray and the Dukes of Argyll (Ian Lindsay and Mary Cosh).
The Royal Burgh of Inveraray (Alexander Fraser).

Name:	Sheriff Court
Address:	Watergate, Rothesay
Category:	B, in Rothesay Conservation Area
Occupier:	Scottish Courts Administration
Use:	Court House
Holding:	Crown

This powerfully modelled, castellated two-storey building is located on a prominent corner site in the centre of the town, east of Rothesay Castle. Designed by James Dempster of Greenock, it was erected in 1832–3 as Bute County Buildings and was enlarged in 1865–7. The Scottish Courts Administration accommodation includes a new Courtroom at first-floor and offices at ground-floor level. The Court House is constructed in coursed yellow sandstone blocks with white ashlar dressings. The main, symmetrical five-bay south elevation is anchored at the corners by slightly higher square turrets. At its centre, the entrance bay rises to form a bold clock tower, surmounted by a heavily corbelled and battlemented parapet with angle turrets. The Tudor-arched ground-floor entrance is recessed beneath a bracketed balcony and five-light oriel. The flanking bays are strongly emphasised, each forming a two-storey panel recessed within the main rectangular frame of the elevation. Tall three-light mullioned and transomed windows light the first-floor. Under these, at ground-floor level, are small three-light sash and case windows with straight hood-moulds. The building returns with one similarly-detailed bay to each side elevation and additional modified bays beyond.

The main entrance hall is lit by an elegant glazed cupola with a stained-glass border. It also boasts a fine open spiral staircase with cast-iron balustrade and hardwood handrail. At the first floor landing, seating is built into a panelled window recess with a foliate cornice carried round the opening. Entrance from the landing to the Courtroom lobby is through a Tudor archway. The rest of the interior has been almost totally modernised.

Reference: Argyll & Bute District Archives: Papers

Region	STRATHCLYDE
District	CLYDESDALE

Name:	Sheriff Court
Address:	Hope Street, Lanark
Category:	B, in Lanark Conservation Area
Occupier:	Scottish Courts Administration
Use:	Court House
Holding:	Crown

Hope Street was laid out *circa* 1830, during a period of great prosperity in Lanark mainly resulting from the economic success of the New Lanark mills. It is remarkable for the number of public buildings in its short length. Besides the Court House, there are the adjacent County Buildings, three churches (one now the Registrar's office), the Library and the Old Meat Market.

The County Buildings were completed in 1836 and housed the local courts until the Sheriff Court House was attached to its west end in 1868. Both buildings are in grey sandstone, two storeys high with rusticated ground floors and matching cornice lines. In detail, however, they display very well the change in mood and taste from conventional late Georgian provincial design to its mid-Victorian equivalent. Whereas the County Buildings have a heavy, placid facade with an emphatic pedimented frontispiece, the Court House elevation to Hope Street is comparatively full of movement and incident. First-floor windows have pronounced consoled pediments and the parapet plays an important part in the silhouette with higher balusters dividing ornamented solid panels above the three advanced central bays, and lower open balustrading at each side. A narrow but pronounced string course at first-floor cill level accentuates the rigorous modelling of the facade. The two buildings are united by a linking bay containing the arched entrance to the Court House.

Inside, a plain stair leads to the first-floor Court Room. Constructed in stone with iron balusters and a hardwood handrail, the stair occupies a square stairhall with a semi-barrel plaster ceiling lit from above by a square roof-light.

The Court Room is also square on plan and of pleasing proportions with a semi-barrelled, panelled ceiling. A moulded centre-piece is pleasingly combined with a ventilator. The area is well lit by three sash and case windows towards Hope Street, complete with panelled shutters. Four doors give access to the Court, including a separate access for the Sheriff and all are identical with shouldered architraves and cornices. The doors, which were originally panelled, have now been faced with veneered plywood to comply with fire regulations. The well of the Court, including the advocates' area and the public benches, have recently been modernised but much of the original character remains.

At the rear of the building is a two-storey former Fire Station, now disused. The County Buildings, superseded by new District Council offices, are destined for use as a Local Museum.

Reference: Lanark (Hugh Davidson).

Region	STRATHCLYDE
District	CUNNINGHAME

Name:	Atlantic Buildings
Address:	Dock Road, Ardrossan
Category:	B
Occupier:	Customs and Excise
Use:	Offices
Holding:	Leased

In 1806 Thomas Telford produced a plan for the Twelfth Earl of Eglinton to turn a bare coastline, with only Eglinton Castle and a few farmhouses inland, into the harbour of Ardrossan with a canal link to Glasgow. At the same time, Peter Nicholson laid out the town. The skeleton of his scheme still survives. In 1815, four years before the Earl's death, money ran out and the canal was never finished. The harbour, however, was finally completed in 1833, largely to Telford's plan, with two tidal basins and a wet dock. Both of these are still in use.

Atlantic Buildings, whose name perhaps reflects the grand pretensions of the project, occupies a prominent position at the V-junction of two roads just inside the dock gates. It may well have been designed by Nicholson, but documentary evidence is lacking. It is a simple late Georgian building on a domestic scale with a wide, shallow bow at the angle, emphasised by the gentle piended "tea caddy" roof and bold chimney-stack above. The central pilastered door supports a brightly painted Royal Arms, and is flanked by sash and case windows, now lacking their original glazing pattern. Built in red sandstone, it is at present painted white, with the bold projecting band courses, cornice and window surrounds contrasting in black, very much in the Ayrshire tradition. The original door is built-up, but it would appear that the ground floor at first consisted of two rooms, one entered direct from the street, and that access to the first floor was at the side. The ground-floor offices were probably used by the harbour master or other dock officials, with domestic quarters above, but the building now functions entirely as an office.

The interior is of no particular interest.

Region	STRATHCLYDE
District	DUMBARTON

Name:	Sheriff Court
Address:	Church Street, Dumbarton
Category:	B
Occupier:	Scottish Courts Administration
Use:	Court House
Holding:	Crown

The earliest part of the Court House is the higher, central section, built in 1824 as the County Buildings. Designed by James Gillespie and Robert Scott, it has a handsome classical facade three bays wide. The original Courtroom, still in use, is on the first floor. The masonry is ashlar, rusticated on the ground floor. In the centre is a Roman Doric columned porch with a small pediment. The first-floor bays are divided by paired Ionic pilasters. There is a simple entablature and cornice at roof level with a plain pediment over the centre bay. The windows in the end bays have moulded architraves with consoled cornices, but the central window, set in a round-arched panel, is unembellished. Part of the 1824 scheme included an adjacent jail, which was demolished in 1973, though its gateway and some other stone fragments have been retained in-situ. The building was sympathetically extended in 1865 by William Spence, who added the lower three-bay wings, terminated by open stone balustrades. Each bay has a centrally placed Roman Doric pilastered doorpiece. Otherwise, its character is similar to that of the original building. The roofs of all three sections are pitched, piended and slated above the low parapets. Police offices and a second Courtroom were added in 1895 and 1898 respectively, to the design of Duncan Macnaughton. The Courtroom block has an impressive Venetian gable window, with Roman Doric columns as dividing mullions. The side lights have Gibbsian architraves.

Internally, many adaptations have been carried out to enable the building to operate as an efficient Sheriff Court. These have partly affected the character of the building, but much of the original classical detail remains. Two rooms are particularly worthy of note. Court No. 1, in the original building, is unique in the V-shaped layout of the advocates' seating, in the well of the court. The Sheriff Clerk's seat is unusually positioned on one side of the bench. The Court is well-lit by large Georgian windows. The wall behind the bench has two access doors with characteristic classical mouldings and pediments above. There is a sounding board over the position occupied by the Sheriff, and a shallow false gallery at the opposite end with false doors. The plasterwork is characteristic of the period and the joinerwork is richly moulded. Court No. 2 has been converted from the 1898 Council Chamber. It has a semi-barrel roof with exposed timber trusses, is top-lit and embellished with delicate plaster detail. The walls are panelled, to dado level, in pine. There are two built-in wall cases, housing relics of a former Scottish regiment which drew recruits from Dunbartonshire. This court is virtually unspoilt by any later alterations. The joinery detail, including the dressings to the tripartite window, is of very high quality. The south stair is the best preserved, constructed of stone but retaining the original hardwood balustrade and richly carved newel posts.

The building now accommodates the two Sheriff Courts, with offices in one wing for the Procurators Fiscal and, in the other, offices for the Social Work Department of the Local Authority.

Reference: Dumbarton, Past & Present (Jones & Taylor).

Name:	Ardencaple Castle
Address:	Helensburgh
Category:	B
Occupier:	Ministry of Defence
Use:	Navigation lights on tower
Holding:	Crown

Today, only the tower remains of a once fine building, the oldest part of which may date back to the time of Walter McAulay, chief of Clan McAulay in 1566. The castle fell into disrepair, was sold to the Fourth Duke of Argyll and, after a fire in 1830, was reconstructed by Lord John Campbell, the Seventh Duke. In 1862 it was bought by Sir James Colquhoun (Fourth Bart.) and in 1923 was owned by Mrs. H. McAulay-Stromberg, a descendant of the original owners. After the Second World War it again fell into decay, and most of it was demolished in 1957–59.

The remaining square tower originally formed the north-east corner of the mansion. It is of four storeys, with a corbelled battlemented parapet and is constructed of flagstone with tooled stone quoins and dressings. The bipartite Gothic windows, set under Tudor-style hood moulds, are now blocked up. A fine carved Argyll coat-of-arms, above the window tiers, is protected from the weather by a boxed-out wire mesh grille.

The tower, still in use by the Ministry of Defence, houses transit lights to help vessels navigate the Rhu Narrows. It is situated in a children's playground in a Naval housing estate.

About 1976, cracks appeared in the tower. At present it is shored up, awaiting permanent repairs.

Reference: Helensburgh & Garelochside in Old Pictures
(Brian D. Osborne.)

R.C.A.H.M.S.

GLASGOW

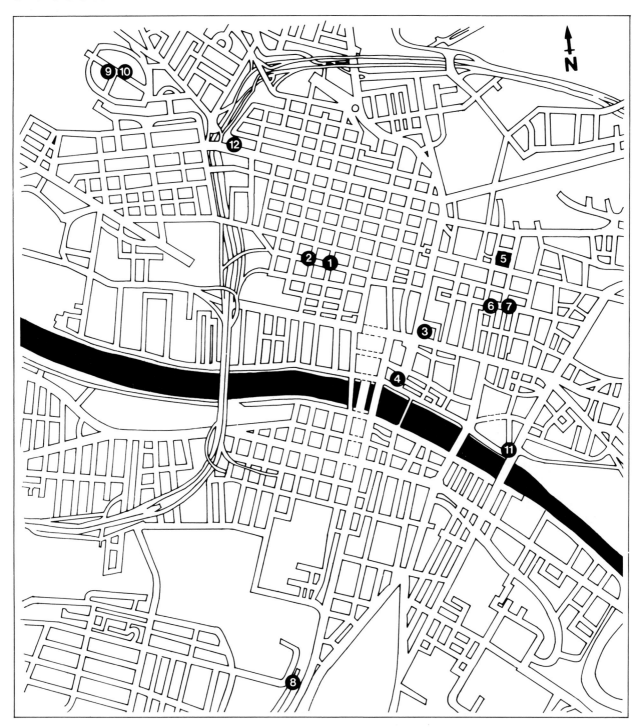

1. Mercantile Chambers, 57 Bothwell Street
2. Scottish Legal Life, 81–107 Bothwell Street
3. 12 Princes Square
4. Custom House, 293–306 Clyde Street
5. Sheriff Court House, 280 George Street
6. Sheriff Court House, 149 Ingram Street
7. Sheriff Court House, 191 Ingram Street

8. 1 Maxwell Road
9. 12 Park Circus
10. 25 Park Circus
11. High Court of Judiciary, Saltmarket
12. Royal Highland Fusiliers Museum, 518 Sauchiehall
Street

| Region | STRATHCLYDE |
| District | CITY OF GLASGOW |

Name:	Mercantile Chambers
Address	57 Bothwell Street, Glasgow
Category:	B, in Central Conservation Area
Occupier:	Vacant
Use:	Offices
Holding:	Leased

Mercantile Chambers was built in 1897 to designs by James Salmon, Junior (familiarly known as the "Wee Troot"), of the architectural firm Salmon, Son and Gillespie. Salmon was a contemporary and friend of Charles Rennie Mackintosh, and second only to him as the most inventive Scottish architect working in the Art Nouveau manner. The sculpture is by T. Derwent Wood of London.

Mercantile Chambers is one of Salmon's earliest large commissions and consists of six floors and attic, constructed in red ashlar sandstone. It has an elaborate symmetrical eight-bay frontage of mixed Renaissance and Art Nouveau design, with a bold arcaded ground floor and an unusual sixth-floor arcaded treatment, which possibly influenced John A. Campbell's finer and more mature design of 1902 at 157–167 Hope Street. The attic floor above the upper arcade creates an interesting skyline with slated, hipped dormers and a lead-roofed ogee cupola in the centre.

Derwent Wood's entertaining, if mannered sculptural scheme is worth study, particularly now that the building has been stonecleaned. Above the entrance is an ornate aedicule, supported on decorative corbelling and with a diminutive bell-like dome. A grotesque figure of Mercury sits within it. Alongside, inscribed ribands bear mottos derived from Glasgow's Coat of Arms: "Trees Grow, Birds Fly, Fish Swim, Bells Ring". At second-floor level, caryatids, representing Providence, Prudence, Industry and Fortune, languidly support a columned frontispiece to the third and fourth floors.

The red-brick rear elevation is of particular note. Its tall oriel windows result from the narrowness of the lane and the need for maximum daylight in the offices. It was probably the prototype for the comparable, and even more advanced designs by John A. Campbell for his 1906 and 1908 office blocks at 124 and 86–90 St. Vincent Street.

The most notable feature of the internal decoration is the original and unusual Art Nouveau design of the column capitals in the ground-floor entrance hall.

References: Architecture of Glasgow (Gomme & Walker). Victorian City (Worsdall).

Name:	Scottish Legal Life Assurance Society
Address:	81–107 Bothwell Street, Glasgow
Category:	B, in Central Conservation Area
Occupiers:	No. 81 Department of Transport
	No. 95 Inland Revenue Office (Third Floor) Property Services Agency (Second Floor)
	No. 107 Vehicle Licensing Office
Use:	Offices
Holding:	Leased

Constructed in 1927 as the Scottish Legal Life Building, this massive edifice occupies a full street block, between Blythswood and West Campbell Streets. The architect was Edward Grigg Wylie, of the Glasgow firm of Wright and Wylie. In style, it is strongly influenced by early 20th century North American designs which, in their turn, owe much to continental Beaux Arts precedents.

The building is eight storeys high, with shop units on the ground floor. The main (north) and side elevations are of Blaxter sandstone from Northumberland, rusticated at ground and first floor and at the angles. The north elevation is symmetrical about the centre axis, and consists of eleven bays, plus wider flanking bays at the corners of Blythswood Street and West Campbell Street. The rusticated base forms the plinth for the bold anta order between the second and fifth floors over the full length of the centre eleven bays. The windows between the pilasters are given vertical emphasis by linking bronze panels with relief decoration. The pattern of windows is different on the two end bays, the second and third-floor windows being linked in an architectural frame with a consoled cornice and balcony. The sculptured coat of arms above the entrance and the other sculptured details at first and eighth-floor levels were executed by Archibald Dawson. The side elevations to Blythswood Street and West Campbell Street are similar.

The entrance to the building is emphasised by a triple arcade, rising through the ground and first floors, with a corbelled balcony above incorporating the company coat of arms and four flagpoles. The open, barrel-vaulted, coffered entrance vestibule has further sculptured stonework including wall niches with shell heads, richly moulded cornices and architraves. The bronze lantern fittings are original. Inside the vestibule is an impressive bronze entrance screen, leading to a marble-floored foyer and stairs with wrought-iron balustrades and brass handrails. Joinerwork is also of high quality, typical of the period, such as glazed hardwood doors with bolection moulds encasing the glass panels.

There have been few alterations to the interior of the building, apart from the erection of demountable partitions in the Vehicle Licensing Office. The whole building is well maintained.

References: Glasgow at a Glance.
Architecture of Glasgow (Gomme & Walker).

Name:	Custom House
Address:	298–306 Clyde Street, Glasgow
Category:	A, in Glasgow Central Conservation Area
Occupier:	Scottish Courts Administration
Use:	Offices
Holding:	Crown

Built in 1840, the Custom House owes its position to the deepening of the Clyde which allowed large vessels to navigate up the river to the heart of the city. The building stands on the north bank of the river overlooking the quay (which is named after it) to the former upper harbour, just east of Glasgow Bridge and Jamaica Street. On the west side of the Bridge is the Broomielaw.

This classical building is attributed to John Taylor, who was also responsible for the Custom House, Dundee. It replaced an earlier Custom House in St. Enoch Square to the north, which was designed by John Dobson. The present building is two storeys high and nine bays wide, the central five bays projecting. Two further smaller, recessed, flanking bays, were added in the present century. Access to a small court behind is through the flanking bay to the west. On the upper storeys of the projecting central bays the five windows are recessed to allow for a row of detached Greek Doric columns. Over the columns, instead of the expected pediment, stands a coat of arms carved in stone and silhouetted against the sky.

A pedimented central doorway leads into a small hall from which a straight flight of stairs rises to the first floor. Apart from this area and a small portion of the first floor, the interior has recently been completely renovated for the occupation of the Procurator Fiscal's staff.

The majority of rooms now have suspended ceilings, only the windows and some shutters being retained, and carpets have been laid throughout.

A two-storey L-shaped building around the court to the rear and an extension clad with facing brick form two further additions to the original building.

Reference: Architecture of Glasgow (Gomme & Walker).

Address:	280 George Street, Glasgow
Category:	B, in Central Conservation Area
Occupier:	Scottish Courts Administration
Use:	Court House
Holding:	Crown

The building is situated at the north-east corner of George Square, across the street from the City Chambers. It was designed by W. W. Robertson of Her Majesty's Board of Works, as offices for the Inland Revenue and was opened in 1885.

The contractors were Messrs W. & D. McGregor, Edinburgh, and the total cost of the building was £25,000.

Three storeys high, with a basement and attic, the building is French Renaissance in style. Its principal facade faces George Street, although the Frederick Street front is architecturally similar. The George Street elevation is divided into three main portions, the central bays being recessed and defined by pilasters rising from above the ground floor to the cornice. All the windows are sash and case, the ground-floor windows being round-arched. The first-floor windows have pilastered architraves and triangular pediments on brackets. Those at the second floor have architraves alone.

There are balconies on the first floor and the building is surmounted with a modillion cornice and open balustrade with pedestals which support ornamental vases. Rising through the balustrading are six dormer windows, five capped with rounded pediments. The dormer over the entrance in George Street has a triangular pediment and recessed shell ornament.

The original telling hall, which was 87 feet×40 feet×23 feet high, has been sub-divided and the main staircase at the entrance from George Street has been enclosed.

More recently, the building has been stonecleaned and completely renovated for use as Civil Law Courts. This has enhanced much of the internal detailing, but the four Courtrooms and the main entrance lobby from Frederick Street all have new suspended ceilings concealing the services.

Both the first and second floors have a variety of office accommodation, but the attic which was used for the caretaker's house is now vacant. The basement houses the boiler room and stores and provides access to the vaulted dry area and moat which runs round the building under the pavement.

Reference: *Building News* 27 February 1885.

STRATHCLYDE/CITY OF GLASGOW

Name:	Sheriff Court, City and County Buildings
Address:	149 Ingram Street, Glasgow
Category:	B, in Central Conservation Area
Occupier:	Scottish Courts Administration
Use:	Court House
Holding:	Crown

This is the busiest court in Britain, if not in Europe, with over 250 sittings a month. It occupies the whole 100 m×40 m block between Ingram Street and Wilson Street and between Brunswick Street and Hutcheson Street. The grand facades of this three-storey neo-classical building are grimy and peeling.

Two Edinburgh draughtsmen, William Clarke and George Bell, won an open competition held for its design, and in 1842 the foundation stone was laid in the original building fronting Wilson Street. Chopin gave a piano recital here in 1848, when the building was still jointly used as the Glasgow City Chambers and the Lanark County Building.

In 1869 the Merchants' Hall, which faced up Garth Street, was converted into a small debt court and a JP court was built behind it. John Burnet (Senior) designed the new Merchants' House, built in George Square five years later. A further extension to the north was completed by Clarke and Bell in 1874.

In 1876 Lanark County moved their offices into Lanarkshire House. When in 1888 the new City Chambers in George Square was completed by William Young, the older building was turned over entirely to the administration of justice. Reconstruction, including the addition of the northern section which extended the building forward to Ingram Street, was finished in 1892 by George Bell (Junior) of Clarke and Bell.

The main public entrance from Ingram Street is through a hexastyle Corinthian portico flanked by projecting corner bays. Immediately inside is an imposing stairhall lit from one of the two wells within the building. The centre of the west facade in Hutcheson Street is emphasised by a giant Corinthian colonnade in antis, with flanking pilasters and a plain entablature, to first and second floors. This was originally the frontispiece to the Merchants' Hall.

The original south facade, on Wilson Street, is emphasised by a deeply projecting six-column Ionic portico of fine proportions, raised on a solid plinth displaying a low-relief pictorial frieze just above eye level. This portico acts merely as a gigantic screen, the entrances being through comparatively insignificant doorways in the flanking bays.

The building is largely unaltered and the twenty sheriffs conduct the proceedings in a rich variety of ornate and dignified courtrooms.

A five-storey replacement building is being constructed on the south bank of the Clyde which will provide twenty major courtrooms and fifty-five cells, making the present Sheriff Court buildings redundant.

References: Architecture of Glasgow (Gomme & Walker).
The Scotsman Magazine No. 1, April 1980.
Glasgow at a Glance.

Name:	Lanarkshire House
Address:	191 Ingram Street, Glasgow
Category:	A, in Central Conservation Area
Occupier:	Scottish Courts Administration
Use:	Court House
Holding:	Crown

In 1752 the wealthy tobacco lord, George Buchanan, built for himself Virginia Mansion at the north end of Virginia Street, with its back to Ingram Street. This was demolished in 1841 when the Union Bank used its site for their premises. Designed by David Hamilton, the main entrance was through a Roman Doric portico facing onto Ingram Street. The Banking Hall at the rear was added in 1853 to a design by James Salmon, Senior. Hamilton's portico to Ingram Street, together with its six allegorical statues, was taken down in 1876 and re-used by James Morrison, the builder, as the frontage to the Royal Princess's Theatre in the Gorbals. It was replaced in the same year by the existing facade designed by John Burnet, Senior, then at the height of his career. This new frontage brought the building forward to the present building line.

When local government was established on a county basis in the 1880's, Lanark County acquired the building as municipal offices—thus accounting for the building's name. They moved to Hamilton in 1964, when the Court took over part, then all, of the accommodation.

The facade to Ingram Street is a clever Italianate design, owing as much to C. R. Cockerell as to Venice. There is a pilastrade at the first floor and a colonnade to the second in which a characteristic mannerist device—spacing the pilasters and columns unevenly—is employed. The colonnaded top floor has deep-set round-arched windows and elaborately sculptured figures by John Mossman, set between the columns of the narrower bays. An open segmental pediment with carved figures embellishes the door leading to the entrance and stair hall, where the Union Bank's crest can still be seen on the mosaic floor. The stair to the right has a heavily carved mahogany balustrade with extended newel posts and is lit from an arched roof-light. There are two main Courtrooms, and one smaller court. A fourth is being constructed.

Much of the original detailing is still intact, including the bank vaults with thick steel doors. Unfortunately, the Banking Hall has been sub-divided into smaller rooms. The suspended ceiling, which covers the entire area, conceals the original magnificent ceiling with its richly ornate plasterwork. Also hidden from view is a dome in fourteen segments, each of which depicts a saint in stained glass, and the original brass light fittings.

References: Architecture of Glasgow, (Gomme & Walker)
The City that Disappeared, (Worsdall)
Glasgow at a Glance.

STRATHCLYDE/CITY OF GLASGOW

Address:	1 Maxwell Road, Glasgow
Category:	C
Occupier:	Royal Marine Reserve
Use:	Offices
Holding:	Crown

About a mile south of the River Clyde, Pollokshaws Road and Eglinton Street/Victoria Road meet in an x-junction from which Maxwell Road runs westwards, creating a wedge-shaped site. Here the Royal Marine Reserve have their Unit Headquarters in a building designed by Robert Miller, one of Glasgow's lesser-known architects, in a plain late perpendicular style. It was constructed between the years 1894-1896 as the Southern Section headquarters of the Glasgow YMCA.

The building's well proportioned street elevations of red ashlar sandstone provide continuity in an area where many examples of 19th century tenement buildings remain. With the demolition of other tenements, however, and their replacement by an assortment of buildings, leaving large tracts still lying desolate, the area lacks any kind of coherence.

The corner block is four storeys high with extensive lower wings returning on both street elevations. Each elevation has gables turned towards the street, the three over the corner block making a particularly effective grouping. On the Maxwell Road elevation the facade is dominated by splendid traceried windows with leaded glass, to the first floor but alterations have been made to the ground floor. Two ornamental ventilators in the arts-and-crafts manner straddle the roof.

Over the main entrance on the corner, a carved stone balcony provides evidence of the building's origins. Its badly weathered Gothic inscription reads 'Glasgow United Young Men's Christian Association—Southern Section'.

Inside, winding stairs give access to the two sections of the building. The Drill Hall is panelled and has a fine timber roof. The other wing contains less significant, smaller rooms. The Dining Room, however, appears to possess an interesting cast-iron roof structure above the present false ceiling.

During approximately thirty years of occupation by the Royal Marine Reserve, many changes have occurred, mostly of a non-structural nature. Much Gothic detailing survives, however, as a reminder of the building's religious origins.

Address:	25 Park Circus, Glasgow
Category:	A, in Glasgow Park Conservation Area
Occupier:	Ministry of Defence
Use:	Careers and Information Office
Holding:	Crown

Park Circus stands on the crest of Woodlands Hill, the climax of the many great crescents and terraces built as the city stretched westwards during the 19th century. The architect was Charles Wilson who, in 1854, had been commissioned with Joseph Paxton to lay out a new park on the west-facing slopes of the hill, and including the River Kelvin. Wilson was also entrusted with completing the work of George Smith, an Edinburgh architect, and of John Baird who had built extensively on the southern slopes.

The Circus was constructed between 1859 and 1863 and takes the shape of a flattened oval, the most impressive central part of the north-east side having a flat centre with a centrepiece projecting in two stages. The south-west side is divided into two quadrants. 25 Park Circus occupies part of the eastern one.

Consisting of three storeys, basement and attic, the proportions are basically those of a Georgian terrace. The detailing, however, suggests a more decorative Victorian approach. The ground floor, for example, has contrasting bands of plain and vermiculated stone, the upper corners of the windows are slightly chamfered and an ornamental string course runs along the cill line of the first floor windows. These windows have architraves and flat pediments, but the second-floor windows only have architraves. The upper storeys are more restrained. To the rear is a yard within a stone wall.

The double door entrance is approached by a short flight of steps and the original railings still guard the basement area. Inside, the small entrance hall leads to a roof-lit stairwell. In the basement there is evidence of the building's residential past in the kitchen/servants' area, where glazed white tiles, varnished timber and the space vacated by the cooking range catch the eye. The main floors are occupied by offices and have a variety of fine chimney-pieces, now blocked up. In the attic is a caretaker's flat with unfortunate, disfiguring dormers.

The original four-pane windows have been replaced by two-pane sashes. Internally few drastic alterations have taken place over the years, although many doors have been panelled over.

References: Architecture of Glasgow (Gomme & Walker)
Glasgow at a Glance

Address:	12 Park Circus, Glasgow
Category:	A, in Glasgow Park Conservation Area
Occupier:	Universities of Glasgow and Strathclyde Air Squadron
Use:	Offices
Holding:	Crown

Situated diagonally opposite no. 25 (q.v.) at the west end of the terrace, the Air Squadron has occupied this building since 1965. The original location was 11 Bute Gardens, but this had to be vacated due to the extension plans of Glasgow University. Formed in January 1941 during the War years, the Squadron was actively engaged in pre-entry training of students from the two Universities for the RAF and continued during peace time to add to these numbers.

This part of the Circus was completed in 1857, but it was to be another six years before it was finished, in the same year as the death of the architect, Charles Wilson.

There is little outward difference between the earlier and later parts of the Circus. The four-pane glazing pattern remains. The layout internally is the same and the recently cleaned stone facade is reflected by a good decorative standard within.

Some modernisation has been carried out, in particular the creation of a bar and social facilities on the first floor by opening up the existing rooms. The other accommodation consists of office space, training and lecture rooms. There is a small garage to the rear with access from a lane.

Name:	The Prince of Wales Building
Address:	12 Prince's Square and 48 Buchanan Street, Glasgow
Category:	B, in Glasgow Central Conservation Area
Occupier:	Scottish Home and Health Department, Scottish Education Department, Scottish Office (Audit), Ministry of Defence, Department of Agriculture and Fisheries for Scotland, Scottish Development Department
Use:	Offices
Holding:	Leased

Built in 1854 to the design of John Baird I, probably as an hotel, this is a four-sided classical ashlar-fronted complex with the main front on to Buchanan Street. The central Buchanan Street block has a rear wing extending into the Square, in effect making it a U-plan building. No.12 forms the most imposing internal elevation of the Square, with the central bays making a bold pilastered four-storeyed frontispiece.

The Government leases about half the building, which at the upper levels continues round all four sides of the square. Some evidence suggests that another opening existed through to Buchanan Street, which would have eased the movement of carriages.

The outside appearance, apart from certain commercial modernisation at ground level, is largely original, with a regular pattern of sash and case windows relieved only by a six-pilastered anta-order centre-piece at the main entrance. Internally, however, modernisation over the years has removed almost all evidence of earlier occupation and the internal plan of the building now resembles a warren.

Reference: Architecture of Glasgow: (Gomme & Walker)

Name:	Justiciary Court House
Address:	Saltmarket, Glasgow
Category:	B, in Central Conservation Area
Occupier:	Scottish Courts Administration
Use:	Court House
Holding:	Crown

Situated on the opposite side of Saltmarket from Glasgow Green, just north of Albert Bridge, the present building of 1913 is by J. H. Craigie of Clarke & Bell, architects of the Sheriff Court in Ingram Street, and is an approximate copy of the earlier town offices, Court House and prison which stood on the same site. These were designed by William Stark and built between 1807–14. Of this building only the portico remains, the first correct Greek Doric portico in Scotland and one of the first in Britain. Public hangings once took place between its two central pillars.

The rectangular building is neo-Greek in style. The portico, facing Saltmarket, is linked by five-bay sections to projecting single-bay wings. Entry is through the portico into the middle level of the building, the lower level being a semi-basement set back behind an area. At both sides and the rear, the height reduces to two storeys. A light-well is positioned on each side of the two courts. Both Court Rooms are similar, and each has an extensive gallery. They are separated by a central lobby known as the 'Lord's Hallway' after the painted mural frieze depicting the course of justice. Little change has been made in recent years, except for the public refreshment room which has modern counter equipment. Elsewhere, examples of the original sanitary ware are still in use.

A plaque fixed to the south wall and visible through the decorative railings which run round the front and sides of the building, marks the height of the great Clyde flood of 12th March 1782.

References: Architecture of Glasgow (Gomme & Walker).
Glasgow at a Glance (McLaren Young & Doak)
Extract from Glasgow 'Evening Times' 13th June 1910.
Glasgow Past and Present (Senex (R Reid)).
The Greek Revival (Crook).

Name:	The Royal Highland Fusiliers Museum
Address:	518 Sauchiehall Street, Glasgow
Category:	B
Occupier:	Royal Highland Fusiliers
Use:	Museum
Holding:	Crown

The building dates from 1903 and was designed in Edwardian Renaissance style by John Keppie, of the Glasgow architectural firm, Honeyman, Keppie and Mackintosh. The front is constructed in red sandstone, four storeys high and three bays wide. Entry is through a shop-front of a later period. On the first floor three windows each have an eight-light upper sash with a plate glass lower sash divided by a central glazing bar. Each window also has a shaped lintel and a mannered pediment. The second floor has three similarly-glazed windows and two corbelled octagonal shafts, possibly intended to support statues at the outer angles. Corbelled pedestals support two Michelangelesque figures in front of a windowless studio floor surmounted by a shaped gable with decorative strap-work.

Originally commissioned by the well known Glasgow firm of photographers T & R Annan and Sons Ltd., it was built in the back garden of a house in Renfrew Street. The Annan firm became renowned, among its other work, for recording the changing face of Glasgow. It still possesses early photographs showing the building as it was; the reception area and shop to the front which is now the exhibition space, the studios on the upper floor, with large north-lights overlooking a light-well, now lying vacant, the display area, now the 'Colonel's Room', and the Printers Workshop, now derelict.

When the Army took over the building after the departure of Annans in 1959 it was used initially as a Careers Information Office but is now a museum. The stair to the front has been enclosed with the wall built tightly against the original wrought-iron balustrading. The lift, caged within the stairwell, no longer works, and there is a suspended ceiling over the exhibition area. However, the 'Colonel's Room' on the first floor, formerly the display area, is reached by a small panelled lift from the ground floor and is still in excellent shape. This room houses many mementoes, as well as the original hardwood floor, chimney-piece and decorative cornice.

| Region | STRATHCLYDE |
| District | HAMILTON |

Name:	Sheriff Court
Address:	Almada Street, Hamilton
Category:	B
Occupier:	Scottish Courts Administration
Use:	Court House
Holding:	Crown

This neo-classical building, originally the County Buildings, occupies a large and conspicuous site at the junction of Almada Street and Beckford Street. It was built in three main stages over an extended period dating from 1834 to 1900. Originally, there was a prison on the site which continued in use until 1882, but was eventually demolished to make way for the third stage of the development. The first stage comprised the nine-bay block in the centre of the Almada Street frontage, built to provide accommodation for the Court and its officials. It also accommodated the Town Council until better accommodation was provided elsewhere, after which the Town sold their interest in the building to the County. The next phase consisted of the central block facing Beckford Street and the single-storey link to the existing building. Dating from the mid-19th century this provided extended accommodation for the Court. The third stage completed the symmetry of the Beckford Street frontage, providing accommodation for the Lanarkshire Constabulary in the plainer, classical block at the end of the site. This included a number of police houses which have since been adapted for other use. The continuous development of the site with successive matching neo-classical blocks, over a period of nearly 70 years, represents a remarkable example of consistent, if conservative planning.

The overall plan is rectangular, comprising a number of separately-roofed sections and light-wells, screened by the main facades. Some of the light-wells have since been enclosed to provide extra usable space. Two storeys high, the building measures approximately 125 feet (nine bays) on the Almada Street frontage and 250 feet (nineteen bays) towards Beckford Street. Massive Ionic porticos emphasise the centres of both street frontages. The detail is fairly simple, some bays being advanced from the main wall line. The bays are defined by Roman Doric pilasters. Otherwise, the treatment is confined to a simple string course, an entablature with cornice and a low parapet. Masonwork generally is in ashlar but the light buff sandstone has not weathered evenly. Some eroded

Beckford Street frontage

Almada Street frontage

stone has had to be replaced. Some of the two-pane sash and case windows have a simple moulded architrave and some, on the ground-floor elevation, are emphasised by architraves and a small cornice. The principal features of both street elevations are the identical tetrastyle Ionic porticos. Both have fluted columns, plain deep entablatures and pediments but neither has any sculpture in the tympanum. On the Almada Street elevation the pediment rises above the cornice of the adjoining recessed bays while on the later Beckford Street elevation, the cornice and pediment are level. The roof is made up of a series of separate pitched and slated sections.

Internally, the classical character is preserved mainly in the entrance halls, staircases and access corridors, since many alterations have been made in order to update the court accommodation. The two main stairhalls, centred on the axes of the porticos, are large well-lit open areas, the stairs being in stone with iron balustrades and hardwood handrails. The flanking walls are panelled in hardwood and the ceilings are richly decorated in moulded plasterwork. Jury Court No. 1 is the best-preserved, although it now has a suspended acoustic ceiling concealing the plasterwork above. The door joinery includes wide moulded architraves and pedimented door-heads. The layout of the well of the court has been preserved. Characteristic moulded plasterwork survives in the smaller Court Rooms.

Reconstruction is in hand to improve facilities for all the functions of this large Sheriff Court, which now houses three Jury Courts, Social Work Officers and Police. An attempt will be made to restore the original character where possible, including the removal of later accretions such as cheap wall linings. A complete new colour scheme more in sympathy with a classical interior of the period will be carried out. Remedial work to the external masonry is already in hand.

Reference: Glasgow and Lanarkshire Illustrated p.63.

Region	STRATHCLYDE
District	INVERCLYDE

Name:	Gamble Institute
Address:	Shore Street, Gourock
Category:	B
Occupier:	Department of Health and Social Security
Use:	Office
Holding:	Leased

This undemonstrative building commemorates the Rev. Henry Gamble of Ashburn, Gourock who died in 1870. His widow, Caroline Anne Gamble, built and endowed the Institute between 1874 and 1876. It was intended as a social centre for the benefit of working men, to provide moral, intellectual and physical improvement. Originally it was managed by a Board of Trustees. Four of these were elected annually and the others were nominated by Mrs. Gamble. The Town Council took over the Institute in 1916, and have continued to operate the building in accordance with its original purpose. The accommodation is sometimes leased to other bodies for social occasions.

The site, on Gourock's sea frontage overlooking the Clyde estuary, is at the corner of Shore Street and King Street. The Institute is ashlar-built in a restrained Italianate style, two storeys high and rectangular in plan. The elevation to Shore Street is symmetrical about the central axis, with a five-window frontage at first-floor level. The elevation to King Street, which is on a steep incline, has an eight-window frontage. The centrally-placed Shore Street entrance has a Roman Doric two-column porch with an ornamental balustraded entablature incorporating a central cartouche. The stepped entrance has recently been provided with a somewhat incongruous modern canopy and plain metal railings. On the Shore Street elevation, the ground-floor windows are rectangular with moulded architraves and entablatures. Those on the first floor are round-headed with moulded architraves and linking bands. There is a plain string course and moulded cill band at first-floor level and a moulded cornice. The roof, above a shallow parapet, is pitched, piended and slated.

Internally, the building has been extensively altered with the addition of screens and partitioning. Some of the original character remains, including plaster cornices and ceiling centre-pieces. There are moulded dado rails in the larger rooms. The stone stair, complete with iron balustrade and hardwood handrail, is well lit by a side window. A plaque commemorating the Rev. Henry Gamble occupies a niche in the wall at half-landing level.

Reference: The Burgh of Gourock 1858–1958. A commemorative booklet.

Name:	Custom House
Address:	Custom House Quay, Greenock
Category:	A
Occupier:	Customs and Excise
Use:	Offices
Holding:	Crown

The history of the Greenock Custom House begins in September 1816, when a feu charter in perpetuity was issued to the Commissioners in Edinburgh by the Burgh Magistrates and Town Councillors. The Commissioners appointed William Burn as architect and the building was complete by 1819. The contractor was Kenneth Mathieson, whose labour force was largely drawn from ex-soldiers of the Napoleonic Wars.

It is a monumentally imposing Grecian Doric, two-storey, basement and attic structure, typical of William Burn's best public work in the classical style. The masonwork is finely dressed ashlar. There are splendid tetrastyle pedimented porticos in the centre of the north and east elevations. The building is thirteen bays wide by seven bays deep. To be in proper scale, the first-floor windows are unusually large with twelve panes in each sash. The ground-floor windows are round-headed and slightly recessed. A Greek Doric entablature carries round the whole building. The heavy parapet conceals a pitched and slated roof. On the rear elevation this parapet is interrupted by timber double doors, presumably intended to allow hoisted contraband to be stored in the attic. (c.f Leith Custom House, (q.v.). There is a handsome, elaborately-painted coat of arms above the main, north entrance door. Its lion, perhaps intentionally, looks particularly welcoming and friendly.

Internally, the spacious top-lit staircase is positioned on the central axis. The iron balustrading is cast from an unusual lyre pattern. The landings are of flagstone. The 'Long Room' on the first floor is the finest internal space. It is entered from the stair-head by a shallow triple-arched, rib-vaulted vestibule and a square top-lit ante-room. The 'Long Room' itself is about 75 feet long and 50 feet wide, with a handsome Ionic colonnade at each end. At the south, it forms a free standing screen; at the north, it consists of attached demi-columns. The double doors off the galleries at first-floor level have prominent architraves with consoles and entablatures. The Collector's Room, like that at Leith, has a curved interior wall with doors made to follow the contour. Doors generally are panelled, and the shutters to the windows are

(19th century lithograph)

of delicate Regency design. The original chimney-pieces have been removed but an original cast-iron fireplace bearing the mark "George III" survives in a stone surround.

The basement, now unused except for the storage of records, was originally used as a tobacco warehouse for cargoes arriving at Custom House Quay.

Reference: Descriptive Note supplied by Customs Officer, Greenock.
Greenock from Old Photographs (Anderson and Monteith).

Name:	Sheriff Court
Address:	Nelson Street, Greenock
Category:	B
Occupier:	Scottish Courts Administration and Crown Office
Use:	Court House
Holding:	Crown

The whole of Renfewshire was served by the Sheriff Court House in Paisley until the year 1815, when a resident Sheriff-Substitute was appointed for Greenock. The Greenock Sheriff Court House was built in 1867 beside the Prison and Governor's House in Nelson Street. The Prison has since been demolished, leaving only the Governor's House, which is now privately owned. The Sheriff Court House stands detached, and looking rather isolated, beside a busy street on the western edge of Greenock Town Centre. Peddie and Kinnear, of Edinburgh, designed the building in their typical Scots Baronial manner.

It is ashlar-built, square on plan, with a symmetrical two-storey and attic, three-bay frontage about a slightly advanced four-storey Scots Baronial tower, which is the most prominent feature of the building. A corbelled superstructure with corner turrets, inset pediment and decorated chimney-stacks forms the base of a square, slated pyramid spire. This is crowned with a spire-topped open lantern. At the base of the tower is a fine semi-circular decorated arched door-piece

with buttresses at either side and a stone balcony above. On the ground floor the windows have segmental-arched heads linked by a moulded string course. There are angle buttresses at the corners of the building. The attic floor, above an ornamented corbel course, features pedimented stone dormers with segmental window heads. These, with the round turrets at the corners, add greatly to the liveliness of the silhouette. All eight turrets have slated conical roofs finished with ornamental iron finials. The building is covered by twin steeply pitched and slated roofs, terminated by crow-stepped gables. It is separated from the pavement by a low wall. The gate and ornamental railings have been removed and only the gate-piers remain.

Internally, the building contains fine woodwork and other decorative features. The Jury Courtroom on the ground floor has remained almost unaltered. It contains a gallery and ground-floor space for the public, with ramped floors for better viewing. The panelling in the Courtroom is constructed in best quality pine. Both the public areas have pew seating with a central division. There is a fine well and a very interesting original, wide Sheriff's bench with a panelled back and sounding board. The witness stand, with its plain curved tester, is also unusual. The courtroom ceiling is coved and richly decorated with delicate plaster cornices. The segmentally-arched clerestorey windows, half-set into the coved ceiling, make a fine geometric pattern enhanced by the moulded architraves. All the other main rooms retain original cornices and panelled doors.

The stair is constructed of cantilevered stone with a handsome decorated iron balustrade and hardwood handrail.

In 1981, the building was updated and extended, in contemporary manner, by a single-storey stone-built addition on the east gable containing a Jury Courtroom with ancillary accommodation. The crowning lantern, missing for many years, was restored at this time, on the basis of Peddie and Kinnear's drawings.

Reference: Peddie and Kinnear Drawings. (Dick, Peddie & McKay, Architects, Edinburgh).

| Region | STRATHCLYDE |
| District | KILMARNOCK AND LOUDOUN |

Name:	Sheriff Court
Address:	St. Marnock Street, Kilmarnock
Category:	B
Occupier:	Scottish Courts Administration
Use:	Court House
Holding	Crown

Two architects produced plans for this building. Those of William Railton, active as an architect in Kilmarnock from the 1850's to the 1880's, were chosen. The Court House cost £1,599. The first court was held on 5th May 1852. Externally, the red sandstone building looks like a two-storey classical mansion with Greek embellishment. Single-storey pedimented wings at each side are linked across the front by a Roman Doric arcade. Grecian detail in the form of acroteria and antefixae, mainly occurs on the skyline. A lofty Courtroom occupies the whole of the central section. The wings formerly housed the sheriff and the usual witness and jury rooms. The internal arrangements have since been re-organised, and temporary, prefabricated court buildings have been erected on both sides. At the rear is an older,

two-storey building with four cells to each floor and a Governor's flat. This, formerly the womens' prison, is now used as police offices.

By way of a narrow passageway, the original central entrance leads to the Court Room. This is an imposing room, well lit on all sides. It has stained glass in the north windows. The handsome plasterwork illustrates Railton's skilful use of the Grecian detail more commonly associated with Alexander 'Greek' Thomson, but devised before Thomson's work had become at all influential. A curiosity is an old strong cupboard with a steel door in the corner of one of the adjacent rooms, perhaps once used for storing valuable police exhibits.

The Court House will soon be superseded by new Court buildings on the opposite side of St. Marnock Street. It seems that external maintenance has not been given high priority. Stonework is crumbling and spalling. A Corinthian-columned portico over the entrance has been removed. It is essential that further deterioration is halted, and that a suitable new use is found for this interesting classical building, before it ceases to house the Sheriff Court.

References: History of Kilmarnock (Archibald McKay, 1909).
Local press items (per Dick Institute Library, Kilmarnock).

Region	STRATHCLYDE
District	KYLE AND CARRICK

Address:	29 Miller Road, Ayr
Category:	C (S)
Occupier:	Crown Office
Use:	Offices
Holding:	Crown

Miller Road was named after Hugh Miller, Provost of Ayr, and was laid out a few years before he demitted office in 1854. Today, the houses are mainly used for offices. No. 29, including the extended attic and a single-storey extension to the rear, forms part of the Procurator-Fiscal's accommodation.

This semi-detached house, echoed by its right-hand neighbour, was built around 1850, as part of the early development along both sides of the road. The ashlar frontage is three bays wide, with a central doorway and flanking stone-mullioned tripartite windows on the ground floor. All the openings to the front are architraved. There are string courses at ground and first-floor cill levels. Coursed rubble is used for the gable and rear wall, with dressed stone coping to the chimney-heads. The roof is gabled, with dressed skews and a moulded eaves cornice at the front. Ugly, flat-roofed dormer extensions spoil the proportions of the front and rear elevations. All windows are sash and case. There is a stone balustrade on each side of the entrance steps, ending in stumpy piers with pyramidal copes and ball finials. The entrance door is panelled with a plain fanlight over, and the vestibule door has etched glazing.

Internally, the decoration is plain with simple cornices. There is a small ceiling rose above the first-floor landing. The stair is constructed of cantilevered stone with plain cast-iron balusters and a hardwood handrail. Most of the original chimney-pieces remain, but the fireplaces are no longer in use and are now blocked up.

194

Name:	Sheriff Court
Address:	Wellington Square, Ayr
Category:	A, in Ayr Central Conservation Area
Occupier:	Scottish Courts Administration
Use:	Court House
Holding:	Crown

This imposing Sheriff Court House stands on the west side of the formal gardens of Wellington Square. Constructed as the Ayr County Buildings, the two-storey Court House faces over the Square in front of the much larger and later extension, now occupied by Strathclyde Regional offices.

Designs submitted by David Hamilton (1813–14) were passed over in favour of plans (1816) by the London-based architect Robert Wallace. The foundation stone was laid in 1818 and the building was completed, with a prison to the west, in 1822 at a cost of £30,000. The main block is eleven bays long by five bays deep, and has a projecting tetrastyle pedimented portico with Ionic columns of Arran stone. The flanking bays also project, but only slightly. Round-headed sash windows are used on the ground floor, with a matching blank recess to each of the flanking bays, perhaps intended for sculpture. The first-floor windows, with six-pane double hung sashes, are set in architraves. All have cornices. A deep, part-balustraded parapet, is broken by the portico. Rising behind the portico there is a large dome with a lantern light.

To the rear and adjoining the Court House is the grand local authority office block, in a similar style. This extension was opened by the Duke of York in 1931, taking the place of the prison building, which contained 149 cells.

Inside the Court House, a spectacular coffered dome dominates the large hall which has a central staircase rising within a ground-floor peristyle of eight Doric columns. The substantial newel is surmounted by an urn. The offices on the ground floor to the left are approached through a corridor with a vaulted ceiling. Upstairs, the circular gallery gives access to three Courtrooms. The two smaller rooms have recently been modernised but the largest of them remains as a well preserved example of a 19th century Courtroom.

Here, Lord Cockburn presided over his last case, which ended with the sentencing to death of Alexander Cunningham on 20th April 1854 for the murder of his wife. After the trial, Lord Cockburn returned to Edinburgh, where he died six days later in his seventy-fifth year. The condemned man outlived the Judge by fifteen days, when he became the last prisoner to be executed in Ayr.

References: Reminiscences of Auld Ayr (Ferguson). Circuit Journeys (Lord Cockburn).

Address:	20 Wellington Square, Ayr
Category:	B, in Ayr Central Conservation Area
Occupier:	Ministry of Defence
Use:	Careers and Information Office
Holding:	Leased

Wellington Square was planned in 1799 by John Robertson, as a palace-fronted residential development. It was eventually laid out, to a reduced plan, in 1806–10. The houses forming the north and south sides were built first, and the side towards the sea was later closed by the County Buildings of 1818–22 (see p. 195). In the Square are monuments to General Neill (Matthew Noble, 1859) the Earl of Eglinton (Matthew Noble, 1865) and Sir James Fergusson of Kilkerran (Sir W. Goscombe John, 1910).

The houses, now nearly all offices, have similar three-bay elevations, each with a central, sometimes porticoed, doorway. There are minor variations of cornice height and window proportion. The style is late Georgian, and they would originally have had twelve-pane sash and case windows. All are built of stone, rendered or harled, and some, including no. 20, have later dormers.

No. 20 retains its original astragalled windows. It has a pleasant Doric-columned door-piece, badly marred by ugly, projecting official signs, and a good six-panelled door with a matching solid panel in place of a fanlight. The Services Recruiting offices occupy only the ground floor and basement. Here, the original domestic character can still be glimpsed, despite some destructive partitioning. One of the ground-floor rooms has an elegant curved rear wall, with matching panelled doors.

Address:	Hamilton Street, Girvan
Category:	B
Occupier:	Department of Employment/ Forestry Commission
Use:	Offices
Holding:	Crown

The Directors of the Commercial Bank must have been pleased with this new branch office when it was built in about 1870. It resembles a small French Renaissance chateau, in a style typical of David Rhind, architect to the Commercial Bank. Although there is no documentary evidence, the design is almost certainly by him. The whole building has now been adapted as government offices.

It is a free-standing symmetrical building, built of red sandstone. Yellow sandstone is used for the architraves, quoins, cornices, and the stone ball finials at the corners of the roof and on each of the balconies over the two doors. These doors, set in the re-entrant angles formed by the projecting central block, are pilastered with key-stoned arched heads. Similar arch detailing occurs in the elaborate dormer set centrally in the mansard roof. This window lights a lofty living room for the manager.

The plan is straightforward. The door on the right gives access only to the ground floor former Banking Hall, safes and Manager's room. That on the left leads to the stone staircase, with barley-sugar pattern cast-iron balusters, which climb past the first floor to the attic flat. The main first-floor Board Room to the front was formerly a handsome room with a well proportioned plaster cornice and central ceiling rose. Now, unfortunately, it has been divided in two. Behind this room is another, almost as large, which has also been sub-divided. From it leads another room which enjoys the use of one of the balconies above the entrances. There are further offices on the same level at the rear of the stair. The second floor is occupied by an attic flat.

Region	STRATHCLYDE
District	RENFREW

Name:	Dargavel House
Address:	Bishopton
Category:	B
Occupier:	Ministry of Defence
Use:	Offices
Holding:	Crown

Dargavel House stands at the centre of a defence establishment which occupies its former estate, and is in use as offices. It is well screened by trees and remains largely unspoiled.

At least three main building periods can be identified. The original Z-plan towerhouse, built by the Maxwells of Dargavel in 1584, is still clearly identifiable as the south-east range of the house, marked by bold, drum towers at the opposing angles. In 1849–51 a slightly larger north wing was added, at right-angles, to the design of David Bryce. This, with the contemporary single-storey service wing to the south, is in Bryce's typical, more elaborate version of the Scots Baronial style. The enlargement was commissioned by John Hall Maxwell, whose initials appear in one of the stone dormer pediments on the west elevation. In 1910, Peter Macgregor Chalmers was called in to restore the interior after fire damage. The single-storey entrance, the top section of the circular tower in the re-entrant angle and the large canted bay window on the west elevation seem to have been added or rebuilt at this time. The Baronial style can thus be seen at Dargavel in its original 16th century form and in 19th and 20th century guises. Many of the windows in the original section have been altered or enlarged, but one remarkable small window high up on the west gable survives unchanged. It has a very pretty moulded surround with a double band of dogtooth ornament. The tower at the south-west angle is also unusual, having an attached, subsidiary bartisan turret, offset on machicolated corbels, with its own steep conical roof.

Inside, the first-floor room in the Bryce wing, now used for conferences, retains a good panelled ceiling with timber cornice. The north room on this floor contains a badly overpainted chimney-piece of classical design and a plaster ceiling in mid-18th century style. This, and the similar plasterwork at the stairhead, very probably dates from the 1910 reconstruction. In the ground-floor room beside the entrance is a large stone Baronial chimney-piece with an iron hood, far too massive for its setting. Presumably designed by Bryce, it must formerly have heated a larger room. The interior of the original section is neglected and under-used above ground-floor level. It was probably used for more menial purposes after the 1850 extension was completed and little or nothing of original interest survives.

An armorial plaque, formerly on the east gable, was removed after the Ministry of Defence acquired Dargavel in 1935. This, together with an early free-standing sundial from the garden, can now be seen in Paisley Museum.

References: Castellated and Domestic Architecture Vol. IV p.21 (MacGibbon and Ross).
Mr. David Bryce (Fiddes and Rowan).

c. 1890

R.C.A.H.M.S.

Name	Territorial Army Drill Hall
Address:	76 High Street, Paisley
Category:	B, in Cross & Oakshaw Conservation Area
Occupier:	Ministry of Defence (Army)
Use:	Careers Information Office
Holding:	Crown

This three-storey and attic drill hall was built in 1896 for the Renfrewshire Militia, later combined with the Argyll and Sutherland Highlanders. It is an excellent example of eclectic design, in a mixture of Scots Renaissance, Baroque and Art Nouveau styles, by the local architect T. G. Abercrombie who was responsible for many of the best late Victorian and Edwardian buildings in and around Paisley. The site, at the west end of High Street, lies between John Honeyman's classical Museum and Art Gallery of 1868 and the massive crown-steepled Coats' Memorial Church of 1894. The side and rear elevations are screened by trees and the symmetrical front elevation is the most impressively composed. Scots Renaissance influence is represented by the corbelled attic storey, turreted twin-bay gables and the three steeply pitched wallhead dormers in sandstone ashlar above the recessed central section. Baroque detail appears in the inventive entrance door-piece which has exaggerated voussoirs and a pediment, broken in the centre to clasp a small window with its own complete segmental pediment. The broad gables are crowned by similar pediments which, with the ogee caps of the flanking turrets, soften the silhouette of the building.

These caps, with their wide overhangs, represent contemporary Art Nouveau influence, which is also noticeable in the deep, projecting eaves on the side elevations and particularly in the extraordinary pagoda-like ventilator in the centre of the ridge, with its emphatic, oversailing roof. The masonry is a judicious blend of squared grey sandstone rubble, in the main walling, and red sandstone ashlar, as dressings and in the upperworks.

Internally only three or four plain rooms are occupied by the Careers Advice Centre. Modern alterations consist of sub-partitioning, hung ceilings and built-in furniture.

Name:	Sheriff Court
Address:	St. James Street, Paisley
Category:	B
Occupier:	Scottish Courts Administration and Crown Office
Use:	Court House/Offices
Holding:	Crown

The Renaissance-style Sheriff Court House in St. James Street was built in 1885, at a cost of £23,000. Clarke and Bell of Glasgow were the architects. In 1890 the large Renfrew County Building was constructed on the corner of St. James Street and Love Street to designs by George Bell of the same architectural firm. The building cost £32,000. The three-storey wing in Love Street is a later extension by T. G. Abercrombie. The two adjacent buildings, originally linked only by a recessed arch at ground level, have recently been joined with a low corridor and secondary entrance. Although both buildings have similar roof and floor heights and other compatible details, the more grossly-scaled County Building, with its giant order tetrastyle Ionic portico, tends to diminish the visual importance of the Court House. Together they form an impressive frontage to a busy road system on the fringe of Paisley Town Centre.

The Sheriff Court House accommodates all the administrative offices required for court work and part of the ground floor of the County Building now houses the Procurator-Fiscal and staff. The County Hall on the first floor is occasionally used as a Summary Court. The remainder of the County Building is occupied by Strathclyde Regional Council.

The two-storey Sheriff Court House is finely decorated and detailed, with an ashlar front and rubble gable and rear walls. The frontage is symmetrical with projecting end bays linked on the ground floor by a Roman Doric colonnade. This forms a prostyle portico below a balustraded balcony, which is carried along the elevation as an apron to the first-floor windows. The ground-floor storey below the balustrade is of channelled ashlar. Tripartite windows in the end bays have bracketted moulded panels below the cills. Above the windows a plain lintel course continues as the frieze to the central colonnade and is decorated with triglyphs over the slightly advanced entrance bay. On the upper floor the end bays are defined by paired Ionic pilasters. Between these pilasters are tripartite windows with finely carved friezes, a feature continued in the centre bays. The eaves entablature is plain with a projecting cornice on which stone urns are strangely situated below the

skyline, in front of the parapet. All the windows are sash and case with single plate-glass panes.

The entrance leads up stone steps to the tall double-leaf panelled entrance door under the central portico. Internally, the building is rich in ornamental decoration. Some alterations have taken place over the years but most of the original character survives, notably in the fine entrance hall, gallery and the cantilevered stone staircase. The gallery, supported on six Tuscan columns, gives access to the first-floor rooms. Its balustrade is of ornamental cast-iron. Decorated plasterwork surrounds the lantern lights. All the main rooms have fine plaster cornices and centre-pieces and good joinery in the panelled window shutters and the exceptionally tall panelled double doors. There are three Courtrooms, one of which is a modern extension. Another has been created by minor adaptation of the original building. The Jury Courtroom is remarkably unaltered and still contains the original raked church pew-type seating made of pinewood. This Courtroom is plainly decorated with a dadoed wall and simple plasterwork between the ceiling coffers. The bench and backboard, with its tester and panelling is a fine example of Victorian woodwork.

The frontage of the two-storey, seven-bay County Building is aligned with the Court House. More purely classical in idiom, it shares a similar treatment of channelled ashlar ground floor, parapet and cornices. It is dominated by the asymmetrically-placed advanced tetrastyle Greek Ionic screen at first floor, the entablature and pediment of which rise above the roof level. Below the entablature, on the plane of the main facade, is a fine sculptured frieze by Frederick W. Pomeroy depicting Greek mythological figures. As at the same architect's Glasgow Sheriff Court House (q.v.), the podium does not contain the main entrance. This is placed at the west end of the block, under an advanced single-storey Roman Doric portico. On the ground-floor frontage and the Love Street extension the windows are all sash and case. The upper-floor windows to the earlier block are mostly casements.

Internally, the building is well ornamented. Most rooms contain fine cornices, centre-pieces, panelled window ingoes and tall panelled doors. The long entrance hall is symmetrical, with staircases at each end, and is decorated with twin Ionic pilasters rising from moulded dadoes supporting a beamed corniced ceiling. Both staircases have fine barrel lantern-lights with decorated drums, cornices and a consoled frieze. An upstairs lobby entered through oak doors, gives access to the County Hall. This is a richly decorated room, finished in oak panelling with richly carved pedestalled twin Ionic columns, a large sculptured centre-piece, open pedimented door-pieces and a semi-barrel vaulted ceiling. This room also contains a massive stone fireplace incorporating the coat of arms of Renfrew County Council with the motto "AVITO VIRET HONORE", and a plaster wall frieze, similar to that under the portico, depicting figures from Greek mythology.

The offices on the ground floor have been partitioned, and alterations made to comply with the Fire Regulations have slightly detracted from the original character.

Reference: *Building News*, October 21st 1887.

Region	TAYSIDE
District	ANGUS

Name:	Sheriff Court
Address:	88 High Street, Arbroath
Category:	B, in Arbroath Conservation Area
Occupier:	Scottish Courts Administration
Use:	Court House
Holding:	Leased

This rather solemn classical building, originally the Burgh Chambers, dates from 1803 and was designed by the architect David Logan of Montrose. A narrow single-bay north wing of three storeys was added in 1844 to the design of David Smith of Dundee. The building must have stood out grandly in the early 19th century High Street. It now has commercial neighbours of similar height and width, but the monumental treatment of the facade still gives it the distinctive air of an important official building.

The plan is rectangular, symmetrical about the central axis, with the accommodation, in two storeys and attic, grouped around the main stair. The three-bay main elevation is in dressed ashlar stonework, rusticated at the ground floor. The central advanced bay is further emphasised by paired Roman Doric attached columns at first-floor level. These frame a recessed tripartite window with a large, plain semi-circular fanlight, and support an entablature with a high attic above. This includes a clock, with a festoon on either side.

The entablature, which is continued along both side bays, incorporates a modified triglyph feature with wreaths above the columns and corner pilasters. Balustrades above the side bays are echoed in the cill bands beneath the first-floor windows. The windows in the end bays are two-pane sash and case. The entrance door is emphasised by a moulded architrave with consoles and cornice above. The roof is pitched, piended and slated. There is a large ornamental iron lamp post at the main entrance.

Some modifications, such as witness accommodation and a Jury Room, have been made to the interior to enable the building to operate as a Sheriff Court. The Courtroom at first-floor level, which runs the full width of the building, is the best preserved interior space. This was formerly the Burgh Council Chamber. It has a semi-barrel ceiling of three bays, in each of which hangs a crystal chandelier. The cornice and frieze are particularly rich in detail. Other fine detail includes a panelled dado to the walls, door-heads with entablatures and two polished marble chimney-pieces. On the long wall is the unusual feature of a shallow high-level balcony, which has a moulded balustrade in painted timber. It appears formerly to have been used for floral displays. The plasterwork and joinerwork in the other rooms is similar, though more restrained. The walls of the stairhall have been lined with veneered plywood. The stair itself, lit by a large Georgian window at half-landing level, has been preserved complete with iron balustrade and hardwood handrail.

Name:	Captain's House
Address:	H.M.S. Condor, Arbroath
Category:	B
Occupier:	Ministry of Defence
Use:	Offices
Holding:	Crown

The Captain's House, formerly known as Woodlands House, is situated two miles north of Arbroath, within the Royal Naval Barracks, (H.M.S. Condor).

In 1800 Hercules Ross, who had acquired a fortune during the American War, purchased the estate of Rossie, near Montrose, and erected the Castle of Rossie to designs by Richard Crichton. It is said that he took down the fabric of his former mansion, and had all the materials carted over to Woodlands, where they were carefully re-erected to form the existing house. Little is known of the house prior to its relocation, but the design of Woodlands appears very up-to-date for its time and can be assumed to be also Richard Crichton's work. It resembles a simplified version of his design for Colinton House, Edinburgh. Such demolition and rebuilding was an unusual event in the early years of the last century, and became something of a local legend. Chisel marks made by the masons for guidance in the reconstruction are said to have survived on the stonework, which, until recently, was whitewashed. The Woodlands estate, including the house, garden, woods and farmland, was acquired by the Admiralty in 1939.

Set in a large enclosed garden, with access through an arched pend in the stable block, the Captain's House is a fine example of a severe, but imaginatively designed, early 19th century country house. It is rectangular in plan, with symmetrical wings, two-storey and basement in the central portion and one-storey and basement in the single-bay wings. It is constructed in dressed red sandstone rubble. On the entrance frontage, the five-bay main block has a slightly recessed three-bay centre, the wings being set back further from the main building line. The simple entrance door with its neat timber canopy and fanlight, is reached from the driveway by a fly-over stair. The handrail is modern. A string course on the main front at first-floor cill level is the only other external embellishment. At the rear of the house, a wide three-bay segmental bow extends through all three floors, with full-height windows on the ground floor. A french window has been formed in the left-hand bay, leading by a modern stair to the garden. The flanking bays contain tripartite ground-floor windows with segmental heads. The pitched roof is slated, with hipped ends. The wings have single-hipped roofs attached to the main gables.

Internally, the ground-floor drawing room is lit by the tall, finely divided windows in its curved, south-facing wall. Within this room there is a delicate cornice and, on the east wall, a fine classical chimney-piece. In the breakfast room nearby there is a two-leaf panelled door and a fine classical chimney-piece with Dutch tile inlay.

The cantilevered stone staircase to the upper floor has a wrought-iron balustrade and hardwood handrail. The upper-floor rooms are simply decorated and the plain basement service rooms have been modernised.

The stables and barns are simply constructed of rubble stonework, their slated roofs matching that of the house.

Address:	11a Panmure Street, Brechin
Category:	C (S)
Occupier:	Department of Employment
Use:	Office
Holding:	Crown

The area including Panmure Street, to the west of Brechin Town Centre, was ready for development in 1837. Named after Lord Panmure, second son of the Earl of Dalhousie and a notable benefactor to the town, the street is remarkably wide and spacious.

No. 11 is on the north side of the street. It forms part of an unassuming two-storey and attic urban terrace, typical of Scottish country town development of the period, and is listed more for group value than for its individual excellence. It has a single-bay door-and-window frontage with a canted dormer to the attic. The stonework is coursed local sandstone, in blocks of unusual length with a stugged finish. Both inside and out the building is largely unspoiled, but no individual features merit description.

Reference: History of Brechin to 1864 (B. Izell).

Name:	Sheriff Court
Address:	Market Street/Brechin Road, Forfar
Category:	B
Occupier:	Scottish Courts Administration
Use:	Court House
Holding:	Crown

Forfar Sheriff Court stands on an elevated site north of the town centre, surrounded by mature conifer trees. It shares this impressive situation with the separate County Buildings, originally the County Jail of 1842–3, rebuilt as offices in 1884. The Court House, designed by James Maitland Wardrop, of Brown and Wardrop, was constructed in 1869–71. It replaced the Georgian Court House in the Town Centre which, in turn, was converted into offices for the Burgh. A high stone wall, which forms the northern boundary of the group, represents part of the former prison enclosure.

The Sheriff Court House is approached up a narrow drive, which focusses picturesquely on an imposing three-storey circular tower. The style of the building is a free mixture of English Tudor with Scottish Baronial elements. It is two tall storeys in height with an attic storey lit by gable windows and timber roof dormers with heavy bargeboards. Construction is in snecked rubble sandstone with numerous ornamental features in dressed ashlar. These include projecting moulded string courses, window rybats and wallhead parapets. The roofline is varied by a vigorous display of gable crow-steps, finials, crockets and tall chimney-stacks.

The front elevation is seven bays wide, with a five-bay recessed centre and advanced single-bay gabled wings with transomed tripartite windows. Hood mouldings over the ground-floor window incorporate armorial panels. The main central entrance is emphasised by a projecting balcony, with a pierced quatrefoil parapet, supported on deep brackets and buttressed piers. The doorway below has a Tudor four-centred arch.

The plan is symmetrical about the entrance hall, which leads directly into the main stairhall. The grand and impressive open-well stair is of stone construction, with an ornate cast-iron balustrade, and is lit by a tall tripartite window. Directly above the entrance hall, behind the first-floor frontage, is the main Courtroom. In this, the most impressive room within the building, the most important feature is the double-tier hammer-beam roof, with a varnished pine ceiling, which features carved foliage bosses at the intersection of the main trusses. The room is lined with dado-height fielded panelling and inset vertical panelling which is continued in the design of the bench and well of the court. Adjacent on the first floor is Court no. 2, a square room lit by windows on two sides. It is also panelled in pitch-pine and has a heavy stone chimney-piece of Gothic design. The furniture, comprising a horse-shoe-shaped oak table with matching chairs, seems to be original. On the ground floor, leading off the entrance hall, is a solicitors' library. This, the only other interesting room inside the building, is lit by a tripartite window and has an ornamental plaster ceiling. The high quality original built-in fittings include a break-front bookcase with metal grilles and a chimney-piece similar to that in Courtroom 2.

Name:	Castle Stead
Address:	Castle Place, Montrose
Category:	B, in Montrose Conservation Area
Occupier:	Department of Employment
Use:	Offices
Holding:	Crown

Now used as office premises, this is one of the most interesting of the numerous 18th century mansions ranged along and behind Montrose's older streets. It occupies a prominent site at the south end of the High Street, where the main road turns through a right angle, and is visible along most of the length of the street. It differs from most old houses in the town centre in having a front garden containing several mature trees which is enclosed by a low wall, formerly fitted with railings. The front block, built shortly before 1821, is single-storey and basement, reached by a flying stair over a railed, sunk area. It is linked to an older rear block, mid-18th century in its present form, which is three storeys in height with an attic. Due to the incline of the site and the modest height of the ground floor of the original building, the ground floor of the front block is integrated with the first floor of the rear section. The site has many historic associations, chiefly connected with the Montrose family.

The late Georgian front block, which is of painted ashlar, is symmetrical about the main entrance. Its two large three-window canted bays retain astragalled sash windows and it has a crenellated parapet over the cornice. The main entrance door is set in an arched recess. The front block has a narrower frontage than the original building, which is reached by a close on the right. It appears as an ashlar-built, pyramid-roofed pavilion squeezed between the front wing and the adjoining property.

Internally, all the former plaster embellishment in the form of friezes and cornices has been removed in the front block and various encased and plastered steel beams have been inserted at ceiling level. The remaining joinerwork consists of panelled doors and architraves and panelled shutters to the bay windows.

The older block, behind it, is harled with a steeply pitched, slated roof with straight skews and end chimney-stacks. The fenestration is irregular, with an early Victorian canted bay added to the lower floors. It has retained more of its original interior character. The most noteworthy feature, known as "The Blue Room", is in the basement, and has a bay window facing the garden. The walls are lined with a richly patterned blue wallpaper. Most of the panelling, including the cornices are of timber, painted in various colours. There is a richly detailed timber chimney-piece and the walls to the bay window are lined in painted tongued and grooved boarding. On the first floor there is one polished marble chimney-piece. Some of the original brass door furniture remains.

Reference: The Closes of Montrose (J. G. Low).

Region	TAYSIDE
District	CITY OF DUNDEE

Name:	Craigiebarn House
Address:	Craigiebarn Road, Dundee
Category:	B
Occupiers:	Home Office,
	Property Services Agency
Use:	Offices
Holding:	Leased

This large, picturesque mansion, originally a private house, is set in garden grounds on the eastern outskirts of Dundee, and has a fine view to the south over the Tay estuary. It was built for his own use in 1911 by Henry Rennie, a Dundee merchant, and designed by Charles G. Soutar, of Maclaren Son and Soutar, Dundee, with assistance from Andrew Patrick.

Its present use is as offices, but seminars and consultations are also held from time to time. The house consists of two parallel rectangular blocks, linked together by service accommodation. It is constructed of random rubble stonework, with harling over certain sections, and is two storeys in height with an attic containing dormer windows.

The pitched roof is finished in mellowed red tiles. The windows are small-pane hinged casements. On the south elevation, there is a painted lean-to verandah constructed in timber, with small Roman Doric semi-columns. The block-topped chimney-stacks are prominent in the design. There is a notable sculptured metal weather vane on the roof over the central gable of the garden elevation. This gable is faced with waney-edged horizontal boarding.

Inside, the most notable room is the first-floor lounge, which runs the full length of the south block. It has a bay window at each end and one at the centre facing south. It is large and spacious, with a patterned plaster ceiling of restrained design. At attic level, the windows at each end are contained in a rectangular gable built out over the bay windows of the first floor below. Joiner-work is distinctive. The architraves and doors are mostly semi-glazed, and the general character throughout is delicate and restrained.

The main entrance from the north is through a small courtyard, with an ornamental gateway through the garden wall. Single-storey prefabricated accommodation has been added, connected to the main building by a low corridor.

Reference: Dundee City Library, Press cuttings of the period 1910–15.

Name:	Custom House
Address:	East Quay, Dock Street, Dundee
Category:	A
Occupier:	Customs and Excise
Use:	Offices
Holding:	Crown

The Custom House and Harbour Chambers is situated at the west entrance to the busy Dundee Harbour complex. Access to the Custom and Excise office is from Dock Street, immediately opposite the fine Sailors' Home and near the north end of the Tay Road Bridge.

This large classical building was erected in 1842–43, for the joint provision of offices for the Customs and Excise and, in the eastern wing, for the Harbour Trustees. The building was designed jointly by James Leslie, then the harbour engineer and John Taylor, an Irish architect who had been appointed Surveyor of Buildings to H.M. Customs in 1830. The London Custom House records show that the plan was Leslie's, but that the elevation design was principally Taylor's. An additional wing was added to the south-east of the building in 1884, by C. & L. Ower for the Harbour Trustees, the original three bays being skilfully increased to five.

The building, very little altered, is still in use by the Customs and Excise Department and the Harbour Board. The facades remain untouched, but stonework repair is now needed, especially to weathered column capitals and mutilated dentil ornament. The front railings were removed as part of the approach roadworks for the Tay Road Bridge.

The Custom House stands independent of other buildings, and is visible on three sides from busy public thoroughfares, making an important contribution to the local townscape. Built wholly of local stone, the main building is rectangular in plan, consisting of three floors and basement. The frontage is thirteen-windowed, with a slightly advanced central portico, and a channelled rusticated ground floor separated by a bold moulded string course from the polished ashlar upper floors. The portico is tetrastyle Greek Ionic, with an entablature and pediment above, elevated on an arcaded ground floor with a balustraded parapet. The entablature and blocking course are carried round at the eaves. The pediment contains the Royal Arms. There are three entrances to the building from Dock Street, the main doorway being in the portico and the others in the middle of each wing. All the entrance doors are panelled with two leafs and fanlights above. The windows are twelve-pane sash and case throughout the building. On the first floor the windows have architraves and cornices, the centre windows in the portico and wings being pedimented. All the windows on the top floor are architraved. The roof is low-pitched and slated, with hipped ends and chimney-stacks at the apexes of the hips.

Internally, the decoration to the Custom and Excise part of the building is plain, reflecting its office function. The large main office on the first floor has a beamed ceiling with moulded detail and a tripartite door-piece. Other offices have simple cornices without decoration. One plain painted wood chimney-piece remains and most of the windows retain the shuttered ingoes. The stairs are of cantilevered stone with iron balusters and wood handrails. Some modern partitions and acoustic ceilings have been inserted. The basement is functional and has no decorative treatment.

Reference: History of Dundee (J. Thomason & J. McLean.)

Name:	The Vine
Address:	43 Magdalene Yard Road, Dundee
Category:	A, in Magdalene Place Conservation Area
Occupier:	Scottish Home & Health Department
Use:	Surgery/Office
Holding:	Crown

This extraordinary little neo-Greek building dates from 1836. It was built by George Duncan, M.P. for Dundee, as a small residence and private art gallery to contain the pictures which eventually formed the original nucleus of the City Art Gallery collection. His architect is unknown. Basically single-storey, the residence was formed by a split-level arrangement at the west end, containing a basement with the living space above. It is now used as a Surgery, and is thus in active public use. Modifications have been minimal.

The building is rectangular, ashlar-built and five bays long by three bays wide. The deep main entrance in the advanced centre bay is flanked by two inset Greek Doric semi-columns. The Doric entablature, which carries round the building, is embellished with elaborate wreath ornament above the wall openings and angles. All the windows on the main elevation have battered, lugged architraves with panels below. The roof above the parapet is low-pitched, piended and slated.

Access is through the centre bay of the east end, leading to an octagonal outer vestibule with dressed stone walls incorporating four niches, which were no doubt designed to hold sculptured figures. This vestibule connects with the main inner hall, which is Ionic in style with eight detached fluted columns and a complete entablature. It is lit from above by a small saucer dome and lantern light. There is much beautiful detail, including acanthus and sunflower ornament in the pendentives. The other rooms, lit by astragalled sash and case windows, are grouped round this inner hall. All these rooms, which are now used as ancillary space to the doctors' surgery, are similar in character, with a wealth of classical detail in the form of plaster friezes and cornices, patterned ceilings and fine joinerwork, including panelled dadoes, doors and door-heads. There are a number of polished marble chimney-pieces and one timber example with a bronze frieze and Dutch-type tiles.

The building, which occupies a corner site, is raised on shallow terraces and surrounded by a pleasant garden with trees and shrubs.

References: Dundee City Library. Press cuttings—article on George Duncan M.P. describing building.

Name:	Sheriff Court
Address:	West Bell Street, Dundee
Category:	B
Occupier:	Scottish Courts Administration
Use:	Court House
Holding	Crown

Dundee Sheriff Court House occupies a prominent position beside a busy road system on the north-west edge of the City Centre. It was formerly at the centre of a symmetrical, neo-classical complex. The Court House was flanked by screen walls, pierced by arched gateways and linked with pavilions comprising, on the west, the Prison Governor's House and, on the east, police offices. The design was the result of a competition in 1833, won by Edinburgh architect George Angus, but only the prison and the police office were then erected. The later central Court House was built in 1863 by Angus' former pupil, William Scott. Scott, then the Town's Architect, faithfully followed his master's design for the facade, but deepened the plan with a rectangular court, instead of the D-plan layout originally intended. Today, the Court House remains, but the greater part of the west wing has been removed to widen Lochee Road. The east wing is now used as a Burgh Court by the Local Authority. New police offices at the rear occupy the site of the former prison. This was removed in 1929–30 to make way for a municipal bus garage, now itself demolished.

The building is rectangular in plan, and consists of two storeys and semi-basement, built in ashlar stonework with a slated, low-pitch, hipped roof.

The frontage is nine bays wide, symmetrical about a powerful central portico, with the three-bay wings recessed between giant Doric pilasters. The massive tetrastyle Tuscan portico rises from a podium. An elaborate carved representation of the Scottish Royal Arms completely fills the pediment. The deep entablature, with blocking course, is carried around at the eaves, giving the building a sharply defined roof line. All the windows are four-pane sash and case. Ground-floor windows have architraved surrounds and are separated from the semi-circular round-arched first-floor windows by a string course, interrupted by the pilasters. A stone-stepped perron gives two-way access to the consoled, pedimented entrance door.

Internally, the Court House has been skilfully updated to modern standards while retaining many of the original features. The entrance hall is largely unaltered, with its original cantilevered stone pen-checked stairs, iron balusters and hardwood handrail. The main Courtroom on the first floor is also still much as Scott designed it, although veneered timber wall panels have recently been introduced. Good quality plaster and joinery work survives in plenty, and the richly decorated panelled and coffered ceiling is particularly notable. This room also contains a visitors' gallery with a fine panelled front. Other rooms contain cornices, original panelled doors and shuttered ingoes to the windows. One further room has been made into a secondary Courtroom with a hung ceiling and wood-veneer panelled walls. Basement rooms are purely functional, without decoration.

Reference: *Dundee Advertiser*, August 9th 1833.

Region	TAYSIDE
District	PERTH AND KINROSS

Name:	Mount Ericht Hall
Address:	Mount Ericht Lane, New Rattray
Category	B
Occupier:	Department of Employment
Use:	Offices
Holding:	Crown

Mount Ericht Hall, erected in 1836 as a Secession church, is situated in the former Burgh of Rattray, now part of Blairgowrie. The church is approached along a narrow lane and occupies an elevated site bounded by a stone wall with iron railings. The church was built for the United Associate Synod, one of several contemporary breakaway groups from the established Church of Scotland. In 1840, this group joined with others to form the United Presbyterian Church. The church appears to have been abandoned as a place of worship before the Second World War, when it was used for civil defence purposes, afterwards taking on its present function as an office of the Department of Employment.

It is a harled rectangle, typical of the simpler type of Scottish church, without belfry or steeple. Two storeys high, it has a steeply pitched slated roof abutting plain skew gables, to which are attached single-storey wings. These appear to be later additions. The detailing echoes the overall simplicity of the building. The principal south-facing elevation is of four bays. The two central windows, flanking the position of the former pulpit, are double-height with arched heads and astragals in the Georgian manner. Transoms have been inserted at the new floor level. The remaining windows on each side are sash and case, circular-headed on the first floor and square-headed on the ground floor, reflecting the horse-shoe galleried plan of the interior. One of the three square windows on the west gable is blind, painted in imitation of the others to create a balanced composition. The gables are terminated by ball finials.

Little now remains of the original interior. Some original ceiling plasterwork survives, including a plain cornice and fretted centre vents. The gallery has been removed and a first floor created by spanning steel beams, supported on brick piers, across the full width of the church. A series of small rooms have been created on both floors, to suit the present function of the building as a Job Centre.

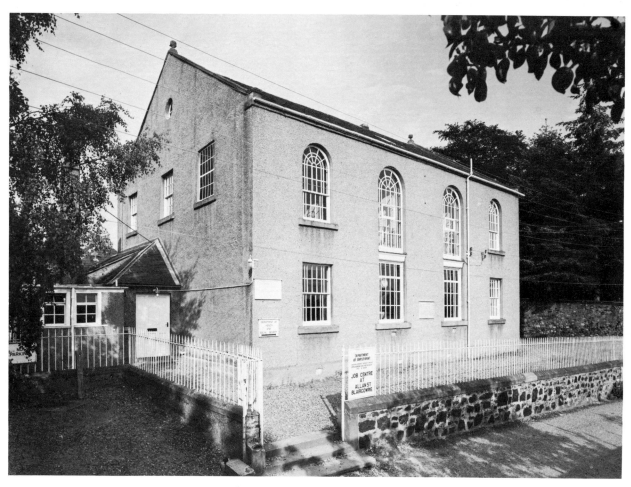

Name:	Balhousie Castle
Address:	Hay Street, Perth
Category:	B
Occupier:	Ministry of Defence
Use:	Regimental Museum
Holding:	Crown

Balhousie Castle is situated on the west bank of the River Tay, overlooking the North Inch. A building belonging to the Eviot family was in existence on this site during the reign of Alexander I, at the beginning of the 12th century. The visible older parts of the present building date back to the 17th century. By 1863, the Castle was in a dilapidated state and only the first floor was tenanted. In 1864, Thomas Hay, the eleventh Earl of Kinnoull, commissioned David Smart to repair, modernise and extend the building, bringing it to its present form. Smart was previously an assistant of David Bryce, and the remodelled building strongly reflects his master's influence, both in composition and in detail. The Castle is in the centre of a landscaped park, with fine old Scots pine trees and an ornamental garden. Though it can be seen from the North Inch, it is not a familiar Perth landmark.

Since World War II it has been used by the Army for a variety of purposes. At present, it serves as the museum of the local regiment, The Black Watch, fulfilling this purpose admirably, the showcase of regalia and relics fitting in well with the character and shape of the rooms.

Externally, the rebuilt Castle is now almost entirely 19th century Scottish Baronial. It consists of three storeys and attic, with single-storey domestic quarters on the north side. It is constructed in rubble stonework with dressed quoins, corbels and crow-steps. The roof-line is broken by a typical Baronial repertoire of pinnacles, square tourelles and dormer windows. On the north face a circular tower, with a conical slated roof topped by a weather vane, rises through four floors. The entrance door, windows and glazing are curved correspondingly. There are neat pediments to the small windows on the top floor. At the extreme corners of this frontage, two turrets are corbelled out at second-floor level, that on the east being circular, matching the tourelles on the south bay. The turret on the west is square in plan and gabled. The other elevations are equally varied in composition, using motifs derived directly from Bryce's country house designs. On the rear, south face there are indications of the earlier building, overlaid by a 19th century segmental bay, corbelled out at first-floor level and crowned at the attic with a square turret. All the windows are sash and case Georgian pattern, except for a recent dormer on the north face, which has a casement window for fire escape purposes.

Entrance is by a studded, curved door leading into a small hall. Access to the first floor, containing the principal rooms, is by a wide spiral stone stair with a panelled dado. The large drawing room, facing south and west, has an ornate cornice and a fine marble chimney-piece. A small circular room, built into the entrance tower, opens from the drawing room. A sitting room on the first floor, with a tripartite window facing west, has an ornate cornice and a fine black marble chimney-piece. Access to the second floor and attic is by a half-turn cantilevered stone stair, with twisted wrought-iron balusters and a hardwood handrail. The attic and basement floors are plain.

In the garden, there are several ornate cast-iron plant holders of French 19th century origin.

Reference: Castellated and Domestic Architecture of Scotland Volume III—MacGibbon & Ross.
Ancient Capital of Scotland Vol. 1, (Cowan).

Address:	43 New Row, Perth
Category:	B
Occupier:	Ministry of Defence
Use:	Careers Information Office
Holding:	Leased

The building, which dates from 1907, is a prestigious exercise in Edwardian baroque by the local architect G.P.K. Young and his brother Cedric, following the style of J. J. Burnet, of Glasgow. It is four storeys high, of eight bays to York Place and six bays to New Row. The ground floor is made up of individual shops. The upper floors contain separate office units. The walls are mainly of dressed ashlar, with richly varied moulded detail. The corner is splayed, rising to an octagonal drum at roof level with a copper-faced dome. This feature has arched and key-blocked windows in pilastered aedicules. The York Place elevation has a single, emphasised window bay on the east, and a similar double window bay on the

west. There are Gibbsian window surrounds on the first floor and blocked columns on the third floor, set in channelled pilasters with raised parapets above. The centre bay is entirely of channelled masonwork. An Ionic columned aedicule with a broken segmental pediment emphasises the third floor. There are flanking chimneys above the cornice. The side street frontage to New Row is of similar character, but simpler in detail with a plainer channelled treatment of the centre bay.

Most of the original elegant ground-floor shopfronts survive, only the Royal Bank unit on the York Place frontage having been radically altered. An Army Careers Information Centre is contained within one of these shop units on the New Row frontage. The original woodwork has been retained and painted. The timber framing is slim and delicate in design, with a recessed, architraved doorpiece including a key-blocked cornice. The base course is of polished granite. The shop front is contained between two channelled granite pilasters.

Address:	3 St. Leonard's Bank, Perth
Category:	B, in Marshall Place Conservation Area
Occupier:	Ministry of Defence
Use:	Offices
Holding:	Crown

This villa is one of several occupying sites which slope gently to the south, overlooking the South Inch. Access is from St. Leonard's Bank, at the rear. It was originally a private dwelling. Built shortly after 1808, it is two-storeyed, in the Regency style, with three bays in the main elevation and the main entrance in the centre. The pretty, white-painted iron entrance porch is also Regency in style, of vaguely Chinese inspiration. Walls are of ashlar stonework, finely dressed. The eaves of the low-pitched, piended and slated roof are projected on timber corbels. Other features of the main elevation include a raised string course at first-floor level and an unusual "eyelid" stone lintel over the two windows on either side of the main entrance. An early 20th century addition is roofed separately from the rest of the house and is visible only from St. Leonard's Bank. Its most notable external feature is a central sash and case window, with arched head and gothic tracery in the top pane, flanked by ornamental monogram panels.

Internally, the main rooms have a rich variety of classical detail in the form of plaster cornices and friezes, panelled shutters to windows and chimney-pieces, some of which have Roman Doric detailing. The stair is in dressed oak with half-panelled dadoes and moulded newel posts. The iron balustrade is richly ornate, with some gilding. The main ground-floor hall is divided from the vestibule by a three-part screen with a leaded glass panelled dado and delicate fanlight. The vestibule ceiling has a plaster centre-piece and cornice. The original Dining Room is panelled in dark hardwood and has an open-timber ceiling. A dressed stone chimney-piece is integrated into this scheme.

The whole building, externally and internally, is in an excellent state of preservation. The site is surrounded with a high rubble wall.

Address:	7 St. Leonard's Bank, Perth
Category:	B, in Marshall Place Conservation Area
Occupier:	Ministry of Defence
Use:	Offices
Holding:	Crown

This two-storey house, which also forms part of the original St. Leonard's Bank villa development, dates from 1825. It is neo-classical in style, three bays wide, with the entrance in the centre of the main elevation. Like the adjacent villas, it is approached from the rear. The main, garden front elevation is an impressive classical design, of finely dressed ashlar stonework, with an unusual verandah treatment of the ground floor and a continuous shallow balcony above. The porch is slightly advanced, incorporating twin fluted Ionic columns with a full entablature. This runs the complete width of the elevation, supported at each end by paired Roman Doric pilasters. The balcony

formerly had a continuous stone balustrade, echoing that above the cornice, but the flanking sections have been infilled. The pitched roof is piended and slated. Two tripartite windows look onto the verandah at ground-floor level. The three windows above are sash and case with finely moulded lugged architraves. The side walls are of random rubble and have none of the fine detail of the main elevation.

The building is symmetrical about the main entrance with two fine ground-floor and first-floor rooms. The roof-lit stair has an iron balustrade with hardwood handrail. The former Drawing Room on the first floor, originally very finely proportioned, has been sub-divided, but classical features such as the coffered ceiling have been preserved. There is a rich variety of moulded plasterwork and joinery in the other main rooms. The inner screen to the vestibule, is semi-glazed, with a fine moulded door-piece.

A kitchen extension has been added to the rear. The site is walled in random rubble and has a gate access to the park.

Address:	1–3 South Street, Perth
Category:	B, in Tay Street Conservation Area
Occupier:	Scottish Courts Administration
Use:	Offices
Holding:	Crown

This building is occupied in part by the Procurator Fiscal's Office, the remainder of the building accommodating local authority offices and those of the Tay River Purification Board. Designed by the Perth architect David Smart, a pupil of David Bryce, it was built in 1863–66 as the Burgh Police Office. It stands on the site of a former merchant's house.

The particular interest of the building lies in the difficulty faced by Smart in creating a design appropriate both for the important narrow riverside frontage and for the long main frontage to South Street. This problem, essentially one of scale, was very successfully resolved. The three-bay gable elevation to Tay Street uses much the same detailing as the South Street facade, which reads as two complementary five-bay buildings, each with its own identical central door-piece. The ridge line of the western half is lower, and a recessed, single-bay link further emphasises the concept of two individual buildings within a single facade. It is Italian Renaissance in style, constructed in ashlar sandstone with projecting chamfered quoins. The three-bay gable elevation towards the riverfront is designed as an impressive frontispiece flanking the eastern approach to the city across Queen's Bridge. Below the cornice it follows the general architectural scheme of the long South Street frontage. Above the cornice is a powerful double chimney gable, supported by scroll brackets and incorporating a pair of arched, key-blocked windows between the two stacks. The eastern, five-bay half of the South Street frontage is distinguished from the western section by having tripartite windows, with very narrow side lights in the end bays and a higher ridge line. Both sections have pedimented Roman Doric central door-pieces. The astragalled sash and case windows have fortunately been retained throughout.

The ground floor still contains the original public Police offices, with vaulted ceilings. A dog-leg open-well stairway rises from the corridor entrance to the first floor, which is divided into a series of rooms and was originally the house of the Superintendent of Police. A separate stairway from the rear of the building gives direct access to the attic flat of the resident caretaker. The basement below the building contains a series of narrow brick-vaulted rooms with high clerestory lighting and access from an area inset into the pavement, now partly filled in or covered over by pavement lights. Next to the Police Office on the ground floor is a series of cells of which three remain in original condition, having heavy brick-vaulted ceilings, narrow windows with steeply sloping cills, stone-flagged floors and stone jambs to the doorways in which are set heavy timber doors with original large rim locks and peep holes. The rest of the interior is generally plain with ornament limited to plain marble chimney-pieces, simple cornices, moulded architraves and panelled doors, all of which remain as original or with minor alterations.

216

Name:	Sheriff Court
Address:	Tay Street, Perth
Category:	A, in Tay Street Conservation Area
Occupier:	Scottish Courts Administration
Use:	Court House
Holding:	Crown

Perth Sheriff Court, built in 1819 at a cost of £22,000, stands on the site of Gowrie House, famous for its associations with the "Gowrie Conspiracy" of 1600, a plot to murder the reigning Scottish Monarch, James VI. The site and buildings were later owned by the Town Council, which gifted them to the Duke of Cumberland after the Jacobite Rebellion of 1745–6. The Sheriff Court was first planned in 1812 by Robert Reid as a County Building with attached jails to the rear. The jails were built at that date, but by the time the County Buildings were commenced Reid had been replaced by the London architect, Sir Robert Smirke. Constructed in fine ashlar sandstone the building occupies an important river-front site in the centre of Perth, and is of great townscape importance viewed from the east side of the Tay. The main elevation, severely classical in design, has an octostyle Greek Doric portico, which breaks forward from a ten-bay colonnade recessed between broad three-bay pavilions with coupled anta pilasters at the ends. Behind the portico, the building is two-storey with square-headed windows to the ground and first floors and three central entrance doorways with semi-circular heads. The windows have projecting architraves capped by a cornice and frieze. The end elevations each have three semi-circular arched tripartite windows with pilaster mullions. The plan of the building is now E-shaped. The central projection to the rear contains the Justiciary Hall (now no. 1 Sheriff Court). This was rebuilt in 1866–7, from the original hemicycle, as a large rectangular galleried court, to designs by David Smart. The north wing contains a second Sheriff Court and the impressive County Hall, measuring 68 ft.×40 ft. is situated in the south wing. A series of Committee Rooms link the former main public areas on the first floor at the front, to provide further Court chambers. A basement to the rear of the building, underneath the Sheriff Court, contains cells with direct access into the Court Room. Over the years various extensions have been added to the rear of the building. These are mostly contained behind the high wall of the exercise yard, which is all that now remains of the former County Jail demolished in the mid 1960's.

The entrance hall beyond the portico has an unusual double stairway, rising in two directions

from the quarter landing. Sombre in appearance, it sets the tone of the building and is constructed in Arbroath stone slabs with solid balustrades in the same material. The double volume of the entrance hall is lit by windows above the heavy, double-leafed entrance doors. The coffered ceiling over the entrance contains an inset lantern light. The principal Court Room, square on plan and symmetrical in design, is lit by a series of circular-headed windows. Arcading is carried round the room as a decorative theme, unifying the wall surface with the fenestration. The timber-panelled public gallery, which spans the full width of the east end of the Court, is supported on cast-iron columns. Above the Judge's bench is a sounding board, supported on corbelled brackets. The heavily ribbed geometric ceiling plasterwork is naturalistic in inspiration and detail. A large centre ventilator has a delicate filigree grille. A water-colour in the Judge's Chambers illustrates the interior when new, showing how little it has altered. Undoubtedly the most interesting interior is the Ball Room in the south wing. Used originally for County functions such as the Perth Hunt Ball, the room was formerly hung with large wall mirrors. The walls are articulated by shallow arcading, very like the scheme of the principal Court Room. There is a remarkable white marble chimney-piece in this room. The mantelpiece is supported by the outstretched wings of eagles carved as capitals to colonnettes which frame the brass fireplace surround. The original dog grate with back-plate remains, as do the andirons within hearth. Heavy chandeliers are supported from the ornate panelled ceiling. Until quite recently a number of fine portraits hung in this room. These included likenesses of the Duke of Atholl and Lord Lynedoch by Sir Thomas Lawrence, and of Lord George Murray by Pickersgill.

References: History of Perth (Marshall).
Ancient Capital of Scotland vol. III (Cowan).

ARCHITECTS, ARTISTS, CRAFTSMEN AND ENGINEERS

Names relate to architects unless otherwise indicated.

BUILDING TYPES BY ORIGINAL USE

1. Banks
2. Bridges and piers
3. Castles
4. Churches
5. Civic Buildings and Public Halls
6. Club
7. Commercial
8. Country Houses and Villas
9. Court Houses and other legal buildings
10. Custom Houses
11. Domestic (Minor rural)
12. Domestic (Urban)
13. Dovecots
14. Farm Houses and Steadings
15. Galleries, Libraries, Museums, Record Offices
16. Garden
17. Government
18. Hotels
19. Military
20. Post Office
21. Schools

1. Banks

Girvan, Hamilton Street (Commercial Bank)	197
Glasgow, Lanarkshire House, Ingram Street (Union Bank)	180
Haddington, 15 Lodge Street, (City Bank)	81
Huntly, 23–25 Gordon Street (substantially altered for Aberdeen Town and Country Bank 1874)	58
Stirling, 1 Corn Exchange Road, (Clydesdale Bank)	13

2. Bridges and Piers

Dreghorn, Old Bridge	158
Inveraray, pier	168

3. Castles

Edinburgh	98
Rosyth	34
Stirling	16, 27

4. Churches

Edinburgh, St. George, Charlotte Square (now West Register House)	88
Rattray, Mount Ericht Hall	211

5. Civic Buildings and Public Halls

Alloa, Burgh Chambers, 14 Bank Street	6
Dunfermline, 79 High Street (built as County Buildings)	29
Fraserburgh, Dalrymple Hall, Seaforth Street	57
Glasgow, Ingram Street, City and County Building	179
1 Maxwell Road (formerly YMCA)	181
Gourock, Gamble Institute, Shore Street	189
Kirkcudbright, Tolbooth, High Street	24
Tain, Tolbooth, High Street	77

6. Commercial Buildings

Aberdeen, 377 Union Street	53
Edinburgh:	
22–24 George Street	100
4 Market Street	108
16 North Bank Street	114
28 North Bridge	115
Queen Street, York Buildings	123
St. Andrew's Square, Prudential Building	134
2 South Charlotte Street	135
Victoria Street, India Buildings	137
Glasgow:	
57 Bothwell Street, Mercantile Chambers	175
81–107 Bothwell Street, Scottish Legal Life Building	176
518 Sauchiehall Street	186
Inverness, 1 Young Street	74
Perth, 43 New Row	213

7. Club

Edinburgh, 3 Queensferry Street (United Services Club)	128

8. Country Houses and Villas

Aberdeen:	
Angusfield House	50
St. Luke's Viewfield	54, 65
Annan, Highburn House	18
Arbroath, The Captain's House, HMS Condor	203
Bishopton, Dargavel House	198
Dundee:	
Craigiebarn	207
The Vine	209
Edinburgh:	
Craigs House	150
Craigiehall	146
Inverleith House	153
20 Inverleith Row	152
Stenhouse Mansion	159
Helensburgh, Ardencaple	173
Montrose, Castle Stead	206
Perth:	
Balhousie Castle	164, 212
3 St. Leonard's Bank	214
7 St. Leonard's Bank	215
Pitreavie Castle	31
Shambellie House and Lodge	22, 27
Stirling:	
Carlton House	15
Forthside House	14
Tulliallan Castle and Blackhall Lodge	28, 34

9. Court Houses and other Legal buildings
(s) denotes Sheriff Court

Aberdeen, (s)	44
Alloa, (s)	7
Arbroath, (s)	202
Ayr, (s)	195
Banff, (s)	56
Cupar, (s)	39
Dingwall, (s)	76
Dornoch, (s)	79
Dumbarton, (s)	172
Dumfries, (s)	19
Dundee, (s)	210
Dunfermline, (s)	29
Edinburgh:	
Cowgate, Solicitor's Building	94
Governor's House, former Calton Prison	130
Parliament Square, Supreme Courts	117
Elgin, (s)	63
Falkirk, (s)	8

10. *Custom Houses*

Coats of Arms: It has been brought to light that the Coats of Arms displayed at some Custom Houses are incorrect. They are those of Scotland showing the Lion Rampant in the first and fourth quarters, but with the shield surrounded by a strap and buckle containing the Garter Motto, "Honi Soit Qui Mal Y Pense", thus creating a bastard achievement, part Scottish, part English. The motto should, in Scottish heraldry read, "Nemo Me Impune Lacessit". The incorrect arrangement first appeared at the time of Charles II. The only suggestion offered for the unusual coats of arms is that the Customs and Excise Department is not purely a Scottish Department. The Lyon Court has noted the inaccuracy.

11. *Domestic (Minor rural)*

12. *Domestic (Urban)*

13. *Dovecots*

14. *Farm Houses and Steadings*

15. *Galleries, Libraries, Museums, Record Offices*

16. *Garden Buildings*

GENERAL INDEX